LEARNING FROM STRANGERS

THE ART AND METHOD OF QUALITATIVE INTERVIEW STUDIES

ROBERT S. WEISS

THE FREE PRESS
New York London Toronto Sydney Tokyo Singapore

The Free Press
A Division of Simon & Schuster, Inc.
1230 Avenue of the Americas
New York, N.Y. 10022

First Free Press Paperback Edition 1995

Printed in the United States of America

printing number

1   2   3   4   5   6   7   8   9   10

Library of Congress Cataloging-in-Publication Data

Weiss, Robert Stuart
    Learning from strangers : the art and method of qualitative
interview studies / Robert Stuart Weiss.
        p.   cm.
    Includes bibliographical references (p.   ) and index.
    ISBN 0-684-82312-8
    1. Interviewing in sociology.   2. Social surveys.   I. Title.
HN29.W42   1994
301'.0723—dc20   93-24464
                                                        CIP

CONTENTS

PREFACE

I conducted my first qualitative interviews while a graduate student at the University of Michigan. I had recently transferred into sociology from a master's program in mathematical statistics and was employed part time by the university's survey research center at the usual marginally adequate student salary. At the next desk sat another graduate student, who augmented her income on evenings and weekends by conducting qualitative interviews for a commercial firm, Ernest Dichter, Inc. I was intrigued not only by her success in income augmentation but also by the firsthand contact with respondents afforded by her method of doing so. My survey center assignment, analyzing sociometric data, brought with it no such firsthand contact. I asked whether the Dichter firm could use another interviewer, learned that it could, and started in.

Ernest Dichter, a Viennese refugee, was retained by American manufacturers and advertisers to tell them why people bought or failed to buy particular products. He called his data-gathering approach "depth interviewing," probably to suggest that it dredged up its findings from respondents' unconscious, where their buying decisions were made unbeknownst to themselves. One of Dichter's more widely reported observations was that people saw prunes as representations of old age. He advised prune packers to put their products in a "sunshine jar" and, in their advertising, to link prunes with children.[1]

I didn't conduct interviews for the prune study, but I did for studies of fiberglass curtains, brands of scotch, and a correspondence school that promised its students it would turn them into artists. Once I received my graduate degree, I ended my work with the Dichter firm to concentrate on what was then my full-time employment, the collection and analysis of survey data. However, I continued to use qualitative interviewing for pilot studies and other small-scale studies. Gradually, I became convinced that the qualitative approach, while quite different from that of survey research, was preferable for some problems. I was particularly struck by the density of information provided by qualitative interview studies and by their usefulness for understanding the complexities of respondents' experiences.

Over the years I learned more about how to do qualitative interview research from many friends, colleagues, and teachers: Carol Kaye, Arlene Daniels, Ira Glick, Peter Marris, Lisa Peattie, Lee Rainwater, Martin Rein, and, through his publications as well as personal contact, Anselm Strauss. Most important for me was Everett Hughes, who brought with him to the Brandeis department of sociology, of which I was then a member, the Chicago School's commitment to firsthand learning about people and their lives. I was the beneficiary of a long tutorial with him under the guise of acting as his co-instructor. I have also had the good fortune to work as a junior colleague with Margaret Mead and David Riesman: with the former on only a few occasions, with the latter for many years.

Despite all this instruction, much of what I have learned about qualitative interview studies has been a product of experience, of trial and error—rather a lot of error—and trial again. Each of the qualitative interview studies I have done—and at this point there have been many, including studies of marital separation, single parenting, bereavement, and the management of work stress—has been an exploration of method as well as of substance.

I have on several occasions been responsible for teaching others to interview or to conduct interview studies. With Everett Hughes I helped establish the field training program in the Brandeis sociology department; more recently, I offered a qualitative interviewing course at the University of Massachusetts in Boston. I have also demonstrated the approach for colleagues with whom I have worked, and I have supervised Ph.D. theses based on qualitative interviews.

This book came about partly as a consequence of my offering workshops on qualitative interview studies at two annual conferences of the American Sociological Association. Those workshops convinced me that a guide to the method would be useful to people in my field and, very likely, in other fields as well.

In this book I try to take the reader from conceptualization of a research project using qualitative interviewing as its method to production of its report. I try to be candid about the problems of this kind of research, but I hope my openness does not obscure my belief in the method's importance for the social sciences. Some issues can be investigated in no other way. I also believe that every investigator in the social sciences should know how to conduct a qualitative interview, just as he or she should be able to interpret a statistical table. Qualitative interviewing is a fundamental method for learning about the experience of others.

Many people have helped me with this book. I want to thank Lisa Peattie for many clarifying discussions of qualitative interview studies, Mark Kramer for his insights into the principles of nonfiction study and writing, and the other friends and colleagues who contributed ideas, observations, and suggestions: Deborah Belle, Arlene Daniels, Uta Gerhardt, David Jacobson, Marie Killilea, Gina Prenowitz, Martin Rein, and Shulamit Reinharz. Erwin Glikes, who was the book's editor and publisher, died not long after the book's publication. His enthusiasm encouraged me to write the book and his editorial skill helped shape it. I remain grateful to him. Mary Coffey and John Drabik, fellow members of the University of Massachusetts Work and Family Research Unit, contributed to the book's production and cheered it on. My greatest indebtedness, as always, is to my wife, Joan Hill Weiss.

CHAPTER 1

INTRODUCTION

WHY WE INTERVIEW

Interviewing gives us access to the observations of others. Through interviewing we can learn about places we have not been and could not go and about settings in which we have not lived. If we have the right informants, we can learn about the quality of neighborhoods or what happens in families or how organizations set their goals. Interviewing can inform us about the nature of social life. We can learn about the work of occupations and how people fashion careers, about cultures and the values they sponsor, and about the challenges people confront as they lead their lives.

We can learn also, through interviewing, about people's interior experiences. We can learn what people perceived and how they interpreted their perceptions. We can learn how events affected their thoughts and feelings. We can learn the meanings to them of their relationships, their families, their work, and their selves. We can learn about all the experiences, from joy through grief, that together constitute the human condition.

Interviewing gives us a window on the past. We may become aware of a riot or a flood only after the event, but by interviewing the people who were there we can picture what happened. We can also, by interviewing, learn about settings that would otherwise be closed to us: foreign societies, exclusive organizations, and the private lives of couples and families.

1

Interviewing rescues events that would otherwise be lost. The celebrations and sorrows of people not in the news, their triumphs and failures, ordinarily leave no record except in their memories. And there are, of course, no observers of the internal events of thought and feeling except those to whom they occur. Most of the significant events of people's lives can become known to others only through interview.

SURVEY INTERVIEWING AND QUALITATIVE INTERVIEWING

Interviews can be as prepackaged as the polling or survey interview in which questions are fixed and answers limited: "Do you consider yourself to be a Republican, a Democrat, or something else?" There is a high art to developing such items and analyzing them, and for years this has been a respected way to collect interview information.

The great attraction of fixed-item, precategorized-response survey interviews is that because they ask the same questions of every respondent, with the same limited options for response, they can report the proportion of respondents who choose each option: 40% Democrat, 38% Republican, 15% Independent, 7% Other or Don't Know. Furthermore, the standardization of question and response permits comparisons among subgroups, so that, for example, the responses of men can be compared with those of women. Categorized responses to fixed-item interviews can also serve as the raw material for statistical models of social dynamics.

Studies whose ultimate aim is to report how many people are in particular categories or what the relationship is between being in one category and another are justly called *quantitative*. They are quantitative not because they collect numbers as information, although they may (for example, in response to the question "How many years have you lived at this address?"), but, rather, because their results can be presented as a table of numbers (for example, in a table entitled Proportions of People in the Labor Force, Grouped by Age, Who Have at Least Some Self-Employment Income).

Quantitative studies pay a price for their standardized precision. Because they ask the same questions in the same order of every respondent, they do not obtain full reports. Instead, the information they obtain from any one person is fragmentary, made up of bits and pieces of attitudes and observations and appraisals.

If we want more from respondents than a choice among categories or brief answers to open-ended items, we would do well to drop the requirement that the questions asked of all respondents be exactly the same. For example, if we are free to tailor questions to respondents in a study of working mothers, we can ask a working mother who has a special-needs child about the quality of the school program she has found, and we can ask a working mother whose children are not yet school age about the worries of leaving her children in day care. And we can make clear to each respondent when we need further examples or explanations or discussions. Furthermore, we can establish an understanding with the respondents that it is their full story we want and not simply answers to standardized questions.

Interviews that sacrifice uniformity of questioning to achieve fuller development of information are properly called *qualitative* interviews, and a study based on such interviews, a qualitative interview study. Because each respondent is expected to provide a great deal of information, the qualitative interview study is likely to rely on a sample very much smaller than the samples interviewed by a reasonably ambitious survey study. And because the fuller responses obtained by the qualitative study cannot be easily categorized, their analysis will rely less on counting and correlating and more on interpretation, summary, and integration. The findings of the qualitative study will be supported more by quotations and case descriptions than by tables or statistical measures.

In general, if statistical analysis is our goal, we would do better to use a survey approach. The survey approach is preferable if we want to compare some specific aspect of different groups: to compare, for example, the job satisfaction of workers in different firms. It is also preferable if we hope to use statistical analysis to identify linkages among phenomena, especially where the phenomena are unlikely to be recognized by respondents as linked. An example would the contribution of parental loss in childhood to vulnerability to depression in adult life.

On the other hand, if we depart from the survey approach in the direction of tailoring our interview to each respondent, we gain in the coherence, depth, and density of the material each respondent provides.[1] We permit ourselves to be informed as we cannot be by brief answers to survey items. The report we ultimately write can provide readers with a fuller understanding of the experiences of our respondents.

We need not restrict ourselves to just the one approach. Standardized items can be appended to qualitative interviews. And usually we can produce numerical data from qualitative interview studies that have explored the same area with different respondents, although we may have to engage in a time-consuming and cumbersome coding procedure and tolerate lots of missing data.

The following excerpt, from an interview conducted for a study of adjustment to retirement, provides an example of the material that can be obtained in qualitative interviews. The respondent is a woman of 66, formerly a department head in a firm in the creative arts, retired for almost 2 years at the time of the interview. This is the third interview in which she was a respondent. The first had been held before her retirement, the second a few months after it.

The interview took place in one of the research project's offices. In this excerpt the interviewer and respondent have just taken a few minutes to recall the project's aims, and now the respondent is describing her current situation:

RESPONDENT: My life is—the euphemism I guess today is "couch potato." I stay home. I try to go out as infrequently as I can. When I say "out," I mean, like shopping . . . um, going any place. I listen to a lot of music. I read a great deal. And I watch television a great deal. I don't see anyone. I do speak to my daughter; I speak to her on the phone. That's it! All the things that I thought I would do, if I weren't in a working situation . . . I'd be writing, I'd create, I'd start a business. I had so many ideas while I was still working. I sort of—now maybe this is fanciful thinking—but I sort of pride myself on being a person who comes up with ideas fairly easily. When I say "ideas," I mean practical, good ideas and creative ideas. But I have no opportunity to . . . Oh, my only hobby is crossword puzzles. [*chuckles*] Which is more of the same, just sitting there in isolation.

I'm not unhappy with my situation. But just that I feel like that the past year . . . wasn't unpleasant—none of it is unpleasant—but it really didn't matter whether I . . . had been alive last year or not. Except in terms of what I can offer to my daughter, who's in Syracuse. I haven't been to visit my daughter and her husband in almost a year. Well, partly it's because of health. I'm afraid to drive a full six and a half hours. Because I do get very, very dizzy and have to pull up to the side of the road. So, you know, it's difficult. But, you know, if I really wanted to open my door, I could take a plane. I could take a taxi over to the airport, and I could fly there. I mean, I could be doing things. I could find alternative ways. But I just don't want to. I don't know if you remember, but I've sort of let myself go. I'm all gray now, practically. Which is okay. If you decide to be. I'm going around in sneakers. I don't have a pair of shoes anymore. It's not a sloppiness. It's just like I'm wearing house slippers all the time, you know, except that it's acceptable in the street. It's like nothing really matters that much. I was going to put on shoes—I mean, you know, real pumps, I mean, the kind that I used to wear—when I came here. And I . . . it was like I was torn between pride in my appearance and the fact that it doesn't really matter. As long as I can be comfortable.

INTERVIEWER: Yeah. It's like you've gone through a metamorphosis?

RESPONDENT: Yeah. But the problem . . . I can understand my reacting this way for a brief time. Hey, I'm going to have the luxury of sloth. And no demands. I'm going to do whatever I want to. If I want to sleep late, I'll sleep late. If I want to stay up 'til two or three in the morning, which I do . . . [*chuckles*] I could understand that as a reaction. The fact that it's extended like almost two years just doesn't worry me. Because if it worried me I'd do something about it. I just don't think about it. It's just that I don't see any changes coming into my life, unless someone knocks on that door for me. And that's not going to happen.

INTERVIEWER: Yeah. Is this a way to capture what you're feeling about it: that it doesn't worry you, exactly, but it perplexes you?

RESPONDENT: Yeah, I just don't understand it.

INTERVIEWER: Is that right?

RESPONDENT: Yeah. I really don't understand why I've become a nothing person. Even just talking to you, now, I'm rambling. I'm not sure I even know how to talk to people anymore, in terms of conversation. I used to be pretty good at it. You know, I would go to all kinds of functions at work. I thought I handled myself fairly well. And now I don't. If I were invited to a party now, I wouldn't go. My nephew's getting married. I just got an invitation last night in the mail. And my first reaction—I have to be honest with you here; I would never say this to anyone else—wasn't joy for him. That was my second reaction. My first was fear. He wanting me to come to Iowa for the wedding, to meet people, to be with my family, friends, and so on. I'm not going to go. I don't want to be seen this way. I don't want to be with people. I had a call from my college roommate about a year ago. And I haven't called her back. I don't call anyone back. I've severed all my phone friendships, even. She's retired . . . just, I mean, at that time she had just retired, and she was sending away for Chamber of Commerce "What's On," and "What's to Do." And I admired her. And I was able to enter into the conversation with her, you know, how exciting it sounded. And once I hung up, that was the end of it. And she's not going to do anything either.

INTERVIEWER: Why do you say that, that she's not going to do anything?

RESPONDENT: Because the first thought that you have is, "Here's an opportunity for a new life." But I think it takes either tremendous confidence in yourself to start a new life on your own without any support or you have to be a certain kind of person who's always been a doer and you keep doing. I think most people don't know how to start a new life. School's told us what to do, bosses've told us what to do, husbands've told us what to do. It's very difficult to tell yourself what to do.

INTERVIEWER: Yeah. Suppose somebody suggested to you, say, volunteer work. What would that mean to you?

RESPONDENT: [*short pause*] My daughter said that to me yesterday. Which is very funny. She despairs, not so much of me, but in terms of my attitude. Which is a non-attitude. Again, I've always hated limits, and here I'm asking for them. Isn't that odd? Freedom, total freedom, is what I've always espoused. But if you were to say to me, "There's a need for some more people to take care of this hospice or to work in this hospital and so on. Could you help out next Tuesday?" Hey, of course. But when I've looked at the volunteer lists—and there's so much need—it's two things. I don't know where to go. Because I don't know anyone. And second, part of it goes back to not wanting to open that door to be among people. I feel that I've gotten so heavy, so gray, I don't even want people to look at me.

INTERVIEWER: Could you walk me through that conversation with your daughter where she made the suggestion to volunteer?

RESPONDENT: We were talking about my mother, who died a couple of years ago. And we used to visit Ma, who lived in an apartment complex for the elderly. And there were all kinds of activities on the premises. You know, they had classes and they had socials and they had dances and so on. And we would try to coerce her into joining. You know: "Don't sit by yourself all day in your apartment. Take a class in ceramics. Do this, do that." And ... and "There's a Thanksgiving Dance; go down and join them." And she wouldn't want to do that. And we felt it would be so much better for her if she were more active, if she did meet other people and did participate. And I said that I ... I suddenly understood how Ma felt. And that we were wrong in imposing our values, just because *we* needed people and we needed activity, on her. And I said, "Now, for the first time, I can really understand why she would prefer reading a book to going to a card game." And my daughter said, "There has to be some way in which you can use your mind and feel that you still make a difference. And why don't you volunteer?" I like the thought of helping others. But I don't know now that I'm as capable of giving as I once was. When I was feeling good, I wanted to share that feeling good. I'm not feeling empty. I still care about my daughter. I still care about the sick person. I still care about what's going on. I still ... even on my pension, I still make charitable kinds of contributions. Because I do care what's happening in this world. It's just that I don't know whether I can give anything.

INTERVIEWER: What did your daughter say?

RESPONDENT: Well, she feels that I ought to try. She feels that I ought to go ... someplace. If I find it unpleasant, I can always stop. It isn't like taking a job. But it's that tremendous inertia. It looks like I'd have to climb a mountain to take the first step out. I think once I made that step I could do it. It's climbing a psychological mountain. [pause] Maybe it's just the fact that I feel so alone. You know, maybe there's a difference when a person is retiring and has someone—or some ones—there to help.

The excerpt displays the depth and development achievable in qualitative interviewing. It also suggests the contribution qualitative interviewing can make to understanding a situation. Although we would need corroboration from interviews with others among the retired to have confidence in generalization, we see in this interview a process by which retirement makes it easy for those who live alone to slide into isolation.

The process begins with the removal, following retirement from work, of the obligation to participate in social activity. To be sure, the newly retired person may for a time find solitude rewarding after the stresses and demands of work life. Solitude can then be a welcome opportunity for reading and lazing and puttering around the house. But as social withdrawal becomes more established, the prospect of having to mobilize energy to interact with others may bring increasing discomfort to the person who is alone. The person may, like the woman in the interview excerpt, be uncertain of having anything to give and so of being worthy of respect, and may think, "Why subject myself to discomfort when it is possible just to stay home?" Withdrawal thus becomes self-reinforcing.

What we have gained from this qualitative interview is an observer's report of one possible impact of retirement. The report could have been provided only by the respondent herself; only she was in a position to make its observations. And the report could have been developed only in an interview that encouraged the respondent to provide a full account.

Qualitative interviews can have different emphases. In this interview excerpt the respondent provided information about her internal state: her mental and emotional functioning, her thoughts, and her feelings. If the interview had been collected in a study with a different focus, the respondent might have given more emphasis to external events, for example, the functioning of the retirement program provided by her company. Qualitative interviews may focus on the internal or the external; what is common to them all is that they ask the respondent to provide an observer's report on the topic under study.

The style of the qualitative interview may appear conversational, but what happens in the interview is very different from what happens in an ordinary conversation. In an ordinary conversation each participant voices observations, thoughts, feelings. Either participant can set a new topic, either can ask questions. In the qualitative interview the respondent provides information while the interviewer, as a representative of the study, is responsible for directing the respondent to the topics that matter to the study. Note that the interviewer in the excerpt asked, about the college roommate, not what her work had been or where she was now living, but why the respondent believed that she too would fail to achieve the active postretirement life she was planning. The interviewer was also responsible for judging when the respondent's report was adequate and when it needed elaboration, and, should elaboration have seemed desirable, for helping the respondent expand her responses without constraining the information she might provide. As would be the case with any interviewer in an interview that was going well, the interviewer here said much less than the respondent. The interviewer at no point engaged the respondent in the small exchanges of ordinary conversation by, for example, matching one of the respondent's observations with an observation of his own. Nor did he at any point introduce his own experiences, not even to note, by saying something like "Yeah, I know what you mean," that he had had experiences similar to the respondent's. It was the respondent's account that was important.

The interviewer was often encouraging. If you were to listen to the tape of this excerpt, you would hear an occasional murmured "Yeah" and "Uh-huh," by which the interviewer not only indicated that he understood but also affirmed that, yes, this is the right sort of material. The interviewer's voice was mostly serious, respectful, interested. The respondent's voice was mostly relaxed, unhurried, reflective, and inward. If you had watched the interview, you would have seen the interviewer smile when the respondent reported an incident she believed comic and become more sober as she described her withdrawal. But mostly the interviewer expressed a desire to understand whatever it was the respondent was saying.

SOME CONSIDERATIONS IN UNDERTAKING A QUALITATIVE INTERVIEW STUDY

REASONS TO CONDUCT A QUALITATIVE INTERVIEW STUDY

Research aims should dictate research method. Here are research aims that could make the qualitative interview study the method of choice:

1. *Developing detailed descriptions.* We may want to learn as much as we can about an event or development that we weren't there to see. For example, we may want the fullest report possible of how it happened that someone began drug use, of what the daily round is like for someone who is retired, or of the events of a prison rebellion. We may well want to interview more than one informant and integrate their reports, but we will in any event want from our informants the fullest, most detailed description possible.

2. *Integrating multiple perspectives.* We may want to describe an organization, development, or event that no single person could have observed in its totality. We may want, for example, to describe the structure and functioning of a federal agency or the impact on a community of a flood. Although interviews are necessary, standardized questions won't work, because every respondent will have different observations to contribute. Historians, biographers, and journalists deal regularly with problems of this sort and regularly do qualitative interview studies.

3. *Describing process.* We may want to know, about some human enterprise, how events occur or what an event produces. Economists assume that retailers set prices to maximize profit. But is this in fact the basis for price setting, and if it is, just how do merchants go about deciding how to maximize their profits? Qualitative interviews with merchants can make evident the processes they use.[2] Or we read in the newspapers about "deadbeat dads" and assume that divorced fathers who withhold child support must be indifferent to the welfare of their children. But is this the case? What leads some fathers who no longer live with their children to fail to contribute to the children's support? Again, qualitative interviews can elicit the processes antecedent

to an outcome of interest. Each of the questions in these examples is a particular expression of the more general question "What are the processes by which an event occurs?" We might also be interested in the consequences of events; for example, how do husbands and wives go about resolving marital quarrels?

4. *Developing holistic description.* By putting together process reports from people whose behaviors interrelate—putting together the reports of retailers and customers or of institutional psychiatrists and institutionalized patients—we can learn about systems. Qualitative interview study may well be the method of choice if our aim is to describe how a system works or fails to work. Thus, we might rely on qualitative interviewing of members of a family to understand the nature of their family life, and qualitative interviewing of members of an organization to understand how the organization works, how it moves toward goals or is paralyzed by internal friction. In general, the dense information obtained in qualitative interviewing permits description of the many sectors of a complex entity and how they go together.

5. *Learning how events are interpreted.* We might want to learn not so much about an event as about how it is interpreted by participants and onlookers. For example, we might be interested in studying responses to a film. Here we already know the "event" but want to learn the reactions of those who were its audience.[3] We might want to know how they thought about what happened in the film, what sorts of causes they identified, and what sorts of consequences they worried about. Qualitative interviewing enables us to learn about perceptions and reactions known only to those to whom they occurred.[4]

6. *Bridging intersubjectivities.* We might want to produce a report that makes it possible for readers to grasp a situation from the inside, as a participant might. Qualitative interview studies can approach the "you are there" vividness of a documentary. They can foster the kind of understanding that might be expressed as "Had I been in that situation, I'd have acted that way too." Quotations from interview material can help the reader identify with the respondent, if only briefly, by presenting events as the respondent experienced them, in the respondent's words, with the respondent's imagery.[5]

7. *Identifying variables and framing hypotheses for quantitative*

research. Qualitative interview studies can provide preparation for quantitative research. Those who do quantitative research require variables to measure, issues about which to frame questions, and hypotheses to test. Variables, issues, and hypotheses can come from prior research, be inferred from theory, or be proposed on grounds of common sense, but where none of these does well enough, qualitative interviewing often is asked to fill the gap. The descriptions of process and system that are likely to emerge from a qualitative interview study can inform quantitative investigators about what matters in their intended topic.[6]

Young investigators are sometimes discouraged from undertaking qualitative research studies because of the time they require and their purportedly limited scientific utility. Let us consider each of these issues.

TIME

Qualitative interview studies have the reputation of being labor intensive. Indeed, if undertaken as a Ph.D. thesis, where there are likely to be large ambitions and limited resources, a qualitative interview study can stretch on and on. Several months may be required for the interviewing, and the analysis of the interviews can take even longer.

But journalists, working against deadlines, find any number of shortcuts available for the completion of qualitative interview studies: They can limit their interviewing to those whom they can reach quickly, and they can do much of their interviewing by telephone. They can not only analyze as they go—most people who do qualitative interview studies do this—but also work out their story in their minds. Once their interviewing is done, they may need to devote only a bit more time to thinking about the meanings of their material before they move to writing about it. A qualitative interviewing study can be enormously time consuming, but it need not be.

It should also be noted that the time required by qualitative interview studies tends to be well invested. Most of it goes into an effort to understand the issues of the research. It is entirely possible for investigators who do quantitative work to end a study knowing more about the statistical packages they have used for computer analysis than about the topic of their study. By contrast, those who do qualitative interview studies invariably wind up knowing a lot about the topic of their study.[7]

VALUE AS CONTRIBUTION TO KNOWLEDGE

As I noted earlier in this chapter, a qualitative interview study is poorly suited to the production of statistics or the numerical raw materials for statistical models. In consequence, economists and others committed to the development of statistical models sometimes disparage the reports produced by qualitative interview studies. They may characterize these results as anecdotal, because they rely on accounts provided by a relatively small sample of respondents, or as impressionistic, implying not only that they are imprecise but also that they are more a product of art than of objective scientific method.[8]

The disparagement is unwarranted. Much of the important work in the social sciences, work that has contributed in fundamental ways to our understanding of our society and ourselves, has been based on qualitative interview studies. Qualitative interview studies have provided descriptions of phenomena that could have been learned about in no other way, including the human consequences of a disastrous flood[9] and the experiences of participants in the women's movement.[10] What we know about the effects of crises in personal lives comes largely from such studies,[11] as does much of what we know about the dynamics of post-traumatic stress disorder.[12] Nor should qualitative interview studies be thought of as only exploratory and ground-breaking, preliminary to other more structured approaches. While it can be valuable for the results of qualitative interview studies to be verified by other methods, it can also be valuable for the results of studies done by other methods to be illuminated by qualitative interview studies.

A COMPROMISE? FIXED QUESTION, OPEN RESPONSE

Investigators who are attracted to the richness of the materials produced by qualitative interview studies but concerned about what may seem to be their looseness sometimes conclude that fixed-question–open-response interviewing provides a desirable compromise. Here respondents are asked carefully crafted questions but are free to answer them in their own words rather than required simply to choose one or another predetermined alternative.

The hope of those who elect the fixed-question–open-response approach is that it will systematize the collection of qualitative material and facilitate the quantitative treatment of the material. In this approach qualitative information (albeit more in the form of summary statements than developed stories) will be collected, but because everyone will have been asked the same questions, the responses to each question can be categorized and worked with statistically. This approach makes it possible to report proportions and correlations as well as experiences and meanings.

Unfortunately, the fixed-question–open-response approach to data collection turns out to sacrifice as much in quality of information as it gains in systematization. The interviewer is not actually free to encourage a respondent to develop any response at length. A very long response, just like a shorter one, will have to be fitted into code categories, and interviewers, aware of this, tend to limit the length of respondents' answers.

Furthermore, the very style of question asking weighs against full response. Not only must interviewers ask every question of every respondent for whom it is appropriate, but they must also follow the same ordering of the questions. The interview is directed by the schedule rather than by the respondent's associations. The result is that the respondent, rather than being free to tell the story of what happened, is forced into a stance of answering a question, waiting for the next question, answering the next question, and so on.

Consider how the respondent in the excerpt given earlier in this chapter would have been dealt with in an interview using the fixed-question–open-response format. The respondent might have been asked, "Could you tell me whether your retirement is satisfactory or unsatisfactory?" Suppose the respondent replied, as she did to a similar question in the qualitative interview, "My life is—the euphemism I guess today is 'couch potato.' I stay home." The fixed-question interviewer would very likely then have asked, "Well, is that satisfactory or unsatisfactory?" On being told it was all right, the interviewer might have gone on to the next question. Suppose, however, that instead of going on to the next question, the interviewer had used the standard probe "Why do you say that?" to obtain further material. Now the respondent might have said, as she did in the qualitative interview, "I'm not unhappy with my situation." Almost surely that would have been the end of the discussion of the couch potato issue. The fixed question–open-response approach would have succeeded in getting a headline but would have missed the story.

The material obtained in fixed-question–open-response interviews has another defect: it tends to be generalized rather than concrete. In our example of the retiree we probably would not have been told the significant detail of the respondent's having traded her pumps for sneakers but would instead learn only that she would "just rather stay at home." Indeed, because the study directors of a fixed-question–open-response survey want a brief response that covers a lot of ground, they write their questions to elicit generalizations. Thus, a typical question would be "Taking it all together, what has been the most important determinant of the way you feel these days?"

Even though fixed-question–open-response interviewing may at first appear to be a systematic approach to qualitative interviewing, it is not. It is a different approach entirely. While studies using this approach may avoid some of the vulnerabilities of qualitative interviewing studies, they also lack their strengths.

THE PHASES OF QUALITATIVE INTERVIEWING RESEARCH

Qualitative interview studies generally begin with decisions regarding the sample to interview, move on to data collection, and conclude with analysis. But more so than is the case in quantitative research, the phases of work in qualitative research overlap and are intermeshed. Analysis of early data contributes to new emphases in interviewing, and the new data collected by the modified interviewing then produces new analyses. The investigator may draft brief reports early in a study, instead of waiting until its report-writing phase, and interviewing can continue even through the report-writing phase. Nevertheless, the focus of the research effort necessarily shifts as the study progresses from its early stages, when recruitment of respondents is likely to be a major issue, to its concluding stages, during which the investigator is primarily concerned with how best to interpret and report the data.

The chapters that follow trace the likely sequence of the investigator's concerns in a qualitative interview study: sampling, preparing for interviewing, conducting the interviews, analyzing the data, and, finally, writing the report.

CHAPTER 2

RESPONDENTS: CHOOSING THEM AND RECRUITING THEM

AIMS AND SUBSTANTIVE FRAME OF THE STUDY

Any research project hopes to make something known that was previously uncertain: to answer a specific question, such as how patients react to a diagnosis of a life-threatening illness; or to illuminate an area, as by showing how the family life of single parents is different from the family life of married parents. In pursuit of its aims, the research project will almost surely have to explore several related topics. To investigate how patients react to a diagnosis of a life-threatening illness, a project might explore how the patient was told, by whom, and within what context, what the patient's anticipations were, how the patient interpreted the news, and how those close to the patient dealt with the news. The set of topics the study explores, taken together, might be said to constitute the *substantive frame* of the study.

The initial step in a study is to decide, provisionally, what its aims will be and what topics will be included in its substantive frame. Once these are decided, who should be talked with, and about what, can be worked out. As the investigator learns more about the area of the study, the study's aims and frame may well be modified. One good reason for doing pilot interviews is to clarify the aims and frame of the study before interviewing its primary respondents. Even with pilot interviewing, however, the boundaries of the study's frame are likely to shift as more is learned, although as the study proceeds they should shift less and less.

The breadth of a study's substantive frame is often a compromise between the investigator's desires for clarity of focus and for inclusiveness. The narrower the substantive frame, the easier it is to say who should be talked with and about what. The broader the substantive frame, the more the study will eventually be able to report and, presumably, the more significant will be the study. Melville included the biology of whales and the technology of whaling within the frame of *Moby Dick.* Doing so enlarged his story from an account of one person's obsession to a mythic enactment of man's self-aggrandizing and self-destructive assault on the wonderfully complex natural order. However, in social research, when balancing clarity of focus on the one hand and ambition on the other, clarity of focus might be given preference. It's hard enough to do a limited study well.

Quite apart from the issue of its breadth, deciding just what areas the substantive frame should include can be difficult. Not only is it likely that an initial listing of areas of useful information would be incomplete, but there may be several different approaches that could be taken to explanation or description, each of which would require development of different areas.

Early in my career I was asked by a consulting group to undertake a study of a university-based executive development program. The aim was to help the administrators of the program understand the program's problems and strengths. Without giving the matter a lot of thought, I defined the study's frame as the experiences of the executives during their residency in the program, and so I investigated relationships among the executives and between faculty and executives, the executives' reactions to classes and colloquia, and the home life of the executives while they were in residency. Only later did I learn that the program's administrators would have preferred a frame that included the use executives made of the program when they were back at their jobs. The administrators, reasonably enough, wanted to know whether the program was doing the students any good. Because I did not develop the study's substantive frame in consultation with members of its primary audience, I omitted issues of critical importance to them.

If there is a clearly defined audience for the study—if, for example, the study has been commissioned, as it was in this instance—the study's proposed substantive frame might be examined from the perspective of that audience. If representatives of that audience are available, the frame might usefully be discussed with them.

The study's substantive frame decides who should be interviewed and what they should be asked. The "Who should be interviewed?" question will be considered in this chapter; the "What should they be asked?" question will be considered in the next.

PANELS AND SAMPLES

There are two distinct categories of potential respondents: people who are uniquely able to be informative because they are expert in an area or were privileged witnesses to an event; and people who, taken together, display what happens within a population affected by a situation or event.

Suppose the aim of our study is to describe an event or development or institution: the management of a political convention, the operation of a nursing service, or the system governing the granting of divorce. We would do best to interview people who are especially knowledgeable or experienced. To enrich or extend our understanding, we might also want to include as respondents people who view our topic from different perspectives or who know about different aspects of it. Our aim would be to develop a wide-ranging *panel of knowledgeable informants*. Each member of the panel would be chosen because he or she could significantly instruct us.

Take the study of a bill that made it through Congress. We might want to report, eventually, on the bill's success as a way of illuminating governmental functioning. To produce a dense description of what happened, we might talk with members of Congress who backed the bill and with people on their staff, with members of Congress who opposed the bill and people on *their* staff, and with reporters who cover Congress. We would try to talk with everyone in a position to know what happened in the hope that each would provide part of the story and that all of their accounts together would provide the story in full.

Our approach would be different if we wanted to study the experiences or behaviors of people who have some common characteristic, people who are, in this respect, in the same boat. Suppose we wanted to know about the experiences with retirement of a sample of former professionals or how single parents manage everything they have to do or what is the impact on people's morale and functioning of going through marital separation. For these studies what we need is a sample of people who together can represent the population of concern. If before we wanted a panel of knowledgeable informants, what we want now is a *sample of representatives*.

Often the study of an issue can be cast in a way that requires a panel of informants but with what seems to be only slight redefinition can be recast to require a sample of representatives. Take the issue of child visitation after divorce. If we define the study's aim as learning what is the institutional structure that governs what is done, we would want a panel of informants: scholars of family law, judges, lawyers, family court officers, and, possibly, a few parents. But if we define the study's aim as learning how divorced mothers and fathers arrange visitation and how they are affected by their arrangements, we would want a sample of divorced mothers and fathers who might together represent the range of parental experiences.

We might, of course, decide to do both studies. We might want a panel of informants to tell us about the institution of child visitation and a sample of parents to tell us how it works in practice. We would then be doing two distinct studies. They would enrich each other, but our work load would be greater.

Sometimes a respondent can be treated either as a representative of a population or as an informant, although not both at the same time. In a pilot study I did of burn victims a respondent was first an informant on the nature of advocacy organizations for burn victims—he was a member of one—and then, in a later interview, a reporter on what it had been like when he himself was burned. My relationship with the respondent was a bit different in the two interviews: in the first he was an expert instructing me; in the second he was a former victim whose story I was helping to elicit.

THE PANEL OF INFORMANTS

The idea in a panel of informants is to include as respondents the people who together can provide the information the study requires. How do we decide just who these people are? The kind of entity we want to learn about makes a difference.

1. *Events.* We may want to report on a happening like a flood, an epidemic, a riot, or a football game; that is, an event that involves people of different backgrounds, with different perspectives, who became involved in different ways. To get a sense of the scope of the event we might begin with professionals or experts: meteorologists in a study of a flood or public health officers in a study of an epidemic. The professionals and experts can suggest the issues that have been attended to in the past and that ought to be attended to now. There may be a literature with which we should become acquainted, and the experts may be able to direct us to studies of similar events. Following this, it would make sense to find people who were caught up in the event, so that we could learn how it was experienced.

2. *An organization.* We might want to study an institution or an organization of coordinated effort: a lying-in hospital, a school, the Navy. Here people in well-defined roles meet to produce planned events. In a study of this sort we can expect to encounter subgroups, or cliques, and politics. Interviews should be held with people in different jobs on different levels, in different relationships to the institution, and from different informal groups.

A study of an organization requires that the investigator succeed in obtaining informants without being perceived as an intrusive foreign presence. How to survive in the field is discussed in books on field methods, but it may be useful here to note that success is dependent on a certain amount of social grace, including sensitivity, considerateness, and tact; self-confidence; awareness of the politics of the institution; and persistence. Of great value is the ability to move through the institution without being blocked by barriers designed to protect its staff from bothersome outsiders. Being unobtrusive can help. It has been said of one brilliant field worker: "Other people have presence; he has absence." But a self-confident presence can also work.

3. *A loose collectivity.* We might want to study a collection of people in touch with one another but not as closely linked as those in an organization; for example, a community, a network of associates, or the residents of a neighborhood. With luck it may be possible to find someone who is central and knowledgeable and who can provide both orientation and sponsorship, like William F. Whyte's Doc.[1] Failing this, any member may provide entry, but the sponsorship of higher-ranking members will count for more.

4. *A social institution.* Many social forms, like marriage or parenthood or the profession of politics, help shape people's lives. To learn about these forms, we have to interview a sample of the people who have been affected by them. In addition, it is likely that there are people who are studying the social institution, and there may be others who serve as therapists for people negatively affected by it. At least a few of these professionals should be consulted.

The Key Informant

A good person to start with in any study requiring a panel is a knowledgeable insider willing to serve as an informant on informants. But others who might help include a knowledgeable marginal or disaffected figure within the system. Such a person may be more willing to describe the system's failings than would someone central to the system and committed to it. Still another possibility would be a retiree, a person who has a career's experience with the system and now has time to reminisce.[2] I myself prefer the informed insider, assuming I can find someone like that who is willing to coach me. But all sorts of people can help.

Orienting figures may need to feel confident of you before they can comfortably be candid. Being vouched for by a mutual acquaintance can be useful. Failing that, it can help to be able to say that someone known to both of you suggested the contact. The implied sponsorship of government or foundation funding for the project may also help.

But it can happen that people you would like to consult prove inaccessible to you; your calls are fielded by a lower-level staff member who turns you away. When this has happened to me, my response has been to think about getting the experience into my notes and to try again. When it keeps on happening, I try to be philosophical about being frozen out, do something else for a while, and then reconsider my strategy. But, in truth, the experience is hard on morale.

Sometimes there is no obvious orienting figure, or there is no need for one because the people to be interviewed are immediately apparent. In a study of a disaster there will be officials and professionals whose job it is to deal with the disaster and the people who are affected by it. Orientation may not seem necessary. Or it may happen that you simply cannot find someone to direct your efforts. How then should you proceed? Two principles suggest themselves: One principle is to start with people who are available to you and easy to interview, especially if having interviewed them will make you more informed and legitimized when you proceed to interview others. A second principle is to have your early interviews with people who are of marginal importance to the study so that if you make mistakes it won't matter so much.

How Large a Panel?

In a study in which there are a great many potential informants it might seem as though interviewing could go on forever. In a study of the functioning of today's divorce laws, with judges and lawyers and divorcees and their families all to be interviewed, when do you quit? When do you decide you have interviewed enough people? The best answer is that you stop when you encounter diminishing returns, when the information you obtain is redundant or peripheral, when what you do learn that is new adds too little to what you already know to justify the time and cost of the interviewing.

Biographers, whose research by its nature requires a panel of informants, regularly have the problem of deciding when to stop interviewing. After having interviewed the occupational associates of the biographer's subject, the subject's close friends, the members of the subject's immediate family, and the people who were close to the subject as a child, should the biographer continue with the college roommate, the distant cousin, the fleeting acquaintance? Even the most indefatigable biographer must call a halt somewhere. In general, when further inquiry will add little to the story, stop inquiring.

REPRESENTATIONAL SAMPLES

Suppose that we want to interview not a panel of people in peculiarly good positions to know but, rather, a sample of people who together can adequately represent the experiences of a larger group.

Probability Sampling for Qualitative Research

One approach is to develop a sample that can be argued on grounds of mathematical probability to be not too different from the population in which we are interested. If everyone in a population has the same chance of turning up in the sample, we have a probability sample.

If the people who make up a probability sample are chosen in such a way that each choice is independent of every other choice, and the sample includes at least 60 respondents, then the sample is likely to be a fairly good representation of the population in the sense that every important characteristic of the population is likely to have one or more representatives in the sample. A sample of this sort and size will, 19 times out of 20, include at least one instance of any phenomenon that occurs at least 5% of the time in the larger population. (The probability that a one-time-in-twenty phenomenon will not appear at all in a simple random sample of size 60 is .046.) Larger samples are still more likely to provide adequate representation.[3]

A sample can be a probability sample only if respondents are selected randomly. Random selection is not the same as haphazard selection. Random means, rather, that the members of the sample were selected by a procedure that could equally well have selected absolutely anybody in the population. One such procedure would be to choose names from a population list. For example, we could draw a sample of the community from the list of names in the telephone book. Our actual procedure might be to let a table of random numbers dictate page numbers, column numbers, and line numbers in the book. We would have to worry, though, about overrepresenting people who had multiple listings and about not representing at all those who had no phones or whose numbers were unlisted. As this example may suggest, designing a probability sample is a fairly specialized activity, and someone who hasn't done it before might do well to consult a sampling statistician.

Often, the list of names we have is limited to a company or a region. Can we generalize to people in other companies or regions? Yes, but not by claiming that the sample is likely, on grounds of statistical probability, to be representative. A sample can be a random sample only of the population from which it is drawn. If we want to generalize beyond that population, we must invoke other rationales.

Samples That Attempt to Maximize Range

We may not want a probability sample from a population even if we are able to obtain one. The larger a probability sample, the more likely it is that it will reproduce in miniature the population of cases from which it is drawn. Instances that occur frequently in the population will occur frequently in the sample. But if instances that occur frequently are very much like one another, the sample will be filled with near duplicates. Precisely because it replicates the population, a probability sample might produce more typical cases, and fewer atypical cases, than we need. We will be learning again and again about the same thing.

Rather than choose respondents randomly, and thus risk unwanted duplication in our sample, we may prefer to select respondents purposively so that we obtain instances of all the important dissimilar forms present in the larger population. We may further want each of the dissimilar forms represented about the same number of times, so that we have the same knowledge base for each. This kind of sample might be referred to as a sample chosen to maximize range.

We are particularly likely to want a sample chosen to maximize range rather than a probability sample if our sample will be small. If we plan to work with samples much smaller than 60 (samples of 30, say) we may not trust random selection to provide us with instances of significant developments that occur infrequently.

With large samples we may choose to maximize range in order to avoid having too many instances of the same type, and with small samples we may choose to maximize range in order to ensure that our sample contains instances of infrequent types. In sum, whenever we conduct qualitative interview studies, we ought to consider sampling to achieve range as an alternative to random sampling. There are advantages to each approach to sampling. Random sampling will provide us with a picture of the population as well as of particular instances, and sampling for range will ensure that our sample includes instances displaying significant variation.

But if in sampling for range your aim is to obtain instances displaying significant variation, you must know in advance what might constitute significant variation and how to find the people who display it. Take, as an example, the problem of learning what the impact is of moving into a new community. You might consider any of the following suggestions:[4]

1. Look for contrast in what may be significant independent variables. If you want to show that adaptation to geographical migration is dependent on the length of time available for planning, make sure you have in your sample instances where there was a good deal of anticipatory time and instances where there was little.
2. Look for contrast in what may be significant dependent variables. If you want to contrast those who have adapted to geographical migration and those who have not, include instances of each.
3. Look for contrast in context. If you suspect that the experience of a newcomer is heavily dependent on the extent to which networks are already established in the community into which the

newcomer moves, do some interviewing in a new development and some in a long-established neighborhood.

4. Look for contrast in dynamics. If you want to show that one of the problems experienced by newcomer couples is that the husband is absorbed by the need to prove himself in his new workplace and so becomes emotionally unavailable to his wife, include in your sample couples in which the husband is unemployed or self-employed or in which the wife has the more demanding career.

If you have a list of possible respondents to work from, you may be able to establish informal quotas that will maximize the heterogeneity of your sample in some respect. You can decide what sort of contrast you want among your respondents and, as you recruit from the list, give preference to the potential respondents whom you need to fill your quotas.[5] To know whether potential respondents have characteristics you want, you can include "filter" questions in the telephone calls you make to arrange for interviews. In our study of retirement, for example, we used the filter question "Might you retire within the next year or so?"

One argument for generalizing to a larger population from a sample chosen to maximize range depends on being able to claim that the sample included the full variety of instances that would be encountered anywhere. If we find uniformities in our sample despite our having adequately represented the range of instances, then those uniformities must be general. If we find differences among types of instance, then those differences should hold in a larger population. We will not be able to say anything about the proportion of instances of different types in a larger population, since the proportion in our sample might be very different from the proportion elsewhere. But we can say what the various types are like, no matter where they appear.

Convenience Sampling

The third approach to obtaining a sample of respondents, in addition to choosing them on a probability basis or choosing them to provide a useful range of instances, is to accept pretty much whomever we can get. This is a sample of convenience.

Some people who do qualitative research are willing to base their reports on informal interviews with friends, family, and chance acquaintances. Their examples are introduced with a phrase like "An acquaintance of mine told me that . . ." Nor is this the approach only of those who have no ambition to contribute to general understanding. In attempting to learn about a group difficult to penetrate—gypsies, migrant workers, the very rich—it can be a breakthrough to find *any* member of the group, any member at all, willing to serve as an informant and respondent.

Sometimes the kind of people wanted for study are unusual in a population and, in addition, not listed anywhere. In the paragraphs below I give some suggestions for nevertheless obtaining a sample.[6]

You may know a few people in the population you want to study. Start with those who are available to you and ask them for referrals. If you don't know anyone in the population you want to study, ask for help from people you think are likely to know such people. Or tell all your friends and acquaintances that you want to find someone who could be instructive about your topic. This use of referrals to build a sample is described by Diane Ehrensaft, who wanted to interview parents who were sharing child-care responsibilities:

> Through word of mouth and my own personal contacts, I began to generate a pool of people who fit the bill of two people, a man and a woman, sharing the position of primary parent in their family. I had no trouble finding potential couples to talk to. People told me eagerly about friends or friends of friends, and I soon found myself generating, both geographically and socially, an arena well beyond my own circles.[7]

If the people you want to interview are likely to know others like themselves, you can ask *them* for referrals. Then the referrals can provide still further referrals. This technique is known as *snowball sampling*.

snowball sampling

Another method of locating respondents is to advertise for volunteers. Better still, you might arrange for a story about your study to appear in a newspaper. In a study of retirement I needed to interview women who had retired from administrative and managerial jobs. A story about the study and my desire to interview appropriate women appeared in a newspaper and brought several volunteers.

You might find a congregating place for people of the kind you want to study. For example, if you want to learn about people who do something illegal, you may be able to find people in jail for the crime—although they will be, by definition, the ones who didn't get away with it. That's how Donald Cressey was able to learn about embezzling.[8]

People who suffer from an affliction may have formed a support group.

Leaders of support groups can suggest potential respondents and are also likely to be repositories of information regarding the condition. It is almost always a good idea to check an encyclopedia of associations to see if a group has been established that specializes in your concern. If the group is in your locale, you might be able to visit.

Social agencies, schools, and hospitals can sometimes provide the kind of people you are interested in. To be sure, you will probably be required first to undergo the scrutiny of gatekeepers, research committees, and committees for the protection of human subjects. It helps to be on the staff or to work with someone on the staff.[9]

These suggestions are not intended to minimize the ingenuity that may be needed to find appropriate respondents. For a pilot study of newcomers to the Boston area I started by asking the gas company for a copy of its most recent list of "turn-ons" and was told that the company guarded the list closely. It took the intercession of a university vice president to obtain the list, and I then discovered that it was several months out of date and thus useless as a list of people who had just moved in. I thought of contacting local newcomer clubs, but before doing so I made connection with a Welcome Wagon representative. She supplied me with names of newcomer couples in her area until the central office of her national organization reminded her that the information she was sharing was proprietary. Luckily, we had by then completed all the interviews we needed.[10]

Arguments for the Generalizability of the Findings of Convenience Samples

A problem with all samples selected only because they are conveniently obtained is that we may not have good bases for generalization. With a probability sample, generalization is straightforward, based on mathematical argument. With a sample in which it has been possible to maximize range, it can be argued that instances of every important variation have been studied. With other sorts of samples other arguments must be relied on. Here are five arguments that might be advanced to justify the attempt to generalize from the findings of convenience samples—and one that should not be, although it sometimes is.

Respondents' Own Assessments of Generalizability. Respondents may be able to judge the extent to which others in their situations behave similarly or differently and have the same or different experiences. Their appraisals are not conclusive. A respondent who says, "I'm like most other people I know in my situation" is not necessarily right. "Pluralistic ignorance", in which people are like one another and don't know it, certainly exists, and so does underestimating the way in which one is different. But knowledgeable appraisals may be more likely. The question to ask about a respondent's appraisal is whether the respondent is in a position to know. I would trust an executive who says that most executives check around to learn the size of the end-of-the-year bonuses being given to others in order to know how to value their own; it is something an executive would be likely to observe. Sometimes respondents can offer evidence for their appraisals: they have talked with others in their situation about the topic or have observed others' behavior with respect to it.

Similarity of Dynamics and Constraints. Insofar as the dynamics of the group we study and the constraints to which they are subjected decide their behavior, we can expect the same behavior from any other group with the same dynamics and the same constraints. On this basis we might argue that what was learned about postdivorce father–child relationships from a study that was conducted in a New England city could be generalized to postdivorce father–child relationships throughout the country. The relationships, it could be argued, would involve the same emotions of parent and child and would be subject to the same constraints of postmarital life.

Depth. An idea that may be intuitively appealing is that underneath the accidents of individuality lies an identity in structure and functioning among all members of our species. As Ralph Waldo Emerson put it, referring to an orator, "The deeper he dives into his privatest secretest presentiment—to his wonder he finds, this is the most . . . universally true."[11]

The problem, of course, is to know when we are dealing with a deep and presumably universal phenomenon. One guide might be to ask whether the phenomenon is necessary to the functioning of whatever it is we are studying or is closely linked to something necessary or is an expression of it. Yet we must be aware that we are working with theory, and we might be wrong.

The study of bereavement provides an example. We might assume that grief results from loss of a relationship of attachment, a relationship in which there is a sense of strong linkage between the self and the other, almost of being augmented by the other. We might also assume that both the capacity to form attachments and the emotions attending their loss are universal or nearly so. We would therefore believe that findings regarding the experience of grief would be generalizable, whatever the quality of the respondent sample. In contrast, we might suppose that mourning practices, the way people display their grief, are easily modified by time and place. We would, therefore, want a representative sample before generalizing about mourning practices. But it should be noted that our belief that we need a better sample for a study of mourning practices than for a study of grief depends on a theory regarding the nature of attachment, loss, and mourning.

Theory Independent of Qualifiers. Akin to the argument based on the purported depth (and therefore universality) of whatever it is we are describing is the argument that there is no justification for questioning the exportation of a theory based on our sample. We might acknowledge that our sample is not representative but argue that there is no reason for the theory to be limited to the sample from which it was developed.

Donald Cressey studied embezzlers in prison to learn about embezzling. His was hardly a representative sample of all embezzlers, since it included only those who had been caught and convicted. (But how else find a sample of embezzlers at all?) Despite this skewed sample, Cressey offered generalizations about the source of all embezzlement, not just unsuccessful embezzlement. He said that embezzling occurs when someone in a position to embezzle can justify violating others' trust in order to solve a nonshareable problem. He argued that his theory could be applied to all embezzlement because it was inherently plausible, it was invariably consistent with his data, and—although he left this implicit—there was no reason his theory should be true only of imprisoned embezzlers.[12]

Corroboration from Other Studies. The findings and conclusions of other studies can sometimes buttress those of our qualitative interview study. They will not be able to corroborate every point of our study—if they could, our study would have been unnecessary. But the more we have of such corroboration for our findings, the more credible our findings become. This is especially the case when the results of a quantitative study can anchor a discussion based on qualitative interviewing. For example, a discussion of single parent overload might be anchored by a quantitative study's findings regarding the disposable time available to parents in various types of households.

An Invalid Argument for Generalization from Convenience Samples

A sample that is not chosen randomly cannot be claimed to be representative even if some of its demographic characteristics match those of the country as a whole. One author described using snowball sampling to obtain a sample of respondents who, with a few exceptions, lived in West Coast urban areas. The author then argued that the sample should be taken as representative of a national population because it matched the national population on age at time of first marriage, number of children, length of marriage, and proportion divorced. However, absence of significant difference between a sample and a larger population on one or on a dozen characteristics does not make a sample representative of the larger population on characteristics that have not been examined. A snowball sample, for one thing, will always underrepresent those who have few social contacts and will therefore underrepresent every belief and experience that is associated with having few social contacts.

Comparison Cases

In qualitative interview studies, anyone who has anything to teach us is a desirable interviewee. Often it is useful to interview at least a few people who might constitute comparison cases. In a study of men in responsible positions, we were several times misled by the filter questions we used to establish that a potential respondent was actually in a responsible job. As a result, we mistakenly selected into our sample men in occupations different from those we wanted to learn about. We interviewed the men anyway and found their contrasting experience to be instructive. And in a study of single parents, we intentionally interviewed people in intact marriages as a way of understanding better what we were being told by single parents.

Should you have a full-scale comparison group? Often, it is all an investigator can do to collect information from an adequate sample of people in a situation; to also collect information from an adequate sample of people *not* in the situation can seem an unmanageable burden. It may also seem unnecessary. Why give time and energy to the study of people who by definition aren't the people you want to learn about?

And yet, how can you be sure that phenomena you associate with the situation you are studying are in fact more frequent there than among people who are not in that situation? In studying single parents it appeared to me that their children were asked to do a great deal. It made sense that this would be linked to the understaffing of the single-parent home and to the special need the single parent would have for the children's help. But, just to be sure, I did some interviewing of parents in two-parent homes. I discovered, to my surprise, that parents in two-parent homes expected their children to do the same sorts of chores that parents in single-parent homes expected their children to do. The difference wasn't in the parents' expectations, it was in the firmness of those expectations. Parents in two-parent homes would excuse their children from chores if the children had something else to do and would accept forgetfulness as an explanation for noncompliance. Parents in single-parent homes could not tolerate their children's noncompliance. In the two-parent home parents wanted their children to help so that the children would learn to be responsible. In the single-parent home the parent needed the children to help because the parent could not manage otherwise. It took comparative data to make this clear.

Judith Wallerstein is properly recognized for her contributions to our understanding of the stresses experienced by children following parental divorce.[13] But many of her readers have wondered whether children whose parents maintained intact marriages might not share some of these stresses and whether children whose parents are unhappily married might not experience still other stresses. Without comparison cases there is no way to be sure.

An investigator who does not have comparison cases may argue, explicitly or implicitly, that a development in the group under study must be peculiar to that group because its presence outside the group has not been noted. Or the investigator may argue that the process leading to a special development is apparent, that the process could occur only in the group under study, or that members of the studied population affirm that they too have noticed that they are different in this special way. Any of these arguments can help, but none is likely to be as convincing as arguments based on comparative study. Is marriage better in couples who share parenting than in couples who do not? Diane Ehrensaft tries to answer this question affirmatively on the basis of her sample of shared-parenting couples.[14] But she did not have a comparison sample of marriages in which couples do not share parenting, so her argument comes close to being, "Well, their marriages look better." She also says that if you consider the logic of the situation, the marriages would have to be pretty good or the couple couldn't keep doing shared parenting. And there doesn't seem to be a high divorce rate among them, although it's hard to know. Without a comparison group, this is the best she can do.

Even if resources have already been stretched by the effort to obtain adequate representation of target cases, it is likely to be a good idea to include at least a few comparison cases. Statistical comparison may not be possible, but even so, the comparison cases can correct what would otherwise be a tendency to exaggerate the peculiarities of the sample that is the focus of the study.

Conceptually Important Cases

Sometimes cases that occur infrequently should be sought out because they are significant conceptually. Take house husbands. I have occasionally presented findings from a study I conducted of occupationally successful men that dealt with, among other things, the division of household labor in their homes. I would report that these men operated from traditional understandings, though with flexibility, and that I imagined that other men did as well. Regularly, it seemed, someone in the audience would ask how I could maintain that position, given the existence of contented house husbands. "I know a man," I would be told, "who stays home and takes care of the kids while his wife goes out to work. And he is perfectly happy with the arrangement."

House husbands, men who devote themselves to child care and home maintenance while their wives work, are statistically unusual. In a random sample of a hundred families you might find two or three.[15] But house husbands play a role in people's thinking about family life, and if you are going to lecture on the division of marital labor, it is probably a good thing to have interviewed a few house husbands.

I found two house husbands by asking around when attending conferences on "men's issues." I later met another house husband through personal acquaintances. I don't pretend now to be an expert on this way of dividing domestic labor, but I do have real images in my mind when I talk about house husbands. Now if I am asked about house husbands, I can make clear my limited information but then describe the adaptations

I have witnessed. I can say that each of the men I talked with had assimilated his roles and responsibilities to a sense of coping, of making things work, that struck me as masculine in style and that, in addition, each maintained a sense of being involved with the world outside the home: one as a writer, the second as a pioneer helping to establish a new form of masculinity, and the third as a former and future head of a small business who had decided with his wife that his wife's greater earning power justified his staying home for now.

An N of 1

Compared with survey research studies, qualitative interview studies collect more material from fewer respondents. Studies of a single case take this to an extreme. The single case may be advanced as valuable because it so effectively displays the complex interplay of particular circumstance and the regularities of the human condition. Furthermore, the density of detail possible in the presentation of the single case makes for drama and immediacy, which can foster an emotional level of understanding based on identification. Authors of studies of single cases may also want to generalize some of their observations. The justifications for generalizability they offer would be those offered for qualitative interview studies done with small convenience samples; for example, that the constraints the subject experienced and the motives the subject expressed were common to all those in the subject's situation.

To these arguments for the single case may be added the idea that the case displays a life significant in itself. Furthermore, insofar as the subject may have been witness to significant events, the subject may provide not only autobiographical material but also a valuable observer's report.

Consider the book *The Narrative of Hosea Hudson: His Life as a Negro Communist in the South,* by Nell Irvin Painter. In it Painter presents edited and rearranged materials from dozens of interviews with a respondent who was "a black workingman in a southern city in mid-century." More than that, he had been a union organizer, a member of the Communist party, a husband and father, and a man with his own ambition to write. His singularities weaken the extent to which he can be taken as exemplary of men in his situation, yet his story makes vivid the economic, social, and emotional problems confronting all black workingmen of that time and place.

One problem in dealing with the case study is to decide to what substantive frame it should be assigned. Helen and Everett Hughes raise this issue in their introduction to Helen Hughes's interview-based life history of a female drug addict: "The story she [the informant] left can be read in a variety of ways: as a psychiatric case study, as an account of the use of narcotics in an American city, and so on. But beyond this, it is a story of one person's journey through the city and of what that journey did to her."[16] The Hugheses here note three frames to which the case study may be assigned: personal pathology, narcotics user, urban dweller. Undoubtedly other frames could also be considered, such as "young woman without family or funds." Perhaps we learn about issues within all these frames, but unless we have one frame clearly in mind, the lessons of the case tend to fade.

Plummer has remarked that case study research tends to be "the strategy of the poor—of the researcher who has little hope of gaining a large and representative sample from which bold generalization may be made."[17] However, case research can absorb as much data-gathering effort and analytic time as would research based on larger samples. Case research is different primarily because it anchors its potential for generalization in the welter of detail of the single instance. Generalization can then become uncertain (and rest heavily on the theory we bring to the case), but in compensation we have the coherence, depth, development, and drama of a single fully understood life.

RECRUITING RESPONDENTS

Having decided on the people you want to interview, you must now gain their cooperation. How do you do it?

key!

Sometimes a telephone call alone can be enough. There can be appeal in a request for an interview. People may welcome the chance to make their situation known or just to have a break in the day. People marooned at home tend to welcome interviewers. So do people with time on their hands, like the hospitalized or the retired. So may people in crisis, such as people going through marital separation, although this is chancy and may change for the same person from day to day. But most people, given adequate assurance about the legitimacy of the interviewer and the confidentiality of what they say, are willing to talk.

yes I agree!

On the other hand, interviewers may need the right sponsorship or topic or approach to avoid being turned down by people whose occupations have accustomed them to asking the questions, including physicians and the police. Indeed, all sorts of things, including geography, can increase the likelihood that a request for an interview will be turned down. In a study of the uses of planned environments such as museums and fairs, my first interviews were on the grounds of the Seattle World's Fair. I found it easy there simply to stop people and ask them about their experiences. My clipboard was a sort of badge, identifying me as a person whose job entitled him to ask questions, and people seemed happy to talk to me. Doing the same thing in the same way at the New York World's Fair a couple of years later, I found people much less willing to talk with me. New Yorkers, apparently, had learned to be skeptical of inquiring strangers—with or without clipboards. But I had no trouble conducting the same sort of interviews at a restored village not far from New York. It may be that in the small space of the restoration it was more evident that I had management approval.

A number of devices can increase the likelihood of recruiting people. We have already noted that it can help in establishing a relationship with an orienting figure in an informant study if you are able to name a mutual friend or colleague and say "So-and-so suggested I call you." The usefulness of a vouching figure extends to members of representational samples. A sociologist found it easier to interview IV drug users after a member of his team who was himself a former drug user spread the message that the sociologist would be around and was all right.

There is a downside to the use of intermediaries that applies, though with less force, to the referrals of snowball sampling. The respondent's presentation of self may be affected by his or her awareness of the intermediary's sponsorship. This may be especially true if the intermediary helps arrange the interview.

Sponsorship by impressive groups or by public figures does not have this drawback. Such sponsorship should, of course, be appropriate to the study if it is to be useful. For a study of businessmen, a business association would be appropriate; for a study of family life, a sponsoring group of priests, ministers, and rabbis. A grant from a government agency is usually viewed as testimony to legitimacy, as is a position at a university. Boards of advisers can serve, in part, as endorsers.

In most of the studies I have done my only sponsorship has been whatever might be implied by government funding and university affiliation. It seemed to me not worth the time it would take to obtain anything more. But studies whose subject is likely to put off potential respondents might be helped by reassuring sponsorship.

When my colleagues and I have tried to obtain the participation of respondents for a community sample of representatives, we have generally sent the potential respondents a letter explaining the study, arguing for the importance of their participation, and saying someone would telephone. Despite the letter, the call from my office to potential respondents often appeared to surprise them. One of the people working with me hit on the idea of starting the conversation with, "We sent you a letter last week. It could easily have gotten in with your junk mail, but do you happen to remember it?"   *Two different things.*

A checklist of items the investigator might be prepared to tell respondents in a first phone call could include the following: who the investigator is (which ordinarily means what the investigator's job or position is), the reasons for the study, the study's sponsorship, how the potential respondent's name was found, why the potential respondent was selected, what the purpose of the interview is, what will be asked of the respondent, whether confidentiality is guaranteed, and whether the interview will be tape-recorded.[18] It is sometimes useful to ask a few questions to decide whether a potential respondent meets a study's eligibility requirements: is in the right age range or occupational bracket.

In a few studies, I have begun with a telephone call and told potential respondents that a descriptive letter would follow. In other studies I have simply telephoned, without any letter sent at any time. People who do survey research tell me that they prefer not to telephone for an appointment, since that makes it too easy for the respondent to refuse to see them. They would rather just show up. I doubt that just showing up would work for qualitative interviewing. But here, as elsewhere, if in a particular study it seems like a good idea, try it. How else can you learn what works?

Where it is especially important to obtain an interview with a particular respondent it can make sense to engage in a concerted sales effort. A writer of books based on interviews wanted to interview me about loneliness, an issue on which I'd worked. The writer's assistant called to tell me that the writer wanted to interview me and that some of the writer's books and articles were being mailed to me. A few days later I received a package containing a paperback collection of the writer's interviews, copies of magazine and newspaper reviews praising the writer's books, and a copy of a magazine story about the writer. A couple of weeks later I received copies of two more of the writer's interview collections. About two weeks after that I received a call from the writer, asking for the interview. I could hardly not agree.

On another occasion an English journalist who wanted to interview me called from England for the appointment. Transatlantic calls get my attention, and I think I am in this regard typical. I wouldn't go so far as to recommend that appointments with difficult-to-recruit respondents be made from a transatlantic telephone, but there is much to be said for letting respondents know that their participation will be valued.

Also important in recruitment success is an ability to keep pitching the study until acceptance is obtained. In the study of occupationally successful men, we wanted to interview our respondents three times over the course of a couple of months. That was a lot to ask of busy men. We began by sending a letter to potential respondents selected on the basis of occupation from street lists of upper-income suburbs. Our interviewers then telephoned the men for appointments. A dozen or so efforts produced discouraging results: about two-thirds of those we contacted turned us down. After a few turndowns interviewers dreaded making the calls.

If we had accepted this low response rate, we would have studied only men who were unusually friendly to the idea of being interviewed. I tried doing recruiting myself. My acceptance rate ran about 50%, but one acceptance for every two calls was still a low response rate. And I too was dispirited by the frequent rejection.

However, one staff member (I will call her Mrs. Adams) seemed to be doing fine with recruiting. She reported the astonishing acceptance rate of 80%. I asked her to show me how she did it.

I role-played a potential respondent. When Mrs. Adams asked me if I would participate, I said I was too busy. Mrs. Adams seemed not to notice. She continued in a pleasant and engaging fashion to describe what the interview would cover. I said, "No, I'd rather not participate." Mrs. Adams said, "Yes, of course, I understand, but I want to tell you why the study is being done and who is doing it." And she went on to tell me about the sponsorship of the study and the kinds of questions that would be asked and how important it would be to have my perspective. She said that the interview would help establish the nature of the stresses in managerial and administrative work and might contribute to their amelioration. She said that I would find the interview interesting and that it would be held whenever and wherever suited me. By now I was intrigued by the study and flattered to be so wanted, as well as just a bit exasperated by being unable to escape. I said, "All right, let's set a time."

Surprisingly, Mrs. Adams, although a demon recruiter, turned out not to be a very good interviewer. Her ability to seem responsive while

continuing firmly on her own track, which made her a wonderful recruiter, produced difficulties for her as an interviewer. In recruiting she
got people to see the world her way. In interviewing she tried to do the
same thing. The transcripts of Mrs. Adams's interviews showed her talking as much as did her respondents. She would continue with a line of
questioning even when the respondent had begun to talk about something
else. She would become impatient when a respondent hesitated and would
supply what she believed to be the thought for which the respondent was
searching; and, because she didn't listen well, her suggestions could be
way off the mark. After enough of this treatment, the respondent's answers would become brief, but Mrs. Adams seemed not to notice.

Mrs. Adams and I had many a struggle before she accepted that it was
undesirable to interrupt a respondent's account. Once she accepted this
principle, she became reluctant to redirect respondents at all, with the
consequence that her respondents could wander into total irrelevance.

And yet Mrs. Adams's willingness to continue an interview despite the
respondent's indications that everything had already been said meant that
several times she obtained important material other interviewers would
have missed. The moral, I guess, is that in social research, as in life, never
undervalue persistence.

CHAPTER 3

PREPARATION FOR
INTERVIEWING

WHAT DO YOU INTERVIEW ABOUT?

I was trying to think through how qualitative interviewers formulate the questions they include in their interviews when I had to break off to go to a lunch with a colleague who has since become a friend. My colleague does a fair amount of interviewing and is, I think, good at it. I decided that I would interview him about how he formulated his interview questions. I could at the same time monitor the source of my own questions.

While walking to the restaurant I could recognize in myself an almost kinesthetic sense of the material I needed for this chapter. I needed dense descriptions that would fully display the process of question formulation. This self-observation suggested that a first step in question formulation is a sense of what would be the right kind of information.

A few minutes after we sat down to eat, and without much introduction, I asked my colleague how he went about learning from respondents. I was about to say that it might be good to talk about a specific incident, but he was already answering my question. However, he seemed to think I was interested not in the pedestrian issue of how he decided to ask this question or that one but rather in the deeper, more fundamental, issue of how he presented himself and his project to respondents. He said, "I show that I want to learn and that I'm worth teaching. That I know something, but not everything. So they can inform me, and I'll understand."

This was not what I needed to know. But I felt too uncomfortable to say, "How, exactly, do you work out what you will ask? Tell me about your most recent interview and how you did it." In ordinary conversation it's rude to pin people down by asking for specific incidents. So I asked the rather general question "How do you get to the questions you actually ask?" After a moment my colleague said, "I try to get to know the person. It isn't like there's just one question I'm going to ask."

Again, not what I needed to know. Now I did ask, "How about the most recent interview you did?" And then, maybe because I wanted permission for my questioning, I added, "Could I ask about that? How you decided what you'd ask?"

Instead of answering my question, my colleague held it up for inspection. "That's a good question," he said. Then he thought about it. Then he told me a story: He had spent a lot of time with the head of a government agency, from whom he hoped to learn about the workings of the agency. He went to meetings with the man and regularly talked with him in the late afternoon. Finally, after one such talk, the official told him that he now understood what it was my colleague wanted to write about, that he could see that the story would be important and valuable. But he wasn't going to let my colleague do the story because it would be an embarrassment to him and his agency. He liked my colleague and wished him well but would see to it that no one in his agency or anywhere else in government would cooperate with him. "And," my colleague said to me, "that was the end of the enterprise."

I wondered if my colleague, in telling me this story, was also telling me that he didn't want to be interviewed and would like to wish me well and send me off. Still, here we were at lunch, with another three-quarters of an hour before it would be time to return to our offices. I thought I would try once more. I noticed that I gave extra effort to being agreeable. I relaxed my voice and tried to make the next question casual, as though my questioning were no big deal, just that I happened to be working on a book about interview studies and found the issue interesting. I said, "I remember your saying, a while ago, that you were going to be doing some interviewing. Can you think about a specific interview? Maybe the one that was most recent. How did you work out what you would ask? Did you work out your questions in advance?"

And now, for some reason, my colleague told me what I wanted to know. He said, yes, he could think of a specific interview. A week before our lunch he had interviewed someone for a book on which he was working. The morning of his interview he had listed the ten to twelve questions he wanted answered. He was able to list them because he knew, in general, the kind of information that would give his account substance. The questions he listed were the ones important to the book that he thought his respondent could answer.

This incident seems to me to display the determinants of the questions we ask:

1. *The problem.* Here my problem was to find out how interviewers work out what questions they will ask.
2. *A sense of the breadth and density of the material we want to collect.* This is the substantive frame of the study plus a sense of the extent to which we want dense detail within it. We may want our materials to be extensive and definitive or neat and narrow or something else. I came to my meeting with my colleague with that almost kinesthetic sense of wanting dense description pretty much limited to the process of question formulation. I didn't intend to learn, for example, whether my colleague's interview practices had changed over the years. I was bringing a narrow substantive frame to my inquiry, but I wanted density within it.
3. *A repertoire of understandings based on previous work, study, awareness of the literature, and experience in living.* That I was myself someone who did interviewing as part of his work made me a more informed and alert inquirer. For one thing, I understood the interview situation well enough to recognize that deciding what to ask about can be a problem.
4. *Pilot research.* This was my first try at investigating how someone else formulated questions. Some of my fumbling might be chalked up to this being my first interview on this topic; I did not yet know what to ask and how to ask it. Had I done a second interview with another respondent, I'd have had a better idea of what to ask.
5. *A sense of what will give substance to the eventual report.* My colleague said he chose questions not only because he thought the respondent could answer them but, even more important, because he anticipated that the answers would give substance to his eventual report.

The last consideration is perhaps the most important: The material we collect is of value insofar as it will contribute to a good report. But what would constitute a good report?

A GOOD REPORT

A good report would inform its audience about matters of importance to them. It would tell them about experiences that affect them, provide them with explanations for things that have puzzled them, and give them maps to situations they may enter. It would contribute to their competence, their awareness, or their well-being.

To do this, the report must go beyond mere provision of information; it must have form, so that its information can be grasped as a whole. A telephone book can be consulted, but not grasped. A good report should make sense as an entity as well as in its items of information; its parts should fit together; it should have coherence.

Coherence happens when the separate pieces of the study fit together so well that we move naturally from one to the next. There is a story or a line of argument or an integrative framework such that each piece of information is the right next one to have as we develop an understanding of an inclusive entity. This inclusive entity may be a story, with a beginning and an end, like the history of an innovative program in an organization, or it may be a functioning unit, like a family. If our report has coherence, our readers will recognize that each piece of the study is important to learn about because it contributes to their understanding of the whole.

There are, in general, two approaches to achieving coherence: One, which uses passage through time to provide structure to the report, can be characterized as *diachronic*. The other, which makes no use of time and so must find some other basis for coherence, can be characterized as *synchronic*.

DIACHRONIC REPORTS

Diachronic reports begin at the beginning and proceed from there. They may describe, for example, how young people leave the vicissitudes of adolescence to enter early adulthood or how stepparents move from wary role-playing to genuine family feeling. They tell stories in which things happen as time goes on.

Diachronic reports may describe phases of development or change; for example, the phases of recovery from grief. They may consider the careers by which people achieve a particular end point; for example, arrival in a mental hospital or in an executive suite. Or they may focus on an event and its impacts beginning, say, with a tropical storm, noting the methods used by the weather bureau to predict its course, then moving to the experiences of sailors on ships caught in what has become a hurricane, then describing the impact of the storm's winds on coastal towns, and on to the cleanups and insurance claims and stories of lucky survival.

Diachronic reports sometimes provide explanation: why applicants chose this particular college or why a disaster occurred without forewarning. They can be responses to our desire to ask the retrospective question "How come that happened?" as well as the prospective question "What happened next?"

Diachronic story lines that attempt to provide explanations have been called "accounting schemes."[1] Suppose we want to explain why it is that some men achieve high business positions. We might include in our accounting scheme a description of the challenges the men confronted, their motivations to succeed, the resources they could call on, and how they finally won through. The story we would end up with would be one of men whose drive, intelligence, and luck brought them success.

Alternative accounting schemes can almost always be devised. To explain why some men achieve success in business we might instead describe how these men learned the interpersonal and technical skills that later aided their rise. The story we could end up with would be one of the familial and educational influences that led to success.

Accounting schemes are not theories about how reality works. They are, rather, sets of categories waiting to be filled by fact. In consequence, accounting schemes are not to be judged as true or false. They should rather be judged by the extent to which they are useful in organizing what we have been told into a story that makes sense and that gives proper weight to the issues that we have learned from our interviewing are important. If we should find in the course of our interviews that a particular accounting scheme doesn't work—the issues it suggests don't seem important whereas other issues seem to matter a lot—then we ought to jettison the scheme. It isn't useful enough.

SYNCHRONIC REPORTS

Synchronic reports attempt to achieve coherence without the armature of time. Generally, they do so by dividing whatever they are about into its significant sectors and moving in logical sequence from sector to sector. A report on the lives of successful men might begin with the sector of their work, since it provides a basis for their participation in the other sectors critical to their well-being. It might then describe the functioning of the men in the sector of marriage, and in their relationships with their children. It might then move outward to their relationships with other kin and to their friendships. In a similar way a report on an organization might describe the functioning of its various departments, perhaps beginning with its leadership, and moving then to the contributions, the internal problems, and the interdepartmental frictions of its operating units.

Contributing to the coherence of synchronic reports can be themes or patterns that underlie developments in every sector. A report might attempt to show, for example, that each member of a family expresses the same unvoiced concern. Or a report might assert a logical connection among an organization's sectors by arguing that one sector is basic to the others or that the sectors are linked by the flow of work.

Sometimes synchronic stories are based on a functional approach. The aim in a functional approach is to explain how something works.[2] The approach requires seeing whatever is to be described—a family, a school, a company—as having goals that it seeks to achieve, or functional requisites that must be met if it is to survive. The members of these entities can also be described as having personal goals, in which event the analyst may be able to describe both the intermeshing and the conflict of personal and communal goals.

One goal of any entity, in this way of seeing things, is self-maintenance: keeping on keeping on. Answering how self-maintenance is achieved could constitute one part of the story. If it is a family that is being described, this might mean giving attention to how funds are brought in and expended, how routines are maintained, and how the work of the family is done.

Every entity will have action goals, ends it wishes to achieve, as well as the goal of self-maintenance. An action goal for the family might be to launch its children into the larger society. A part of the story of a family might be a description of its efforts to achieve its action goals and its success or lack of success.

Some aspects of the entity could be taken as fixed for the period of the study. They might include, for example, the roles and relationships of members. The story could describe how these arrangements facilitate and impede goal attainment.

The risk in synchronic reports is that they will lack a strong conceptual framework, and so will appear to be merely a collection of observations. True, stories that show how a system works can be interesting and may be what a particular study requires, but it is easier, all else being equal, to hold a reader's attention with the sort of plot-unfolding story line that a diachronic approach makes possible.[3]

FROM SUBSTANTIVE FRAME TO INTERVIEW GUIDE

Suppose the aim of our study is to learn about and report on the visitation experience of separated or divorced parents. As we think about the story we want to tell in our report, we find that we give it a diachronic form. We anticipate beginning with the parental relationships maintained by respondents when they were married. We would then trace the changes in the parents' relationships with their children as the parents moved toward separation. We would describe what led the parents' marriage to dissolve and what arrangements the parents made then for their children's care. Finally, we would describe how the parents' custody and visitation arrangements evolved over time.

We might have considered other frameworks for the report. We might have considered using a diachronic approach in which we would contrast the histories of visitation arrangements that produce repeated appeals to the court with the histories of visitation arrangements that seem more satisfactory to the parents. Or we might have considered using a synchronic strategy of contrasting the parents' and children's experience in conflict-free visitation arrangements with their experience in conflict-laden visitation arrangements.

But let us suppose that we have decided that our report will move from the parents' early familial relationships to their relationships with their children after the ending of the parents' marriage. Let us further suppose that our interests, experience, hunches, or preliminary work make us want to include as one area within the project's substantive frame the level of parental investment in the children. One reason we might want to learn about parental investment is that we believe it can affect how the parents arrange custody and visitation.

To develop information about parental investment, we must first decide the narrower components of the area about which we can question respondents. We also have to keep in mind that parental investment and its possible expressions could include enough topics to fill an interview all by itself, and if we want our interview to deal with other matters as well, we will eventually have to limit ourselves to the aspects of parental investment most relevant to custody and visitation. But let us begin by being inclusive. We might arrive at a list of topics-to-learn-about like the following:

1. The parent's thoughts and feelings regarding the children when the children were born and on any later occasion when the parent became aware of emotional investment in the children.
2. The parent's present thoughts and feelings regarding the children, including fears, worries, hopes, gratifications.
3. The extent to which the parent's planning and activities are organized around the parent's relationships with the children. Are the children central or peripheral in the parent's planning and activities?
4. The extent to which the children play a role in the parent's self-image and self-presentation.
5. The parent's thoughts and feelings when separated from the children.

Each of the topics in the list suggests lines of inquiry that can be pursued with respondents. By listing these lines of inquiry we can construct a guide for the interviewer when exploring this area with a respondent. The listing of lines of inquiry might look like the following:

1. *Past thoughts and feelings.* What were R's [the respondent's] thoughts and feelings regarding the children when the children were born? [Possible questions: "Can you remember when your child was born? Could you walk me through what your thoughts were? What your feelings were? Did you say anything to anyone? To the other parent? Do you remember when you first held the child? How did that happen? What went through your mind? What were your feelings?"] Was there a point where R really felt like a parent? What happened to produce this?
2. *Current thoughts and feelings.* Ask about occasions when R is with the children. What goes through R's mind at such times? What are R's feelings? Ask about most recent time R had worries

about the children. What was the incident, what were the worries? Has R had fears in relation to the children? When? What did R fear? Has R had hopes? Ask about most recent time R was gratified by the children. What was the incident, what were the gratifications? Ask for times when R was dismayed or embarrassed by the children, when R was angry with them, when R felt burdened by them, when R was proud of them.

3. *The children and R's plans and activities.* To what extent is R's daily routine organized around the children's needs and activities? Ask about R's most recent workday and most recent weekend. How much are the children in R's mind while R is at work? At other times? Does R have any impulse to telephone? What happens in telephone calls? In the most recent telephone call, what was said? Does R make a special occasion of the children's birthdays, milestones at school? Ask about most recent such events.

4. *R's self-image and self-presentation.* Ask for incident when R has felt most like parent. Ask for most recent incident when R talked to friends or family about self as parent or about children. Was there such an incident in the last day or two? Is an incident of this sort frequent or infrequent?

5. *Separation from children.* Ask R about times of separation from the children. How did the separation occur? What were R's thoughts and feelings? Did R attempt to maintain contact by telephone? What were R's feelings on rejoining the children?

The study's substantive frame would, of course, require investigation of other areas as well as parental investment, including, at the least, the history of the parents' visitation arrangements, the parents' experience with the visitation arrangements, and the reactions of the children to the arrangements. For each of these other areas we would work out, just as we did here, the narrower issues and topics about which we might ask questions, and then work out lines of inquiry for the interview.

It might be that interviewing in the area of parental investment would fill all the time set aside for a single interview and, to learn about other areas we would either have to narrow what we ask about in the area of parental investment or schedule more than a single interview with respondents. If we were devote an entire interview with respondents to discussing parental investment, the preceding list of topics might serve as an interview guide. If we intended to cover other areas as well in the interview, we could reduce the number of topics in our guide which deal with parental investment.

An *interview guide* is a listing of areas to be covered in the interview along with, for each area, a listing of topics or questions that together will suggest lines of inquiry. The guide functions for the interviewer as a prompter might for an actor. If the interviewer is fully in control of the interview topics, the guide itself can remain unused. But if the interviewer begins to be uncertain about what questions might come next, or whether an area or a topic has been skipped, the guide is there to be consulted. The interview guide may also be consulted at the very end of an interview as a last check that everything has been asked.

One of the functions pilot interviews can perform is field testing a draft of the interview guide. A single pilot interview can suggest where a guide is overweighted or redundant and where it is skimpy, but three or four pilot interviews might be the minimum for safety. Even with such testing, the guide is likely to undergo modification as more is learned through interviewing about the area of the study.

The best guides list topics or lines for inquiry so they can be grasped at a glance, with just enough detail to make evident what is wanted. The guide may suggest specific questions to start discussion in important areas, but that isn't necessary. Where the interviewer is thoroughly familiar with the study's aims, guides can be sketchy, listing only topic headings. Where interviewers cannot make independent judgments regarding how best to direct their inquiry, as when the interviewers are not part of the investigative team, the interview guide must be developed in more detail. The amount of detail in the example above might be about right for an interview conducted by someone not fully aware of the study's aims. But still more detailed and dense guides seem to me difficult to use in an interview setting. It wouldn't do for an interviewer to have to say to a respondent, "Would you wait a moment while I read again what I'm supposed to ask?"[4]

When the guide is more fully detailed, interviewers may have to be cautioned not to shift from qualitative interviewing to survey-style interviewing in order to cover everything. Focusing closely on the guide, at the cost of attention to the respondent and the flow of the interview, is always a mistake. Some of my worst interviews have been produced by a conscientious attempt to cover the topics in a guide. Permitting the respondent to talk about what the respondent wants to talk about, so long as it is anywhere near the topic of the study, will always produce better data than plodding adherence to the guide. Even though the interviewer should try to cover the guide, the interviewer should be prepared to concentrate attention on matters on which the respondent is especially able to report, even at the cost of skimping on other matters.

Years ago, before tape recorders, when I was taking interviews in shorthand, the interview guide would be the last page of my shorthand book. Now it is a page or two on a clipboard. Sometimes, if I know an area well or if the interview is entirely exploratory, I do without a written interview guide, although I have one pretty well worked out in my mind. But I like to have a written guide available to me, even if I do not use it in the interview. It is there to provide preparation for the interview, before the interview begins, and it can be a checklist to be used at the end of an interview to ensure that nothing has been missed.

Here is a guide intended to direct the first of three interviews with occupationally successful men. It provides the basis for discussing the meaning of work and the nature of work stress in the men's lives.[5]

1. A DAY AT WORK

   a. Ask R [the respondent] to walk you through a day at work— the previous day, if possible. When did R get in? What happened then? When did R leave? What thoughts on leaving? Did R take work home?
   b. Develop indications of emotional investment, tension, stress, and distress.

2. TASKS AT WORK

   a. Where is R in the work flow system? How does R's work come to him—who brings it or assigns it, and how? How does what R does involve him with others?
   b. Describe R's relationships with superiors, peers, subordinates, and clients—as they are typically, as they are at their best, and as they are at their worst.

3. HOW R CAME TO THIS WORK

   a. What led R to his current line of work? (We don't need a detailed work history; a summary is good enough.)
   b. Find out how R came to his current job and what his feelings about his current job are.

4. GRATIFICATIONS AND BURDENS OF WORK

a. What is R going for in his work? Obtain incidents in which R's work was gratifying to him. What were the gratifications? If not noted, ask about challenge, achievements, contributions.

b. What does R have in mind as he does his work? Instances of "flow"? Ask, if appropriate, "Can you think of a time when you lost yourself in your work?"

c. Obtain incidents in which R was unhappy at work and when work produced distress.

d. Obtain incidents of stress. How did these incidents develop? What was their outcome?

5. RECOGNITION AND REWARDS

a. How does R see his standing at work? How does he come to know it?

b. Obtain incidents in which R's work was responded to by others. If not volunteered, ask about performance reviews, salary and bonuses, verbal recognition.

This interview guide generally led to interviews of 2 hours or a bit less. Usually between four to six areas can be covered adequately in a 2-hour interview. If we want to cover more areas—or if one or more of the areas requires extensive discussion—we would probably do best to anticipate having more than a single interview session.

QUANTITATIVE ITEMS

Often, as I noted in chapter 1, there is good reason for including quantitative items in qualitative interviews. Quantitative items can help anchor a qualitative discussion. Without quantitative information we might have to make imprecise statements like "Many of our respondents felt their present circumstances to be undesirable." With quantitative material we instead can say, "Asked to rate their present circumstances on a scale going from the best time in their lives to the worst, over 30% of respondents rated their present circumstances in the lower third of the scale." The second is by far the stronger statement.

Furthermore, quantitative items—or, at any rate, items asked of everyone—make it easy to segment the population of respondents, for example, into those 40 and younger and those over 40, or into those who say their marriages are very good and those who say they are only good or fair. Quantitative items also can be a basis for further qualitative exploration. In the study of occupationally successful men I found that standardized questions about stress symptoms and depression symptoms provided a useful starting point for learning about times of stress and depression. At the end of the third interview we asked the men we were interviewing to respond to our symptom list. If in response to the item ''Has there been a time in the last year when you felt low or depressed?'' someone answered yes, the interviewer could then ask what was happening at the time. Important information often emerged.

I don't like beginning qualitative interviewing by asking for census data (''What was your age at your last birthday?'' and ''Would you say you work at paid employment full-time, part-time, or not at all?''). It sets the wrong tone. Questions of this sort suggest that you want ''just the facts, ma'am.'' Once such an understanding is established, it becomes that much more difficult to establish that you want a full and detailed narrative account. But when an interview is over, it doesn't hurt to ask for whatever census data you think may prove useful. It is then natural to say, ''Could I ask a few more questions, about your age and the like?''

KEY! [handwritten annotation]

STANDARD GUIDES AND TAILORED GUIDES

A standard interview guide should do for interviews with respondents who are representative of a population. While each respondent may elaborate part of the interview in a way no other respondent does, this need not be anticipated in the guide. People who are informants on some part of an event, on the other hand, must be interviewed on what they know that no one else does. If you are interviewing a panel of informants, you will probably have to draft a new guide, with the particular respondent in mind, for each interview. And the interviewer should be prepared to drop the guide entirely if the interview takes an unexpected direction.

EARLY INTERVIEWS AS LEARNING EXPERIENCES

When we try to imagine developments in a situation we don't know firsthand (such as what it is like to be a member of a submarine crew), we must adapt images from experiences we have had. We construct our initial understandings from the heroes, villains, and other characters who are

members of our internal repertory company; the places we have been ourselves or have read about or have seen on television; and the plot developments our lives have taught us to anticipate. Our construction is never
exactly right. When we actually interview someone in the situation, we
inevitably discover that we didn't understand fully, and perhaps not at all.

In virtually every new study I do I am thrilled by the surprise of things
turning out to be different from my expectations and yet just the way they
should be. This can be the case even when I have myself experienced the
situation, because I find that others have experienced it differently in ways
I could not guess. Interviewing is our only defense against mistaken
expectations. Anyone entering a new conceptual area should make every
effort to obtain, early in the study, images and ideas based on experience
rather than surmise. As soon as possible, the investigator should conduct
pilot interviews.

Just because initial expectations are so likely to be inaccurate, interview guides for pilot interviews can be largely misdirected. Areas asked
about can turn out to be dull and unproductive while areas not included
in the guide turn out to be critical. The interviewer, especially in the first
pilot interview, may experience bad patches, where it is hard to make
connection with the respondent and hard to know how to proceed. However, after only a first or second interview, the way things are begins to
fall into place. Eventually, it will be obvious what is important; initially,
it rarely is.

One implication of these observations is that pilot interviews are highly
desirable. Another is that even when interviewing for the study proper
starts, interview guides should be seen as provisional and likely to change
as more is learned. In a study of a representative sample, where the same
guide is to be used with the entire sample, the guide may not stabilize
until the fourth or fifth pilot interview. Even then the guide may undergo
further modification as the study develops. In my study of well-
functioning men it wasn't until we were halfway into our interviewing
that I realized we weren't learning nearly enough about marital quarrels
and other problems of personal life.

Just as interview guides take a while to stabilize, so too can research
aims. Every funding agency requires that investigators know what they
are after and be able to list the aims of the study in their proposals.
Sometimes there are indeed specific questions the investigator hopes to
answer. Yet it is often the case that the investigator knows only that the
area of study is attractive, possibly because it is important and yet murky,

possessed of mysteries. It is as though the area dares the investigator to discover what is going on. You couldn't very well write *that* into a research proposal.

When the investigator's reason for undertaking a study is not much more than a belief that a situation is intriguing and worth studying, one of the problems of the research enterprise will be to find the research problem that justifies the research. Findings and problem may emerge together. An investigator's initial aim in a qualitative interview study of blue-collar marriages might be simply to know more about blue-collar marriages. Eventually, the investigator might be able to define the study's aim as learning what happens in situations where the husband's ability to provide an income, and in this way to be a reliable husband and father, is always in question. There must be some aim for the study to begin, but sometimes it is only toward the end of a study that its focus becomes well defined.[6]

TO TAPE OR NOT TO TAPE

Investigators' policies regarding the use of tape recorders vary enormously. At one extreme is the investigator whose books are compilations of interview excerpts, who brings two tape recorders to an interview, each with its lapel mike, clips each mike on the respondent's shirt front, and sets both machines going. At the other extreme are investigators who treat a tape recorder as an intruder in the interview.

Tape recorders remind people that there will be a record of what they say. Even when people seem to have stopped attending to the tape recorder they can feel constrained by its presence. Most experienced qualitative interviewers have had a respondent who, upon using a word that is obscene or vulgar, turned to the tape recorder to apologize to the transcriber. And almost every qualitative interviewer has had a respondent who hesitated before sharing a confidence and then said something like "Would you mind turning off the tape recorder, because there is something I want to tell you I don't want to have on the tape?"

And what do you do with the tapes when you've got them? They take hours to transcribe, and then you find that the important material is hidden in the paragraphs and pages of verbiage. Nor do you really need it all. Some first-rate investigators insist that they can remember enough after an interview to write an adequate report.[7] And one investigator I know believes that there is a useful discipline in taking notes. A tape recorder, she believes, encourages you to let your mind wander because you know the recorder will capture what the respondent is saying; note taking requires you to focus.

My experience is different. I find that using a tape recorder makes it easier for me to attend to the respondent than when I take notes, just because I don't have to worry about getting down all the respondent's words. (To be sure, I am sometimes instead distracted by worry that the recorder has failed.)

But most important to people who tape-record is that notes never capture exactly what was said. Note taking tends to simplify and flatten respondents' speech patterns. The conversational spacers ("You know what I mean?") are dropped in note taking; so are respondents' false starts and stray thoughts and parenthetic remarks. The vividness of speech disappears.

Content is likely to be lost as well. While I have a fairly good short-hand for a nonstenographer, when I try to take verbatim notes I regularly omit the unimportant and much of the parenthetic ("I shouldn't be telling you this, but . . ."). Often, I am also forced to omit detail. Suppose a retiree is describing a morning routine: "I get up earlier than my wife and go down to start breakfast and then put it on a tray and bring it upstairs. And we just sit in bed talking and having breakfast and reading the paper and my wife will start the crossword . . ." If this is given to me rapidly and I am taking notes, I will get down the very first words but will surely miss a good part of what follows. Indeed, if a respondent is speaking rapidly, I will often have to skip material to keep up.

I now regularly tape-record.[8] I do this because I am accustomed to working from verbatim transcripts and value the fidelity of the transcripts of tape-recorded material. I also value being spared the drudgery of transcribing shorthand notes. I began doing qualitative interviews before portable tape recorders were in general use, and I have done more than my share of transcribing shorthand notes into a typewriter or desk tape recorder. It is a time-consuming and wearing job. Although my shorthand has improved, I wouldn't want to have to do all that transcription again.

Whether to tape-record or not depends on what you intend doing with the interview material. If you want verbatim transcript, because you intend to quote respondents' comments in your report, then you should make every effort to use a tape recorder. You will very likely later edit what the respondent said, but you will have control of the editing. Note taking enmeshes editing and recording and leaves you with no way to know what changes you have made in the respondent's actual comments.

You should also consider tape recording if you want not so much to learn about events as to capture how a respondent saw them or reacted to them. Then the nuances and complexities of speech that are likely to be missed in note taking may be important for you. And certainly if you want a record of what was said because your version may some day be questioned, you would do well to use a tape recorder.

But if all you want are facts and you don't care about phrasings, you may be better off with notes. And if a tape recorder would be intrusive, then of course you should take notes and let the tape recorder go. For example, a study of how small entrepreneurs organize their business, where there is no anticipation of writing a report using quotations and where the respondents might be put off by a tape recorder, would be better done from notes.

Tape recorders can be, for some people in some circumstances, deterrents to candor. If your study requires you to learn things about people that could discredit them—let alone get them indicted—forget about using a tape recorder. Indeed, if you want to learn about actionable mistakes at work (such as the kinds of errors by physicians that would make them vulnerable to malpractice suits), even taking notes can put respondents off. You might do best, should you enter such an area of study, to slow your note taking and instead try to remember what you're being told—and then write down as much of it as you can immediately after leaving the interview.[9]

TRANSCRIPTION

If you do tape-record, you must decide how much you will transcribe. Only as much as you need, of course, but how much is that? And how can you know whether you will need something until you see it?

One approach is to transcribe everything and use the transcripts as a set of materials to be mined, accepting that a good deal will be dross. This approach puts the analyst's convenience before the time and money required for the transcription, and in an ambitious, well-funded study it is the way to go.

If a study's budget is limited, consideration might be given to listening to a tape once, transcribing only what seems likely to be useful and paraphrasing the rest or noting something like "From minute 24 through 29 discussion of relationship with boss." Another approach is to take notes on what is contained on the tape, never transcribing at all except for quotations to be used in the report. Still another approach is to take notes during the interview even though it is also being tape-recorded. The notes, when typed, can provide an index to the tape, and transcription can be done as needed.

Not long ago I participated in a study whose budget was too tight to fund the costs of transcription of interviews, let alone the travel costs of face-to-face interviews with respondents spread across the country. The aim of the study was to diagnose the source of a malaise within a national organization and to prescribe its remedy. I conducted taped telephone interviews with half a dozen organization members. I took sketchy notes on the interviews but did not transcribe any of the tapes. While writing my part of the report I listened to a couple of the tapes to remind myself of their contents and also drew from them a few telling quotations. Mostly, I relied on what I had learned while conducting the interviews and could consult my notes to be reminded of the remainder.

As in so much else in qualitative interview studies, there is no single right way. Everything depends on what is to be accomplished, the level of resources, and the nature of constraints.

HOW LONG SHOULD AN INTERVIEW LAST?

Most survey studies try to keep interviews to an hour or less. But qualitative interviews can run as long as 8 hours—with breaks, of course. If the interview is easy and sustaining, the respondent interested and cooperative, and the material instructive, and if there are no time constraints, a reasonable expectation is that the interview will go for an hour and a half or 2 hours. I do not often observe respondents getting tired or restless at the 2-hour point unless something has gone wrong in the interview. I may be tired, but respondents seem more often to be enlivened.

If there is tension in the interview because the respondent is ambivalent about being interviewed, then holding the interview to an hour might be right. If you don't know what to anticipate, you might ask respondents to plan on an hour and a half, with the option of ending earlier or going on for a bit. Half an hour seems about the minimum time for an interview. Although any interchange, no matter how brief, can produce an interesting observation, I find it difficult to develop a coherent account in an interview of under half an hour.

Once in a while a respondent seems willing to go on longer than I am.

I believe it is good policy to support the fullest report a respondent can give and to continue an interview as long as it is productive. Nevertheless, interviewing can be wearing, and I can only do it for so long. When I become too tired to be fully in touch with what I am being told and it is possible for me to schedule another interview, I call a halt and make another appointment. But if the respondent lives far from me, and I'm not up for another two-hour drive out and two-hour drive back, or if there is no possibility of rescheduling, I'll stay with an interview as long as there is material to cover.

HOW MANY INTERVIEWS WITH THE SAME RESPONDENT?

It is almost always desirable, if time and costs permit, to interview respondents more than once. You have to keep your frame pretty narrow if you plan to cover it all in a single sitting. Furthermore, a first meeting is partly about establishing the research partnership. Interviewer and respondent get to know each other, get a sense of the rhythm of interchange, and establish the outlines of the respondent's story. When they meet again they know each other better. Also, in the intervening time the respondent may have begun thinking about the areas discussed, and memories may have surfaced. Or the respondent may have been made more sensitive to the issues of the interview and may therefore have newly noted incidents worth reporting.

With increasing contact and increasing confidence in the research procedure respondents are likely to be more willing to report fully. In the study of occupationally successful men it was only in a fourth interview that a respondent talked about his wife's alcoholism. In a study of women who were single parents, where we interviewed a small sample every 2 weeks for about 5 months, we normally did not learn about the emotional ups and downs in relationships with boyfriends until the fifth or sixth interview.

Only infrequently does the cost of a second interview with a respondent outweigh its usefulness. Third interviews are generally also worth doing. Of importance here is the number of areas to be covered in the interviewing. Fourth and fifth interviews are likely to produce a sense of diminishing returns, except when they provide information on continuing stories in respondents' lives. It is not that nothing at all is learned from fourth or subsequent interviews; respondents can always report on new events or new aspects of already described events. The question is whether the investigator might not gain more by interviewing additional respondents.

Sometimes it is desirable to interview a few respondents many times but most respondents only a few times. That can provide the study with both extensive case reports and a reasonable sample size.

DO YOU PAY RESPONDENTS?

Some funded studies now pay respondents for their time. A New York City study of drug users, for example, paid respondents twenty-five dollars plus two subway tokens for completed interviews. My impression is that with very low income respondents the opportunity for payment can be an important incentive for participating in a study.

In a study with middle-income respondents we acknowledged the contribution respondents made to the study by giving them a gift certificate to a restaurant after our first interview. Most were pleased and it may have aided rapport when we returned for further interviews, but I doubt that it was necessary for us to have done this.

My guess is that in most studies the reward for a respondent is the interview itself and the contribution he or she can make to the study. Payment doesn't seem to make a difference in a respondent's willingness to participate. If the interview goes well, payment is largely irrelevant to the respondent's experience, except for those who truly need the money; if it doesn't go well, payment won't make the experience better. Still, a gift to acknowledge a respondent's contribution is likely to be appreciated.

WHERE DO YOU HOLD THE INTERVIEW?

An argument can be made for interviewing people in the investigator's office: if you interview people in their home you're not going to hear much that is inconsistent with their commitment to their home roles and if you interview people in their offices they are less likely to discuss problems with coworkers. Since most people seem to prefer your coming to them, most of my interviewing has been in respondents' homes. Some investigators think that's fine; they can observe the setting within which the respondent lives, may meet members of the respondent's family, and may observe the respondent in interaction with them.

On the rarest of occasions the safety of interviewers may come into question. Interviewing respondents within their homes can pose a slight but nevertheless real risk, perhaps especially for women. I have told people who have interviewed for me to trust their intuitions, and to end the interview if they feel uneasy. Once a woman who was interviewing for me did not want to return for a second interview with a male respondent. She had no special reason; she just hadn't felt comfortable with him. That feeling of discomfort was enough to go on. She may have been responding to minimal cues she was not able to identify, or she may have developed a sense of the respondent that told her the situation was dangerous. We found a male interviewer to take over for her.

With few exceptions, however, respondents who have agreed to be interviewed in their homes will go to some effort to be hospitable. Indeed, by far the most common response to a stranger within one's home is friendly interest and desire to be of help.

TELEPHONE INTERVIEWS

Reasons of economy may make it seem desirable to interview by telephone. I have conducted many telephone interviews and regularly find that useful information can be developed. It helps for me to have met the respondent or at least to be able to identify myself with a project the respondent recognizes, so that the respondent knows I am who I purport to be. But even with my identity established, I don't feel as much in touch with the respondent in a telephone interview as I do in a face-to-face interview. My shallower connection to the respondent generally produces a shorter interview. In one study in which I did both face-to-face interviews and telephone interviews, the face-to-face interviews ran an hour and a half or more, while the telephone interviews ran about 45 minutes, and sometimes less.

A research project that compared telephone and face-to-face interviewing found that telephone respondents broke off contact more quickly, were both more acquiescent and more evasive, and were more cautious about self-revelation.[10] But a team that has done a great deal of telephone interviewing describes it as "the next best thing to being there."[11] This strikes me as right: it's better to be there, but telephone interviews are the next best thing.

CHAPTER 4

INTERVIEWING

GETTING STARTED

You have called the respondent to confirm that you are expected. You have checked your tape recorder. You have put your interview guide, fastened onto a clipboard, in your briefcase, first glancing at it to remind yourself of the interview's aims and content. You get in your car, a street map beside you. You find the respondent's home, park, ring the doorbell. The respondent comes to the door. You introduce yourself and are directed to a place to sit.

Your first concern should be to establish a good interviewing partnership. The way you act and what you say should communicate that you expect to work with the respondent to produce the interview. For example, as you bring out your tape recorder, you might ask, "Is using the tape recorder okay?" The point isn't the particular remark but, rather, the assumption of a collaborative relationship. *yes!*

I bring two signed copies of a consent form to interviews. I give both to the respondent and say, "These are two copies of our consent form. Could you read one of them, and if it is all right would you sign it and give it to me and then hang on to the other?" Then I ask something like "Is there anything about the study you would like me to tell you before we begin?" Sometimes respondents want to know how they happened to be contacted. I then describe the sampling procedure. I almost always also say something about the general goal of the study, such as "We're trying

61

to learn about the experience of retirement and so are talking to people who know about it because they're doing it." I usually name the study's sponsor or give my academic affiliation to provide additional evidence that the study is legitimate.

When I can, I begin the interview where the respondent seems already to be. In a study of retirement, if a respondent mentioned, before I turned on the tape recorder, "I'm not actually retired; I've got a couple more weeks to go on the job," I might ask, after starting the tape recorder, "What's it like, being two weeks before the end of the job? Is that something you think about?" I might then go on to ask how the issue of retirement had arisen while the respondent was on the job, how other people had indicated that they were aware that the respondent was leaving, and how the respondent's job had changed since he scheduled a retirement date. If there is no evident place to start, I might begin by asking how the respondent happened to enter the situation about which I want to learn. "I would like to ask what your experience has been in retirement, maybe starting with how you happened to retire when you did."

In a pilot study of people who are HIV positive I generally started with how it happened that respondents got tested rather than how it happened that they became HIV positive, since their experience as people who were HIV positive actually began with the testing, not with the infection. Here is the start of my interview with one HIV-positive respondent:

TRANSCRIPT EXCERPT

INTERVIEWER: The idea of the study is to find out what happens to people as a result of their being tested and finding out that they are positive. What effects, if any, does that have on how they think, how they see the world, what they do. It's the kind of information that nobody has except the guy who's going through it. Nobody else has it.

RESPONDENT: Right.

I: I'm a sociologist at the University of Massachusetts, downtown.

COMMENTS

The setting is a small office in a testing station. The respondent has been told by his counselor that a study is being done and he has said he would participate. I want to establish a research partnership with the respondent.

TRANSCRIPT EXCERPT

And what I'm doing is talking to people who are in your situation, because you know what is going on and nobody else does, but it is important for other people to understand as well as they can. And so I'm going to ask you to work with me to tell your story. And that's it. That's what I'm doing.

KEY

R: Tell you what happened, huh?

I: Exactly.

R: Sure. That's a good idea. And it's about time.

I: Yeah. It's amazing, with all the AIDS research, this hasn't been done. Anyway, here is a consent form for you to read. It describes the study, and if it's okay with you, you sign one copy and let me have it, and keep the other.

R: Oh, yeah. I have no problem. So, will it be used in, like, kind of segments, something where it's like people will be able to listen to us? Or is it strictly for doctors and psychologists?

I: Nobody will be listening to the tapes except for people on the project.

R: It doesn't matter to me.

I: What we'll do is, we'll transcribe it. We'll be reading the transcripts of your interview and the

COMMENTS

Now I explain what my role will be as interviewer and propose to the respondent that his role will be to provide information about "what is going on" in his life, to tell his story.

The respondent indicates that, yes, this makes sense to him.

Here I try to get in tune with the respondent by extending his comment "And it's about time." I then ask the respondent to read and sign the consent form.

This suggests to me that the respondent may feel threatened by the form. "I have no problem" may mean that the respondent first felt discomfort, then rejected it. This, plus the question about who will listen to the tapes, makes me think that reassurance might be called for.

My guess is that confidentiality might be an issue.

The respondent says confidentiality is not an issue.

Just to be on the safe side, and to forestall the respondent's later feeling uncomfortable about what

TRANSCRIPT EXCERPT	COMMENTS

transcripts of interviews with other people we interview and we'll compare them and summarize them and say this is what goes on. We might quote people, but if we do we will drop out identifying information.

he's bought into, I go into detail about how his tapes will be used.

R: Well, I don't care. I mean, if you do quote me and you have to use my name, it may be more effective, by using my name and saying what it is. But that's neither here nor there.

Again the respondent says he doesn't care. Looking back, I think he wanted his story told.

I: It's just our practice that we don't do it.

Maybe I should have gone on to the interview at this point instead of staying with this, but I felt more had to be said about the ground rules.

R: Yeah. I just figured that one or the other, it doesn't bother me.

Respondent is holding his ground.

I: Okay.

"I accept your position."

R: Really, it doesn't. It has no effect for me, for some reason. Denial or something.

This could be interpreted as saying, "I'm going to be vulnerable to exposure but I don't care, although maybe I should."

I: Also, if it is possible, it would be good if we could talk again, maybe next week or two weeks from now.

I direct the respondent's attention to the interview at hand and its continuation.

R: Yeah, sure.

"Okay. I'm ready for the interview now."

I: I guess I'd like to start by asking how you happen to be here. Could you just walk me through how you happened to get tested?

And so we start. The phrase, "Could you just walk me through . . ." suggests the level of detail I would like the respondent to provide.

In this excerpt I made explicit the terms of the interviewing relationship. After introducing the study and myself, I said, ''What I'm doing is talking to people who are in your situation, because you know what is going on and nobody else does. . . . So I'm going to ask you to work with me to tell your story.'' Often, I don't describe in such detail the interviewing relationship I hope to establish, because it seems to me already pretty much understood. In this case the respondent must have struck me as uncertain of what would be expected of him.

THE INTERVIEWING RELATIONSHIP

The interviewing relationship is a research partnership between the interviewer and the respondent. The terms of this research partnership are ordinarily implicit, but if I were drafting a contract between myself and a respondent, I would include the following clauses:

1. The interviewer and the respondent will work together to produce information useful to the research project.
2. The interviewer will define the areas for exploration and will monitor the quality of the material. The respondent will provide observations, external and internal, accepting the interviewer's guidance regarding topics and the kind of report that is needed.
3. The interviewer will not ask questions out of idle curiosity. On the other hand, the interviewer will be a privileged inquirer in the sense that the interviewer may ask for information the respondent would not make generally available, maybe would not tell anyone else at all.
4. The interviewer will respect the respondent's integrity. This means that the interviewer will not question the respondent's appraisals, choices, motives, right to observations, or personal worth.
5. The interviewer will ensure, both during the interview and afterward, that the respondent will not be damaged or disadvantaged because of the respondent's participation in the interview. In particular, the interviewer will treat the respondent's participation and communications as confidential information.

There are other ways, besides the research partnership, of defining the interviewing relationship. Sometimes interviewers present themselves as the means by which the respondent can tell his story: ''Through me you can make your story known.'' This might be the approach of someone doing life history studies or of a reporter in an interview with the famous or the notorious.

It is also possible for the interviewer to take the role of the respectful student, awaiting instruction. One woman, an excellent interviewer, said she tried to make the government officials she interviewed feel that she was ready to admire their knowledge and authority and was, indeed, already awed to be in the presence of someone so important. She believed that disguising how much she knew and how perceptive and skeptical she was disarmed her respondents.

Some interviewers are willing to act as the respondents' antagonists. If they suspect the respondent is holding back information, they are ready to confront the respondent: ''You say you haven't ever used drugs. But you hung out with drug users. There must have been a time when you experimented.'' Interviews in police stations, of course, take on this quality, as do some employment interviews. Journalists sometimes read up on respondents, the better to confound the respondents' efforts to dissemble.

In my experience the research partnership definition of the interviewing relationship works best. It is the most easily sustainable, both for the interviewer and the respondent. And it is consistent with the reasons for having research interviews.

SOME INTERVIEWING GUIDELINES

Being a good interviewer requires knowing what kind of information the study needs and being able to help the respondent provide it. Here are some guidelines.

WHAT IS IT YOU WANT TO OBTAIN IN THE INTERVIEW?

In the great majority of research interviews you will want the respondent to provide concrete descriptions of something he or she has witnessed. This includes both scenes and events external to the respondent and the respondent's own thoughts and feelings. A task in almost every interview is to communicate to respondents that this is what is needed. Here is an interview excerpt that suggests the kind of information that is wanted and how it can be obtained. It is from an interview with a divorced father who was involved in a dispute with his former wife over his times of visitation. I conducted the interview as part of a study of the usefulness of a program for helping parents deal with visitation problems.

TRANSCRIPT EXCERPT	COMMENTS

RESPONDENT: It really appalls me that they [in the court] think that I'm some . . . some, I'm some symbol of money. That is the only reason that I even go to court and the court has any use for me is because I am a symbol of money. That is the only reason. They don't . . . they could care less if I saw my son. Okay? It's a different story if the mother wasn't seeing him. But they could care less if I didn't see him. They could care less if I didn't have a roof over my head. They could care less that I wouldn't be able to take my son because I don't have any money to feed him when I have him because I pay all the money out. They don't care about that.

This response, a description of the courts as the respondent views them, is generalized. That it is so emotional may obscure the fact that it summarizes the respondent's experience rather than presents any specific experience. Note the respondent's use of "they" when he insists that "they" don't care about his relationship with his son, only about obtaining money from him for his wife. Later, when the respondent describes a specific incident, he will talk about specific people.

INTERVIEWER: Could you walk me through the last time you went to court, just what happened?

This is a way of asking for the concrete incident that led to the generalized emotional statement. The phrase "walk me through" is intended to communicate the level of concreteness wanted. "The last time" is intended to specify a particular incident.

R: The last time I went to court was just before I went to see the counselor. Basically, I went down to go over custody and payments. Now think about it. I got to pay rent. I live in an apartment. I got to pay rent. I got to put food on the table, you know. I got to make payments on the car. I make three hundred dollars a week, gross. Take out my taxes, I make two hundred and forty-seven dollars.

The respondent provides a time reference for his last time in court and a reason for having gone there but then returns to his outrage.

TRANSCRIPT EXCERPT	COMMENTS
They want seventy dollars. Who pays for my rent?	
I: Okay. When you came to court, were you waiting around before you . . .	*I bring the respondent back to the court appearance, to what is likely to have been its beginning—waiting around.*
R: Oh yeah, wait around for hours, hours.	
I: Where were you waiting?	*I ask for specifics to keep the respondent in the incident.*
R: You wait downstairs in a lobby, waiting to be called. And then you go through this shenanigans.	
I: What happens while you're waiting to be called?	*I'm asking for the concrete details of the incident. Notice that I ask about what happens in the present tense. This is an error, because it encourages a generalized response. (I say more about this later in this chapter.)*
R: You sit. You sit. You sit. You don't even get called. I had the lawyer go stand in line. You don't even see a judge. You see some person who shuffles a million people around a day. And then you sit down with a mediator. He's my mediator. He's not my mediator. He's telling me what I'm supposed to do like he's a judge. He's telling me, "This is what you have to do."	*The response is generalized, quite possibly because of the present-tense question.*
I: Was your wife with you when you were seeing the mediator?	*I now supply a specific detail to bring the respondent back to the incident.*
R: Oh yeah.	

TRANSCRIPT EXCERPT	COMMENTS
I: So it's the three of you—you, your wife . . .	*Again, requiring the specific.*
R: Me, the lawyer—I might just as well have left the lawyer at home. I mean, I might as well have left him at home. I mean, I mean, the lawyer couldn't do anything.	*The respondent is now in the incident. It only remains to ask about it.*
I: So what happened?	*Which I now do.*
R: What happened is, you know, it's like this. I want three weeks. I want three weeks vacation with my son. Not all at once. Three weeks.	*I can't tell if the respondent asked for this or if it was only in his mind.*
I: So did you say that or . . .	*For clarification.*
R: I mean, what's this guy? What's wrong with three weeks? What's the problem with three weeks? One week, three times a year. Spring, winter, and summer. You know, what's the big deal? I don't see any problem with that. Oh, no. The mediator says, "Two weeks." I say, "No, I want three weeks." I mean, I don't know what the problem is. What's wrong with three weeks?	*Apparently, the respondent asked and was refused. And then the respondent argued.*
I: So what did he say then?	*I ask the respondent to continue reporting on the level of what actually happened.*
R: He says, "Well, I'm only giving you two weeks and come back in a year and a half and we'll negotiate again." What do you mean, come back? I'm not coming back to this court again. Negotiate? What are we negotiating? This is my son. It's not a negotiating thing.	*The respondent is now providing a description of the incident, both what was happening in the event and what was happening internally. This is the level of concreteness needed for the study. Note how it develops further useful detail.*

TRANSCRIPT EXCERPT	COMMENTS

I: Did your lawyer say anything?

R: My lawyer. My lawyer's like . . . he says, "Well, why can't we have the three weeks?" But, you know, it is the mother. I'm like, "Well, I'm the father. Without me there wouldn't be a child." Well, I'm like, well . . . nothing. Nothing. And I say, "I love my son and I love seeing my son and I love spending as much time as I want with my son. And I don't like you telling me when I can spend time with him."

This is an instructive account of the frustrations of the noncustodial father and the feelings of helpless rage that develop. Note the respondent's anger at being told when he can see his son by someone who doesn't know him or his son.

I: What did he say when you said that?

Again phrasing the question on the level of the concrete event.

R: "Well, that's the way it is."

The respondent says that he was essentially just turned away by the mediator, not attended to.

I: What were you thinking . . .

Asking for the internal experience.

R: What am I thinking? I want to kill the guy. I want to kill her. You know, 'cause she's sitting there smiling and smirking. I mean, I tell you, I tell you, I'm a very rational person. But when I left that day, I tell you, and I watched the news, right? And I see these guys and I'm sitting there going, "There's something going on behind the scene. You're not seeing the whole picture."

A statement of the level of rage the experience induced. Notice the shift into the present tense. Here it is not generalized; instead, it describes a past incident as though it were occurring now.

I: What do you mean by "these guys"?

The respondent is alluding to thoughts. I ask him to develop them further.

R: These people that are on TV and they're killing their wives. I

This is a description of murderous rage. The respondent self-

TRANSCRIPT EXCERPT

COMMENTS

mean, nothing should ever be
drawn that far. All right, beating
your wife—I never did any beating. I never had any restraining
order. Because I'm—you know.
But I tell you, if I was that type of
person, the way I felt when I got
out of there, I tell you, I could
have knocked her off. 'Cause I was
pissed.

*control is good enough so that
he will not harm the mediator or
his ex-wife. But this is the feeling
that underlay the diatribe with
which this excerpt began.*

This excerpt began with a generalized statement of the court experience of a noncustodial father. I wanted the respondent to move from this
to as close to an observer's report as he could provide of his experiences,
internal as well as external. Only that sort of concrete description of just
what happened could constitute interpretable data regarding the experiences of noncustodial fathers in court.

Generalized descriptions can be good enough if they are about an issue
of peripheral importance to the study. A respondent's statement that "I go
to work about nine in the morning" would be acceptable if the study isn't
especially concerned about the respondents' use of time. But if respondents' use of time is important to the study, the interviewer should attempt
to obtain a concrete description of what happened the morning of the day
preceding the interview.

We obtain descriptions of specific incidents by asking respondents to
particularize. In the foregoing excerpt I asked, "Could you walk me
through the last time you went to court, just what happened?" Other
questions that might also have served to elicit a concrete description
include: "Could you tell me about a time that displays that at its clearest?"; "Is there a specific incident you can think of that would make clear
what you have in mind?"; and "Could you tell me what happened,
starting from the beginning?"

It can sometimes seem to an interviewer to be an untrustworthy sampling of respondent behavior to ask only about the last time an incident
occurred. To check this, it might be useful for the interviewer to ask if that
occurrence was very different from previous occurrences and, if it was, to
ask for the occurrence that preceded the most recent one as well. Often,
however, the discussion of the most recent occurrence will produce so

much instructive particularity that it will be of secondary importance whether it is a typical event or not.

TENSE AND SPECIFICITY IN THE INTERVIEW

It is useful to bear in mind that reports of actual events are ordinarily made in the past tense: "I did . . . ," "He said . . . ," and so on. However, respondents may also make reports of actual events in the present tense to give their accounts a sense of immediacy and drama, as though the events were happening now. The respondent just quoted did that when he said, "My lawyer's like, he says, 'Well, why can't we have the three weeks?' "

A more frequent use of the present tense might be called "the generalized present." This is the tense respondents most frequently employ for a generalized description. It summarizes developments that occurred in the past and continue through the present. This is the tense used by the respondent in the excerpt just presented when he said, "You sit. You sit. You sit. You don't even get called." Notice that the respondent used the generalized present in response to a question by the interviewer that was itself in the generalized present: "What happens while you're waiting to be called?" This question assumed the generalized present and so pulled a response in the generalized present. A better question would have been, "What *happened* while you were waiting to be called?"

The generalized present is often requested in studies using a fixed-question–open-response format. Such a study might ask, for example, "What are the issues about which you and your wife tend to disagree?" As was exemplified in the excerpt, when a question is phrased in the generalized present, the response is likely to be in the generalized present.

There is a second generalizing tense, which I call "the generalized past." A respondent can signal this by use of the auxiliary "would," as in "I would sit there for hours." The respondent could also signal this tense by using "used to" or an equivalent: "I used to spend a whole day sitting there." Here too the respondent is summarizing, not describing a specific incident.[1]

Respondents often prefer to provide generalized accounts rather than concrete instances. One reason for this is that they can feel that they are being more responsible reporters if they remain general, since they are describing an entire class of events rather than a single idiosyncratic event. The generalized material, they may think, is more inclusive and so constitutes better information. Actually, when respondents provide generalized accounts, their description expresses a kind of theory of what is most typical or most nearly essential in the class of the event. By doing this, respondents preempt the investigator's task of analysis; it is they who have decided what is important.[2]

In addition, a generalized account permits respondents to minimize elements about which they feel diffident. Respondents may feel that generalized accounts are appropriate for a report to someone like the interviewer, whom they don't know that well. Generalized accounts are more nearly public information, with none of the potentially embarrassing or revealing details of private life.

Interviewers, in qualitative interview studies, like their respondents, may imagine that the generalized present or generalized past will provide an overview that saves interview time and is less subject to the idiosyncrasies of the specific event. In addition, the interviewers may unconsciously prefer to phrase a question in the generalized present or past because it seems less prying, less intrusive, than a question that asks for a specific past event. The question, "What's it like when you and your wife quarrel?" can feel easier to ask than "Can you tell me about your most recent quarrel? Could you walk me through it?" Asking about a specific past event can make interviewers uncomfortable because it seems as though they are putting respondents on the spot.

But just because questions phrased in the generalized present or generalized past appear less intrusive, the interviewer should be wary of them. The point of qualitative interviewing is to obtain from respondents a field report on their external and internal experiences. This does require the respondent to provide a density of detail that would not be provided in ordinary conversation. If asking for detailed, concrete information in an interview constitutes an unacceptable invasion of privacy, the interviewing partnership is faulty.

QUESTIONS TO ASK

There are no magic questions. Any question is a good question if it directs the respondent to material needed by the study in a way that makes it easy for the respondent to provide the material. Sometimes the best question is one that in a very few words directs the respondent to give more detail or fill in a gap: "What happened then?" Sometimes it is one that takes the time to tell the respondent just what is now needed: "Could you give me a concrete instance of that, a time that actually happened, with as much detail as you can?" Any question that helps the respondent produce the material you need is a good question.

On Phrasing the Question

Should every question be phrased in an open way, or might a question be a leading one in that it anticipates a response? Do you ask "What were your feelings then?" or "Were you unhappy about that?" Or might you even offer "You must have been unhappy"?

Most often, you will not want to affect the respondent's report by offering anticipations in your questions. If you have no reason to anticipate a particular response, you would ask, "What were your feelings when that was happening?" But sometimes you can help a respondent provide a full report by demonstrating your understanding, and one way to do this is to name the respondent's state. In this situation the right thing to say might be "You must have been unhappy about that." Or if you don't want to supply the characterization, "unhappy"—after all, if you do, the characterization of the feeling isn't the respondent's own—you might try "It sounds as though you had a pretty strong reaction." You don't have to be compulsively nondirective, but you should make sure that the words and images you may eventually quote in your report are the respondent's, not yours.

There may be a few points in an interview where you want to check on a surmise you have come to. One way to do this is to say, "It sounds like you are still pretty upset about that." But if the respondent agrees with this, you might do well to check whether the agreement comes because of politeness or because you have been right. I have sometimes asked "Is that exactly right?" just to make sure.

Helping Respondents Develop Information

Most important in an interview is obtaining concrete information in the area of inquiry. Once a respondent has alluded to an actual incident, perhaps in response to your asking, with respect to something of importance to the study, "Could you tell me the most recent time that happened?", you may have to help the respondent develop the incident adequately. Here are forms of development you might want to obtain and some ways you might ask for them.

1. *Extending.* You might want to know what led to an incident. Questions that ask for this include "How did that start?" "What led to that?" Or you might want to know the consequences of an incident: "Could you go on with that? What happened next?"

2. *Filling in detail.* You might want more detail than the respondent has provided. A useful question often is "Could you walk me through it?" An interviewer who worked with me used to add "We need you to be as detailed as possible," and that seemed to work for her. Another approach to obtaining increased detail is to go to the beginning of the respondent's story for which you want detail and ask what followed, exemplifying in your question the density of detail you want: "So you were sitting there, talking with your guest, and this other fellow came over. What happened then?" You could even add "Can you walk me through it?"

3. *Identifying actors.* You might want to learn the social context of an incident, the other people who were there. You could ask "Was anyone else there when that was happening?" "Who else was there and what did they do?"

4. *Others the respondent consulted.* Especially in a study whose concerns include how respondents dealt with problems, you may want to ask whom the respondent talked with about an incident and what the respondent said: "Did you talk to anyone about what was going on?" This may also produce information about the respondent's view of the incident at the time.

5. *Inner events.* You will generally want to obtain information regarding some of the inner events that accompanied the outer events the respondent reports. Inner events include perceptions, what the respondent heard or saw; cognitions, what the respondent thought, believed, or decided; and emotions, how the respondent felt and what strivings and impulses the respondent experienced. They can also include the respondent's preconceptions, values, goals, hopes, and fears. You will usually want at least the cognitive and emotional events. Imagine a respondent reporting, "My boss called me in and told me he wanted me to fire one of the people working for me." After the respondent developed what happened, you could ask the respondent to de-

scribe his or her cognitive reactions by asking, ''When that was happening, what thoughts did you have?'' Then you might obtain emotional reactions by asking, ''What were your feelings when he said that?'' or ''Can you remember how you reacted, emotionally?''

6. *Making indications explicit.* Respondents may indicate by a gesture, a grimace, or an expressive shrug feelings they haven't put into words. You won't have the gesture, grimace, or shrug in your transcript when you are analyzing your data, nor can you quote it as supporting material for your report. The problem is to communicate to the respondent that you sort of understand what he or she is indicating but that you want to be sure. To convey the message that the respondent's feelings are worth developing in words, you might try suggesting, perhaps by a nod, that you understand, and then ask for elaboration by the question, ''You had some pretty definite feelings?'' or ''What were the feelings you had?''

Handling Difficult Questions

Some questions are hard to ask. People in survey research sometimes say that income is the most private of matters, more difficult to ask about than sexual behavior. Perhaps, but sexual behavior is difficult enough. However, often there is a relatively tactful way of entering a difficult area. To learn about men's extramarital experiences, in the study of how occupationally successful men organized their lives, we sometimes began by asking respondents about their experience of loneliness and then moved to questions about friendships with women other than their wives. Still, despite our efforts to be as tactful as possible, a few men responded by saying that they didn't want to get into that area. That told us something—although not very much.

In general, if there are difficult issues to be developed, it is important to establish a reliable research relationship before entering the area. It is also important for interviewers to know why the information is needed. Interviewers in any study should always understand its goals, so that they can know which of a respondent's leads to develop; but if they are to ask about sensitive issues, it is especially important that they know why they are asking. And they must thoroughly believe in the study's right to know. Otherwise they will communicate their absence of confidence in the questions.

Markers

I define a marker as a passing reference made by a respondent to an important event or feeling state. One respondent whom I interviewed in the study of retirement reported, "We went to our place on the Cape a couple of weeks after my mother died, and my husband spent all his time working on the house. He always has one more thing he has to do." The point of this response was to communicate how occupied the respondent's husband was, despite his retirement. The reference to the death of the respondent's mother—not previously mentioned by her—was a marker. The respondent was indicating that this was something significant for her, by which she dated events; that she understood that it might not be important for the study; and that if I wanted to pick it up, well, there it was.

After the respondent had finished developing the material about her husband's full schedule, I said, "You mentioned earlier that your mother had died. What happened?" The respondent then described how devoted she had been to her mother. That devotion explained why her inaccessibility to her husband had been an issue in his retirement. Now, with her mother dead, there were indications that things might be different. This was material important to the study.

Because markers occur in the course of talking about something else, you may have to remember them and then return to them when you can, saying, "A few minutes ago you mentioned . . ." But it is a good idea to pick up a marker as soon as you conveniently can if the material it hints at could in any way be relevant for your study. Letting the marker go will demonstrate to the respondent that the area is not of importance for you. It can also demonstrate that you are only interested in answers to your questions, not in the respondent's full experience.

Sometimes interviewers feel it is tactful not to pick up markers. This may, on occasion, be true, especially if the marker was dropped inadvertently. But most often respondents are in enough control of their report that if they don't want you to know about the area, they won't drop markers.

Respondents sometimes offer markers by indicating that much has happened that they aren't talking about. They might say, for example, "Well, there was a lot going on at that time." It is then reasonable to respond, "Could you tell me about that?" It is different when a respondent clearly states that an area is off-limits to the interview by saying something like, "There was a lot going on at that time, but I don't want to talk about that.'' Now you can't possibly ask, ''Could you tell me about that?'' Still, if the topic appears relevant to the study and you have a good interviewing relationship, you might ask, ''Can you tell me anything about what sort of thing that was?''

MANAGING THE INTERVIEW

Intrusions

The first rule of interviewing is that if the respondent has something to say, the respondent must be able to say it. If you find yourself talking over the respondent, interrupting, or holding the floor while the respondent tries to interrupt, something is going wrong in the interview. You might want to withdraw some of your attention from the respondent for a moment or two to figure out why you are competing for the floor. But whether you figure it out or not, you ought to stop doing it.

It is easy to intrude in an interview. You can interrupt the respondent. You can finish the respondent's sentences. You can offer your associations to what the respondent is saying. You can suggest explanations for observations about which the respondent is perplexed; for example, if the respondent shrugs and says, ''I don't know why he said that,'' you could propose, ''Well, maybe he was trying to defend himself.'' You can insist on completing your question even if the respondent has already started to answer. You can hop from issue to issue following your own train of thought rather than the respondent's. With any and all of these, don't do it.

Never, never fight for control of the interview. The interview is a collaboration. If it should happen that a respondent is developing an irrelevant topic at great length, you may have to interrupt to say that there's another topic you would like to get to. But that should be done in the spirit of the collaboration; it's your responsibility to set topics. You can usually manage the redirection without discouraging the respondent from talking freely. In the retirement study a respondent who was nearing retirement wanted to talk about the details of his business and how hectic things were. His discussion was interesting but not useful for the study, so at a pause I asked, ''With all this going on, is it possible for you also to plan for retirement?'' We then moved to discuss the respondent's planning for his retirement.

Talking About Yourself

The interview is about the respondent, not about the interviewer. In my view, at least until the interviewing has ended, the interviewer should do only as much self-reporting as is consistent with the interview situation. It is usually enough for the interviewer to give business card information—location and profession—along with the study's aims and sponsorship.

If a respondent asks about some aspect of the study, the question should be answered fully—although not so fully that the respondent's attention wanders. If a respondent asks a question of the interviewer such as whether the interviewer had a difficult time finding the respondent's home, the question should be answered in a way that will satisfy the respondent's concern, but briefly. If a respondent asks a specific personal question, such as whether the interviewer had an experience similar to the one the respondent is describing, the interviewer should answer honestly rather than seem mysterious. But again the response should be brief; it's the respondent's experience that's important.

Some interviewers believe that self-disclosure fosters disclosure by respondents. I don't have much experience with self-disclosure as a facilitative technique, but the experience I do have leads me to question it. My own experience is that self-disclosure complicates an interview situation by shifting the respondent's attention to the interviewer and altering the respondent's relationship with the interviewer.

Monitoring the Information the Respondent Is Providing

You must carry into the interview a general idea of what you want to learn about. The interview guide is one statement of this. Your ability to judge what else might contribute to the study's report should make it possible to recognize when material not anticipated in the guide could be useful for the study. Even as you are listening closely, you should be assessing whether the material might be useful for the study's report. The guiding question is "Does this material help illuminate experience in the area of the study?"

Suppose your study is on the psychological and emotional concomitants of being engaged in a lawsuit. Your concern is what it feels like to be either the person sued or the person doing the suing. In an exploratory interview you find yourself being told by a plaintiff about his experiences as a father when his son got into a dispute over ownership of baseball cards. Is this relevant material? Should you ask for its development in the interview? Or should you be thinking about how to redirect the respondent? If I could imagine any use for the material, I would want the respondent to develop it. It might occur to me that the stance of being a father protecting his child, or teaching the child to deal with conflict, carries over into the respondent's present adversarial action. For me, that possibility would be enough to justify encouraging the respondent to develop the material.

It can be hard to know what is relevant, especially in early interviews, before the frame of the study is firmly established. My policy is: If in doubt, see what's there.

Adequacy of the Respondent's Account

Suppose what you are being told is in exactly the right area. How do you know whether you are being told enough, whether you are being given enough development and enough detail? One test is visualizability. Can you call up the scene and imagine who is there in the setting being described and how the participants relate to each other? If you were to stage the scene in a theater, would you know what people to put there? Would you know who is saying what? Would you be able to move the plot forward? Actually, you'll never get enough information to do all of this, but you ought to be able to identify the major figures present on the scene, know the important things that were said, and maybe understand how the scene came to be or what happened next. If an event is of critical importance for your study, you should try to get as much information about what happened as your respondent can supply, up to the point where the respondent becomes restive.

Managing Transitions

The best questions fit in so well with what respondents are saying that they seem almost to be continuations of the respondents' own associations. They encourage respondents to say more about what is already in their minds. Transitions to new topics require respondents to stop and think, to relocate themselves; they may be necessary, but they tend to be unsettling.

Suppose that after a respondent has told an anecdote about his children, the interviewer nods and then asks, "How about at work, what is a typical day like?" The respondent will require time to reorient himself. He must redirect his mind from his relationship with his kids to his work situation. For a few moments, the respondent is apt to flounder. The verbal expression of this might be, "Well, ah, well, ah, the way it goes, I guess . . ." The interviewer has flustered the respondent.

I used to tell interviewers who worked for me that they could fluster respondents three times in an interview. Anything more and the respondent would wait for the next question, answer it briefly, and then wait for the next question. This is how respondents act in survey interviews. It isn't at all what is wanted in qualitative interviews.

Actually, how many times a respondent can be flustered and yet remain ready to give a full report depends largely on the quality of the interviewing partnership. A fully cooperative respondent can be flustered more than the three times I would tell interviewers was their limit. But where there is initial resistance—for example, where a respondent isn't sure he or she wants to be interviewed—even a single flustering can lead to responses that are stiff and sparse.

It is good practice to try to follow the respondent's associations so long as they remain within the interview's frame. The interviewer will still have a great deal of influence on the direction the respondent's associations take. The interviewer will be constantly communicating—by nods of agreement and understanding as well as by questions and comments— what is of value to the study and what is not. Even if few directive questions are asked, the interview will be an interactive product. Usually, without introducing new topics more than three or four times in the interview, the interviewer will find that the issues that have to be covered have been dealt with.

There are, however, a few ways of phrasing transitions that can prepare respondents for redirection. When it is evident to the interviewer that a particular line of inquiry has been adequately developed, the interviewer might say, perhaps nodding affirmatively, "Okay. Now there is another issue I wanted to ask you about. It is . . ." The respondent may still be flustered but will have warning that a question requiring reorientation is about to be made.

How Well Is the Interviewing Partnership Going?

Be alert to indications by the respondent of discomfort, antagonism, or boredom. If there is any suggestion of any of these, your immediate aim should be to restore an effective partnership. A way of doing this is to listen sympathetically to whatever the respondent wants to offer so long as it is within the study's frame. Often the respondent will have talked easily and comfortably in an area dealt with earlier in the interview, such as challenges at work and how they were overcome. Returning to that area may improve matters.

Use your own feelings in the interview as a guide to what is going on. If you are being bored by the respondent, something is wrong in the interview. The respondent may be avoiding emotional material or may be defensively providing only superficial elements. Chances are, if the respondent's account were rich and alive, you wouldn't be bored.

Sometimes in an interview I have felt sleepy, almost to the point of being unable to keep my eyes open; the same, I think, has happened to other interviewers. This is boredom to an extreme. Almost never, I believe, is it an indication of fatigue or sleep deprivation. Rather, it suggests that the interview has become lifeless and that the interviewer has bought into an unspoken agreement with the respondent just to get the interview over and done with.

If you find boredom with the interview setting in, find a topic with life in it. If the respondent becomes engaged, you will too. There is little value in mechanically plodding on, obtaining still more material that challenges your ability to remain awake. Keep in mind that you are at least as interested in the topics of the interview as a reader of the ultimate report will be. If you are bored by the material, you can be sure its readers will also be bored. The contrary is also the case: if you are fully engaged by the material and drawn in by it so that you feel your understanding is being enlarged by it, then others will be also.

One approach to finding engaging material, should an interview become boring, is to ask yourself what may be concerning the respondent that the respondent isn't expressing. If you attend closely, you may pick up clues to emotions underlying the respondent's account. Respondents may show their emotions in the phrases they use or in the stories they tell or in their posture or voice tone. Should you get a clue about which you feel fairly confident, you might try to check it out—tactfully. A phrasing

I use to check out such clues is "It sounds like . . ." (as in "It sounds like you're saying that you don't feel you've been properly recognized"). Other introductory phrasings for getting beyond superficials are "Sometimes people who are in situations like the one you're describing have feelings like . . ." or "I wonder if you might have been thinking . . ."

But if you're not comfortable making potentially facilitative comments of this sort, don't do it. And if you should run into an interview that becomes draggy, do as well as you can with standard techniques and keep in mind that not every interview can be stellar.

EXAMPLES OF INTERVIEWING

EXAMPLES OF GOOD INTERVIEWING

Interview I. *Working with a Respondent to Produce Useful Material*

Here is an example of effective interviewing, from the study of occupationally successful men. It shows how a good interviewer and a cooperative respondent can work together to produce material useful for a study.

The respondent had completed a brief first interview the week before. One aim of this second interview was to learn about stressful incidents at work—how they happened and how they were managed. The interview took place in the respondent's office.

TRANSCRIPT EXCERPT	COMMENTS
INTERVIEWER: Can you think of what has been the thing that has been most troubling of all the things that you've had to do while you've been here?	*The interviewer asks the respondent to find an instance of stress produced by a work assignment.*
RESPONDENT: [*pause*] Well, I think the most difficult task I've had at [firm name] was when I was . . . I've been here five years and it was my first year, and my task, which was really . . . ah . . . im-	*The respondent describes his first year as having been difficult because he felt unequipped to deal with an important client. The account is a bit distanced, with details smudged, but that's all*

TRANSCRIPT EXCERPT

plicit, because I had to learn what we did . . . I was hired as someone who will manage people who did know—and they did. A fairly large group. And the greatest source of revenue this company had at the time was this one client. And I don't know—I mean, I didn't have a vague idea [*chuckles*]—but it turned out that I understand . . . well . . . what . . . ah, what we did from a conceptual standpoint. But I had absolutely no technical knowledge at all, and in this medium not having technical knowledge impairs your ability to do creative work. So I was in a severe disadvantage. And I found that to be very difficult, a very difficult situation to go through.

right. The time at work the respondent is talking about seems genuinely to have been difficult, and continuing this line of questioning seems likely to produce useful material.

And in addition to that, I was . . . I was brought in because the whole client relationship with this one client was a mess. And, uh, it was run by a person who at the time was a vice president of marketing for the company and someone else who was very creative but resented the fact that I was brought in to try and get this thing organized and sort of be the people person and get morale back up and, you know, all this other stuff.

Here's something that may be interesting; the respondent was brought in to remedy problems with the client.

So I got very . . . I got no support from them at all. Quite the contrary. So the—plus I hated the client. It was, uh, the combination of all this I felt was pretty awful.

Conflict with the incumbents and dislike for the client. If this isn't a setting for stress, what is?

I: Was there any incident where it

The interviewer asks for a criti-

TRANSCRIPT EXCERPT

COMMENTS

surfaced or crystallized, and now you can remember that as a time when you really had the, uh, the height of feelings of whatever distress there was?

cal incident. He asks for an incident that will display the elements that made the respondent feel awful.

R: Well, I . . . I can . . . [*pause*] I don't know, there were so many instances. I mean, I inherited this team. I found out . . . I had been here three days, and I found out that one of these guys that worked for me, an account supervisor, was just dishonest! You talk about dishonest subordinates, this guy was just dishonest. And he created . . . he was terribly destructive to the whole organization. He . . . I mean . . . again, in a technical environment, he lied about things that were . . . were not happening. And I thought, "This is awful!" And there'd be days when I'd know, without a doubt, that this guy cannot stay. So I fired him.

The respondent is flustered. Maybe he's unwilling to experience the discomfort that would be associated with talking about a critical incident of trouble with colleagues. He shifts away from the tensions with the vice president and his creative colleague to describe something else, a problem with a subordinate.

I: What was it like . . . uh, you know, going through that decision, that "I've got to get rid of him"?

The interviewer accepts the story, although it is out of the area initially identified, and asks for the internal experience that accompanied the decision.

R: [*pause*] Uhm . . . he . . . he was so blatant it was really not a . . . it wasn't a difficult decision, and it wasn't a, uh, an agonizing one in any sense. [*Spring in swivel chair squeaks.*] This guy was so blatant. And the thing that amazed me was that he'd been allowed to stay here. Why have you people not done

Ah, here's the connection to the preceding material: the vice president (the fellow who had been in charge) and his sidekick (the creative colleague) should have fired the subordinate. This is further evidence for the respondent's side in the conflict with them.

TRANSCRIPT EXCERPT	COMMENTS

anything about it? And I
thought . . . I remember feeling a
little resentful that—this is interesting, you know—you bring in a
new guy and give him some pretty
difficult tasks right off the bat!
You know, you could've cleared
house for me before I showed up.
But you didn't. But that was consistent with the way these two people worked.

I: Yeah.

Encouraging further develop-
ment.

R: It was a certain amount of—it's
interesting because one of them,
the guy who was vice president of
marketing, he and I are equals in
this company now. He runs a division and I run a division. And actually we're quite good friends.

The respondent is skipping to the
end of the story. A lot must have
happened between the respon-
dent's first showing up (and fir-
ing a subordinate who needed
firing) and this outcome.

I: Back then things were not so
good between you?

The interviewer takes the respon-
dent back to the beginning.

R: [*laughs*] They weren't good at
all!

I: What did it feel like, realizing
that you had opposition on a higher
level?

Picking up R's comment and
asking for the feeling state that
might underlie it.

R: Well, I thought . . . this guy's
personality . . . he's real slow talking . . . his values and mine were so
different. And he was so clearly
hostile—subtle in his own way—
but to me clearly hostile. Uhm
. . . that [*pause*] I never . . . well, I
never . . . I guess . . . You know,
I'm trying . . . trying to describe
how I felt. I guess I never doubted
my own self.

Note the mixture of perception of
the vice president and personal
feeling state.

TRANSCRIPT EXCERPT	COMMENTS

I mean, I didn't know what was going on—but why should I? I just got here! [*chuckles*] Uh, and I, you know . . . so his . . . the way he treated me was just annoying, but never made me feel—I never doubted myself.

And, uh, I made friends quickly here, and the team of people who worked for me rallied around me real quick because I fired this guy who was such a destructive force. Early on, uh, I got this whole team into, uh, one of the conference rooms, and, uh—I don't know whether I really planned this, I just sort of did it—but I sat them down and I said, you know, "I'm so-and-so and this is . . ." I was kind of introducing myself to them. [*chuckles*] No one had introduced me. And I said, "I'm so-and-so and this is my background and this is what we're supposed to do and, frankly, I will not pretend that I know the techniques." I said, "I really don't. And, uh, because I don't, uhm, I'm going to ask you to really help. And, uh, if you help, I'll learn and there are things that I do know, and I'll be able to, uh, I'll be able to do something for you as a team."

It would be possible for the interviewer to now say, "You said something a moment ago about the way the vice president treated you. Could you describe that? Maybe describe a particular incident?" However, the interviewer doesn't interrupt, and the respondent now goes into how he established alliances with his subordinates. Firing the incompetent subordinate seems to have helped him establish himself.

This is an unasked-for critical incident. The respondent describes how he presented himself to his subordinates in an initial meeting. He asked for their affiliation and pledged himself to function as team leader, with loyalty returned for loyalty given. The story is useful for understanding supervisor–subordinate relationships. There seems no need to develop it further.

And, uh, then I subsequently, you know, pretty soon got rid of this other guy, so they believed that. And they supported me. You know, so it wasn't . . . I wasn't in a total vacuum. I mean, at least not in my group. You see they trans-

TRANSCRIPT EXCERPT	COMMENTS
ferred their loyalty over to me right away. So that was good.	
It was easier to deal with Alden Brown.*	*When respondents name people, it can be assumed that their thoughts are moving closer to memories of actual incidents.*
I: Was he the vice president?	*The interviewer checks that his assumption that this is the vice president, not the creative colleague, is correct.*
R: Yeah.	
I: So you could rely on the people that you were working with?	*Asking for confirmation, but also communicating the message "Yes, I understand, I'm with you." But the phrase "working with" misses a point the respondent had made, namely, that the respondent was accepted as the leader of the team by his subordinates, as the boss, and not merely as a coworker.*
R: I could rely on the people who worked for me.	*The respondent corrects the interviewer's phrasing.*
I: Anybody else that you . . . sort of thought to yourself, "Well, I've got *that* person as a friend"?	*Since we're talking now about allies, we may as well develop that element. We ought to know if others were involved in addition to those identified so far, and it may be difficult to return to this scene later.*
R: Uh, no. No, not really. [*pause*] But just the people who worked for me. I didn't really know any others.	*This completes the picture of the respondent's interpersonal situation at work at the time. He was in command of the loyalty of his subordinates but otherwise on his own in confrontation with a hostile vice president and colleague.*

* This name, like all names of respondents and the people to whom they refer, is an invention.

TRANSCRIPT EXCERPT	COMMENTS

I: Can you remember back when you had an interaction, where you got bad vibes?

The interviewer now asks again for a critical incident. Note that the respondent has now established that the vice president and his creative colleague were derelict in at least one respect—they didn't fire a dishonest subordinate—and that he had successfully won the loyalty of his subordinates. He may be ready now to talk about what happened between him and his antagonists.

R: [*chuckles*] Well, I can remember one . . . uh, trying to come up with the most dramatic example. I . . . I was so mad. I was. This is awful. Uh, the client was [X Corporation]. Yeah. And we used to have to go down to have monthly meetings in [small town], which is in the middle of nowhere. And, uh, we went down there for a meeting. And it was always a very hostile environment. They didn't like us, we didn't like them. And here were two different groups, creative groups, working together, but we really used to compete with each other.

Note the hesitancies. The respondent is not entirely comfortable reporting this incident.

And the two guys that I worked with were Alden Brown and Dennis Ealing, who's since left. And, uh, Alden and Dennis—I'll believe this to this day—really kind of set me up.

The interviewer assumes that the "two guys" are the vice president (Alden Brown) and the creative colleague (Dennis Ealing). The interviewer is confident enough of the identities to feel no need to check. But it's odd that the "two guys" should be referred to now as though they hadn't already been talked about

TRANSCRIPT EXCERPT   COMMENTS

extensively. It's as though the respondent, in describing this incident, has moved to another area of his mind.

They said, "Well, in this meet-   *The respondent is recapturing*
ing . . ." You know, maybe thirty,   *how isolated, disoriented, and*
forty people and I'd been here a   *vulnerable he was.*
short time and this is in [small
town], so I felt displaced in the
sense that there's no . . . I was with
them and staying in some crummy
hotel, you know. So it's really sort
of—and I'm feeling very uncomfortable with the clients and the
whole bit. And, uh, they kind of
set me up by saying, you know,
"In this meeting you should really
propose this," knowing darn well
that it was going to get shot down
and be torn apart. And I, not having . . . not having the technical
knowledge or . . . or experience
really to be able to distinguish
whether or not this was a good
idea. So it was . . . I said it at the
meeting, haltingly—because I
didn't have confidence to really do
it from conviction. And it got torn
to shreds. And I remember sitting
back down and saying, "That was
amazing. Boy, this was awful."

I: Did you realize what it was?   *The interviewer is asking the*
                                    respondent what was going on in
                                    his mind. The interviewer could
                                    also have asked for information
                                    about thoughts and feelings in a
                                    more open way: "While this was
                                    happening, what was going on in
                                    your mind?" That probably

TRANSCRIPT EXCERPT

R: Oh yeah. I kind of realized it halfway through what I was saying. You know, sometimes your perceptions are heightened when you have to speak publicly. [*chuckles*] And I remember thinking, "This is not going to work." Well, maybe I read it in the faces of the people. Whatever it was.

I: Could you sort of develop it from there? What happened? You're sort of talking, you look at the faces of these people in front of you. And they're starting to get uncomfortable?

R: Very. Everybody started squirming, and I guess I have another two minutes to go with this idea and it's failing. It's, uh, I suppose it's like the comedian with a bad joke! It's just—that is what it was like. A bad joke! And, uh, I . . . Yeah, I could read everybody's face and I just sort of kept on talking and I eventually did it mechanically and I'm sure I condensed it as much as I could so I could end.

COMMENTS

would have been fine. But the phrasing used here is less distancing, more in touch.

The respondent is describing both self-monitoring and his monitoring of others. One of the issues included in this study's substantive frame was the way respondents deal with challenge. Self-monitoring seems to be part of that process.

The interviewer has decided the previous response was good enough as a description of what had happened to produce the respondent's sense of failure. Now the interviewer asks for extension of the story: What happened then? Note how the interviewer tries to establish the level of concreteness he wants by bringing concreteness into the question: "You look at the faces . . . and they're starting to get uncomfortable?"

TRANSCRIPT EXCERPT	COMMENTS
I: Can you remember what it felt like internally while you were dealing with that?	*The respondent has come to the end of his description of the event. Now the interviewer asks for his internal state while it was happening.*
R: Oh, I felt like a fool. I felt mad. I felt—I really resented being set up. I mean, I thought, "What a cheap shot! What a son of a bitch." I mean, that's rotten.	
I: Then you knew it was set up?	*This sort of leading question can reassure the respondent that the interviewer is thinking and feeling along with him and can therefore encourage the respondent to continue. But an argument could also be made for asking a more open question such as "Did you have any thoughts now about your colleagues?"*
R: Oh yeah! And I said, "I would never have done that to you, you bastards." You know. But I also realized you've got to be pretty desperate to do this crap.	
I: Yeah.	
R: You know, . . . and, uh . . . so I sat down. And when I sat down, at first I just felt sort of, you know, just dread, just feeling, "What did I just do? This is awful! I feel like such a fool." And everybody's sort of, you know . . . and they very politely said, "Well, I'm sure your idea may have some merit." And this other company guy, he was sort of sarcastic and . . . and so	*This is the right level of concreteness and the right density of detail. The interviewer may well be nodding to signal understanding and assurance that this is important material.*

TRANSCRIPT EXCERPT

condescending. And he said,
"Well, I'm sure once you gain a
little more experience in this field,
you'll realize that that idea
wouldn't quite apply to this particular situation. Although, you know,
on its own merits it might . . .
might've been all right." But it
was a real put-down. A real put-
down. Yeah. And I knew, you
know . . . I instantly recognized,
"Well, my credibility with *these*
people . . . gee, why did you set me
up? Why did you do this?"

I: Yeah.

R: It was rotten. "Why did you
ever do this?"

I: Yeah. Why had they done it?

R: Ah, well, I thought there was
a . . . From their standpoint it probably was more or less, uh, very
shortsighted, but, uh, it ensured
that as far as this one client was
concerned, which was the company's most important client, I'd
never have any credibility with
them. And that's true! I haven't.

I: What happened after that? I
mean, could you sort of . . . ?

COMMENTS

*On the surface this question asks
for information about the motivations the respondent attributed to
the pair who had set him up. It
also is a way of getting at the
kind of threat the respondent felt
himself exposed to.*

*The respondent thought that his
colleagues had wanted to queer
his reputation with the firm's
most important client, and in fact
they had succeeded in this. He
might reasonably have feared
that his job was in danger. This
suggests a high level of threat.*

*The interviewer asks the respon-
dent to extend the story. The description of the stressor
situation is adequate; so is the*

TRANSCRIPT EXCERPT

COMMENTS

characterization of the level of threat. Now the interviewer wants to know what this level of threat did to the respondent and how he dealt with it. The open phrasing here ("What happened after that?") seems to me exactly right. Let the respondent tell the story, and get him to fill in the blank areas later, if necessary.

R: Well, for the rest of the meeting I just sat there, you know. I just . . . I don't know . . . tuned out. I mean, I paid no attention to that. I just sort of sat there and said, "Well, why did they do this?" And I realized, you don't do this unless you're scared of me. You wouldn't have to go to these extremes. It's really unfair.

This is a description of trying to achieve mastery of self in a situation of what must have seemed catastrophic failure. Note how many leads there are, in this one brief passage, to an understanding of responses to threat. First there is the respondent's focus on the threat, then his attempt to work out the aims of his enemies, then his disparagement of his enemies together with an effort to reassure himself of his own potency, and finally his protest of the wrong done him.

I: Now you've got—you were going to have dinner with them that evening and . . . ?

The interviewer decides not to seek further elaboration of this scene and instead goes on to the next scene. Again, note the level of concreteness in the question.

R: No, we had to fly back on this tiny little plane.

I: What happened?

The interviewer encourages the respondent to continue the story.

R: I just sat by myself. I didn't talk to them. I didn't want to go to them and say, you know, "You set

TRANSCRIPT EXCERPT	COMMENTS

me up.'' I wouldn't give them the pleasure of it. Just sat by myself. And, uh, when we got to the airport, I just walked . . . walked away.

And, uh, we came to work the next day, and I decided, well, I'm not going to—because I was trying to be their friend! You know, I was trying to get the . . . get on the good side. I was trying to, uh, please them, trying to get along with them. Go and ask them questions. Show them that I was interested even though I wasn't completely knowledgeable. You know, that was the end of that.

The respondent has not before described having attempted to ingratiate himself with the vice president and the creative colleague.

I: What happened the evening you got home? After . . . after you got off the plane?

The interviewer asks for further extension of the story. Instead of asking about a nonspecific time ("after you got back"), the interviewer refers to a concrete event ("after you got off the plane").

R: [*pause*] I didn't share it with my wife.

Mentioning that he didn't share the incident with his wife is a marker. Why else mention something that didn't happen? The interviewer must decide whether to pick it up. It could have been picked up with the question "How come?" Had the interviewer done this, the respondent very likely would have talked about problems in his marriage. Instead of detouring in that direction, the interviewer properly continues the story of the job trouble. Later in the interview the in-

TRANSCRIPT EXCERPT	COMMENTS
	terviewer could return to the marker by saying: "Earlier you said that when you returned from that client visit, you didn't tell your wife about it. Do you remember thinking about telling your wife?"
I: Can you remember how you felt?	*The interviewer asks the respondent to describe his internal state on return. Here, as is often the case, it is valuable to learn not only what happened, but what the respondent thought and felt about what happened.*
R: Mad. Angry. I was angry. Yeah. I was feeling—I was also glad to be out of [client company's town], it was such an awful place. Hated it! [*chuckles*] I mean, the whole environment. Something like that to happen in that kind of environment. It was just sort of . . . so distasteful. But, I don't know, I was just angry. Like I couldn't wait to get to work the next day. I probably didn't sleep very well.	
I: Why couldn't you wait to get to work?	*Maybe it would have been good here to ask the respondent about what kept him awake: "What was going through your mind?" The interviewer may have moved too quickly to the return to work.*
R: Because I wanted to do something about it, you know. [*pause*] And I . . . I can't remember specifically what I did. I can just remember how I felt. And I felt like, I'm	*The respondent says he wanted to do something about the incident, but can't remember what he did. He goes on to describe what seems to have been an ef-*

TRANSCRIPT EXCERPT	COMMENTS
certainly more honest than you are. My intentions are better. And uh, [the firm] was right to hire me because you couldn't run an organization where other people would report to you. So they won't. From now on they'll just report to me. And, you know . . .	*fort to reassure himself that despite his disastrous presentation to the client, the company had been right to bring him in and should continue to value him.*
I: Did you have some sense of damage done?	*The interviewer wants to know to what extent the respondent felt his standing in the organization had been damaged. But the respondent hadn't yet said anything about believing damage had been done to his standing. The interviewer should first have learned how the respondent thought the incident would affect his standing at work by asking something like "Did what happened in your presentation affect your situation at work?"*
R: To me personally?	*The respondent is floundering a bit. He is not sure what the interviewer has in mind. Damage to the firm? Damage to him personally? What sort of damage?*
I: To your . . .	*The interviewer, recognizing that the question was too vague, starts to specify that he wanted to ask about damage to the respondent's situation at work.*
R: To my reputation?	*But the respondent is continuing with his review of what might have been damaged. So the interviewer gives the respondent the floor.*

TRANSCRIPT EXCERPT	COMMENTS

I: To your reputation in the firm.

Now the interviewer says that yes, he wants to know whether the respondent had been aware of damage to his reputation in the firm.

R: As far as I was concerned, that was such a clear setup that any . . . anybody should've recognized it. I'm sure everybody did. Emmett Franklin, the man I now work for—and he is one of the founders—yeah, I think Emmett . . . I never talked to Emmett about it, but I think he understood.

Despite the interviewer's problem in directing the respondent, the interviewing partnership is sound, and the respondent continues to work with the interviewer to produce useful information.

The respondent's reference here to Emmett Franklin was a marker, although the interviewer did not recognize it. Later in the interview, the interviewer asked the respondent how he had managed to maintain himself in the company despite the failure of his presentation to the company's most important client. At that point the respondent said he had gone to Emmett Franklin and told him that he needed him as a mentor or he would never last. Franklin, who apparently thought well of the respondent, did agree to act as the respondent's mentor and helped him obtain accounts of his own. But here the respondent discouraged questioning about Emmett Franklin by saying he had never talked with him about the incident and by neglecting to mention that he nevertheless had gone to him for help.

I: Looking back now, uh, how long . . . could you say how

The interviewer is asking about the aftermath of the incident.

TRANSCRIPT EXCERPT   COMMENTS

long that incident stayed with you
emotionally?

R: Oh, as far as Alden Brown's
concerned, it will always stay with
me. I mean, he and I do get along
very well now. We're good friends,
but I'd never work with him!

I: How about the other man?

R: Dennis Ealing? He went to
work with the client company.
[*chuckle*] He's its director of marketing. He was an odd duck. Very
brilliant guy. Absolutely brilliant.
And I don't like him.

Interview II.   Negotiating What the Respondent Will Report On

Particularly early in a first interview, the interviewer may have to search
for the areas in which the respondent can provide useful material. The
interview guide will tell the interviewer the areas in which the study needs
information, but the respondent may have little to offer in some of the
areas, a great deal in others. Or the respondent may feel uncomfortable
about reporting material in some areas, and their exploration might be
postponed until the interviewing partnership is better established. The
following excerpt displays the process of searching, in the beginning of a
first interview, for the areas to discuss.

The respondent was an IV drug user who had learned a few months
before the interview that he was HIV positive. The interview was one of
several conducted in a pilot study of reactions among present and former
IV drug users to the results of testing for HIV. The interview took place
in the HIV clinic of a hospital in which the respondent was an outpatient.
The respondent had mentioned, in a brief discussion with the interviewer
that preceded the interview, that the medical staff at the hospital were not
giving him information he wanted. The interviewer began by asking about
this.

TRANSCRIPT EXCERPT	COMMENTS
INTERVIEWER: You were just saying you wanted information. Can you say what kind of information you wanted?	*The interviewer begins where the respondent is.*
RESPONDENT: Well, essentially knowing what to expect. To me that seems to be the greatest problem right now about this whole thing, being HIV positive, about having this. To know what comes next. You know, everybody talks about AIDS. Okay, AIDS is going to kill you. There's no cure for it. But how? And when? I mean, can I expect to get up every morning? Am I suddenly going to be struck down one morning, I can't get up anymore? Am I going to lose my sight? Am I going to lose my mobility? What's going to happen? How is it going to happen? Is it going to be painful, is it not going to be painful, what? Even having the experience of seeing other people having died from it, it still doesn't tell me a lot about what to expect.	*This is vivid, but it's hard to know where to go with it. The response suggests both dread of what may happen and discomfort because so much is uncertain. It might be worth learning, perhaps, whether worry about what might happen is always in the respondent's mind. But the reference to "seeing other people having died from it" sounds like a marker.*
I: You've seen other people die from AIDS?	*The interviewer picks up the marker.*
R: Yeah. I've had a lot of friends who've died from it, and I know that most of them became very debilitated at the last stages and went to the hospital. They began to lose a lot of weight, and they became very ill. And so I'm wondering, "Is this the kind of thing that's in store for me? Am I going	*But the respondent doesn't now describe a particular incident. This is generalized: "a lot of friends." The respondent might intentionally be avoiding being specific because he doesn't want to talk about a particular person or might rather have something else on his mind. The interviewer*

TRANSCRIPT EXCERPT	COMMENTS
to end up in a hospital somewhere, [having] to be cared for, or whatever?'' There are a lot of aspects to this thing, in my case particularly. I'm thirty-nine years old. I don't have any kids.	*might possibly ask for specifics by saying, "Of the friends who've died, could you tell me about the one who died most recently?" But that question would not connect with the respondent's worry about himself. In any event, by the time the respondent stops talking, the respondent has moved to not having kids. This is both another marker and apparently another aspect of the respondent's worry about his own situation.*
I: You don't have any kids?	*The interviewer picks up the marker and asks the respondent to develop the thought of not having kids in any way that feels right to him.*
R: No. I don't have any children. And at present I'm not really going steady with anybody, not living with a woman or anything like that. It's difficult to maintain the single lifestyle now. I mean, I'm out having a drink or something and I run into a woman, start talking to her. I feel somewhat obligated to make sure that nothing goes on but conversation. It kind of puts a real strain on me.	*The respondent extends not having kids to not going with a woman—with whom, presumably, he could have kids. Then he moves to his feeling that when he meets a woman he cannot allow a relationship with her to develop. The respondent seems to be alluding to actual events.*
I: Are you thinking of a special time, a particular time?	*Again the interviewer picks up what seems to be a marker.*
R: This is any time right now. I can't afford to have a relation with a woman right now.	*The respondent refuses the interviewer's implied suggestion that the respondent is summarizing*

TRANSCRIPT EXCERPT	COMMENTS

actual events. He says that there are no such events; he isn't establishing relations with women now.

I: When was the last time this happened?

Nevertheless—mistakenly—the interviewer tries again for a particular event. The vividness of the image of "nothing goes on but conversation" may have made the interviewer believe that the respondent did have a particular incident in mind, despite his disclaimer.

R: Shit. I mean, at least three, four months now since I had a relation with any woman. I mean, I'm in a stage where I'm just looking. That's all I *can* do, is look. Because, what am I going to do? They say, well, okay, use condoms. But even condoms are not a hundred percent safe. There's too many possibilities of an accident happening. And so what I've done is more or less I've just gone to where I don't have any sexual relations with women. Now that . . . phew . . . is a real change, a real upsetting thing. You know, there's still a relationship based on friendship and conversation. But, I don't know, it's just not enough for me.

The profanity here may express exasperation at having to say again that there isn't any woman, or it may be a way of introducing further detail of a repugnant situation. What follows is a vivid description of the respondent's sense of having to turn away any chance for a sexual relationship.

I: It means you're alone.

Partly to strengthen the interviewing partnership, partly to attend to the feeling tone of the respondent's report, the interviewer establishes that yes, he does understand that the respondent is talking about how his HIV status has forced him to isolate himself.

TRANSCRIPT EXCERPT	COMMENTS

R: Yeah. Yeah. A great deal, a great deal. And it's adjusting to it, accepting the fact that I will never have kids. That entire aspect of my life is through. I'm thirty-nine. And how am I dealing with that?

The response "Yeah. Yeah. A great deal, a great deal" acknowledges that the interviewer has understood his feelings. Now the respondent goes on to elaborate what it means to be alone. He indicates that not having kids is an expression of being alone.

I: What do you think about that?

The interviewer asks for further thoughts about dealing with not having kids. The question is a bit awkward, but gets the idea across.

R: It's fucked up. It's real messed up. It's *real* messed up. . . . It seems like it's difficult, very difficult to deal with.

The respondent seems to be saying that the situation is so appalling that it cannot be grasped. Here the profanity seems to express movement from a more public self to a self closer to emotion. The respondent uses intensifying words to convey the depth of his despair.

I: How's that?

The interviewer is asking the respondent to continue the theme of "it's difficult."

R: I have a lot of friends, a lot of acquaintances, a lot of people I'm meeting who don't know me that well, and I know they're wondering, like, "What's it with him? Why is he not with anybody?" Which brings up a whole thing about people wanting to know what's up with you. . . . It puts a strain on family relationships. All my brothers and sisters, they've got wives, girlfriends or boyfriends, or whatever. And just the whole concept of . . . anytime you see me,

The respondent fears that he is suspect because he is alone. He must deal not only with being alone, but also with the suspicion that his being alone creates in others.

TRANSCRIPT EXCERPT	COMMENTS

I'm always by myself. There's never a woman involved. I've got nieces and nephews that are getting to the age where I know that they're beginning to look and say, "Well, gee, Uncle Al never has a girlfriend. He's never around any woman. He never brings anybody around like that." Dealing with that whole aspect of it, knowing that people are wondering and that some people are not saying anything out of respect. They're not being nosy, they're not asking it outright.

I: When's the last time something like that happened? Like you were with somebody and this thing came up?

The interviewer is here trying for a concrete incident that would display the respondent's "knowing that people are wondering." But the interviewer's phrasing asks for such an incident in too open a fashion.

R: Well, probably have to be before the tests. And then it wasn't an issue. It never did come up because it wasn't an issue. Since the test I have not been involved sexually with anybody. Okay? And that's simply because I just have chosen not to. It's just on my mind so heavy. To think about that. It would be easy to do that. I could get away with it real easy. I mean, I could fool somebody right quick. But what would that involve? That involves taking a chance on infecting somebody else. Cutting somebody else's life short. Why would I

The respondent misinterprets the interviewer's question as asking about his being HIV positive in connection with a possible sexual relationship. He says he hasn't been with anyone since before the tests, and then he didn't know he was HIV positive. But now "It's just on my mind so heavy."

TRANSCRIPT EXCERPT	COMMENTS

do that? Or why even want to do that? I don't have the heart to do anything like that. Just don't have the heart to do that. I really don't feel like I could do that to somebody, that I could pass this on to somebody else.

I: It sounds like it's made you feel sort of a pariah, like.

Here the interviewer could have picked up the ethical issue or the self-restraint the respondent is describing, but that would probably have led the respondent to repeat what he's already said about not wanting to put someone else at risk. Instead the interviewer makes explicit what may be the theme underlying much of what the respondent has been saying: no kids; being seen as suspect by friends and family; having no access to sexual relationships. The interviewer is, in effect, checking a hypothesis, while at the same time suggesting an issue for development. And the interviewer is also again establishing that he understands what the respondent is saying. Note that the interviewer offers his guess at the underlying theme in a tentative, "sounds like . . ." statement that the respondent can reject.

R: Yeah. Yeah.

The guess seems to have been right.

I: Is that it?

The interviewer is giving the respondent a further opportunity to

TRANSCRIPT EXCERPT	COMMENTS
	reject the guess if it doesn't strike him as exactly right.
R: Yeah, it definitely made me feel like a pariah. The old-style lepers, I guess. Way on the outside now. Always looking, but you never touch. Never let anybody get that close. It's tough, man. It's very tough to be that lonely. To not have the affection, the closeness. Just not be there anymore. To always be backing out of things, always on your guard to never let a situation get that developed. Or somebody may want to be with you—you can't let that happen. Can't let it happen to you. You just can't let them get that close. At the same time, doing it in such a way as not to just come right out and say, "Hey, I got AIDS." Like to get the message across that you just don't want that kind of relationship.	*The respondent corroborates that he is talking about feeling like a pariah. He now explicitly links this feeling to his earlier statement about not being able to touch, but only to look. Note that now, instead of skittering from issue to issue, the respondent speaks coherently and with vivid emotion. He is now talking about matters of great importance to him.*
	The respondent and the interviewer have together located what the respondent can best contribute to the study at this point in the respondent's interview: a statement of how isolating it is to be HIV positive and how lonely it is to be so afflicted.

The interviewer made a couple of mistakes in the course of this excerpt. He failed to recognize that the respondent had disclaimed any potentially romantic relationship and went ahead to ask for an instance; and he phrased an appropriate question in so open a fashion that the respondent entirely misinterpreted it. Nevertheless, the interviewer paid close and unfaltering attention not just to what the respondent was saying, but also to what might underlie what he was saying. Fairly quickly the interviewer found an important underlying issue that had been expressed in much of what the respondent had said and that had to be recognized if the respondent's situation was to be understood. The interviewer's recognition of this underlying issue was not only valuable for the study in its own right, but also strengthened the interviewing partnership.

EXAMPLES OF POOR INTERVIEWING

A bad interview can often be identified just from the look of a page of transcript: the ratio of words said by the respondent to words said by the interviewer will be nearly one to one. However, a preponderance of respondent material doesn't guarantee a good interview. An interviewer can produce a bad interview not only by talking as much as the respondent but also by permitting the respondent to develop at length material of no value to the study.

Bad interviews are more frequently of the sparse-response type than the runaway respondent type. Leading to the sparse responses, often, is what seems to be questioning by the interviewer that is unrelated to the respondent's train of thought; instead, the interviewer's questions are directed solely by the interview guide, or they express the interviewer's own train of thought.

Interview III. An Interviewer with an Unshakeable Assumption

In this first example of bad interviewing, the interviewer seems to be trying to control what she is being told. She has a preconceived notion of what the respondent ought to tell her, a notion she doesn't permit the respondent to influence.

The general topic was relationships at work, and the interviewer was searching for instances of stressful relationships. The respondent had been talking about other members of his work group.

TRANSCRIPT EXCERPT	COMMENTS
INTERVIEWER: In relationships with any of these people or anyone else you would interact with regularly at work, would there be anything about the relationships that . . . were there any times when the relationships themselves were bad or were a source of distress for you personally or . . .	*The question doesn't adequately direct the respondent to a specific relationship—a boss or subordinate or peer. And the final phrasing, "times when the relationships themselves were bad or were a source of distress," has a vagueness that makes response difficult. In its favor, the question does get the respondent into the area of relationships at work. In*

TRANSCRIPT EXCERPT   COMMENTS

addition, it asks for concrete instances.

RESPONDENT: Well, I find that, for the most part, the kinds of . . . I never had any bad relationships myself with anybody in the group.

The respondent starts on something, then changes course to reject the notion that he had had bad relationships.

I: But within the framework of the people you were speaking with . . .

The interviewer doesn't recognize that the respondent has rejected the idea of having had bad relationships with anyone in his group. Now the interviewer begins to argue ("But . . ."). My guess is that the phrase "bad relationships" suggests being unable to get on with others and the respondent wants to deny being that sort of person.

R: Within the framework of the people with whom I worked, I did not have any relationships which grated on me, no.

The interviewer should now recognize that the respondent wants to close out this line of questioning. The respondent is saying, firmly, that there is nothing to report.

I: Or which caused . . .

The interviewer keeps going on the issue of bad relationships. The interviewer seems to have been determined to complete the earlier question, even though its premise has already been rejected by the respondent.

R: Some of them had relationships which were grating . . . which grated on each other, which I was pretty much aware of and probably could deal with more effectively than anybody else, because I never wound up with a situation in which in order to resolve this I had to make an enemy out of any one of them.

The respondent offers a compromise: he acknowledges that other people had trouble with each other, a situation he was able to help with. The interviewer should accept this and let the respondent develop the material, perhaps by asking, "Could you tell me about one of those times?"

TRANSCRIPT EXCERPT	COMMENTS
I: Uh-huh. That was just your own style.	*The interviewer doesn't recognize that there is a story being alluded to here. Instead, she takes the respondent's comment as a statement about managerial style.*
R: Yeah, that's more a matter of leading them rather than telling them what to do. If you can convince them and convince the whole group by consensus that this is what we ought to be doing, then they all go out, back to the trenches, and do it.	*And now we have a bit of management philosophy of little obvious use to the study. It is quite distant from the topic of relationships at work. The interviewer has fostered this by her reflection in the previous comment.*
I: Basically, you never got into a stress or distressful situation, then, with any of your people that you're related to or felt closer to?	*Now the interviewer returns to the bad relationship line the respondent has flatly rejected. This approaches badgering. In actuality, the respondent may have been in stressful or distressing situations with one or more of his people—most managers at some point are—but this isn't the way to get a description of those occasions.*
R: No. The other thing I would say is that I typically manage the group by calling the whole group in and asking them to explain what they are doing. Just going through . . . each guy says what's going on in his area, and then, sort of by consensus, it all helps steer the consensus as to what we do next, fellas. But that way, pretty much, people as a group understand as a group what they were trying to accomplish, and you could shift responsibilities around to match the skills, and so on.	*The respondent is now speaking in the generalized present. At this point it would make sense to accept where the respondent is and ask him to become concrete: "Could you tell me about the last meeting? Walk me through it?"*

TRANSCRIPT EXCERPT	COMMENTS
I: What about your "boss"? I mean, do you have some kind of relationship?	*The interviewer's question suggests an absence of interest in what the respondent just said. My guess is that the interviewer is continuing to search for stressful or distressing experiences and has hit on the idea of asking about specific relationships. But to introduce this now abruptly shifts the interview away from where the respondent is.*
R: My present boss?	*The respondent is flustered—as well he might be. He tries now to reorient himself. He asks a question partly to gain time until he can get a grip on the new interview topic.*
I: Well . . .	*And, in stumbling fashion, the interview goes on.*
R: . . . or my past boss?	
I: Your . . . maybe we can talk about both.	
R: Well, my past bosses were two people for whom I had a great deal of respect.	
I: Yes, you did mention . . . perhaps we can go into that a little bit.	

In this interview excerpt the interviewer was determined to get an interesting story of troubles with a coworker and refused to accept the respondent's unwillingness or inability to come up with one. The interviewer also refused to accept the respondent's indications of material he could develop comfortably. I find it remarkable that the respondent continued to be cooperative, despite the interviewer's competing with him for the floor, disregarding his comments, and abruptly shifting topics.

Interview IV. Refusing Respondent Leads

Here is another excerpt from an interview in which the interviewer did not listen well. In this excerpt the respondent tried to contribute usefully to the study, but the interviewer failed to elicit from the respondent the meanings of a critical incident. The interview topic was the way that recognition and informal evaluation affected the respondent.

TRANSCRIPT EXCERPT	COMMENTS
INTERVIEWER: I was wondering if, you know, what sort of an audience you have for your work? Is there some sort of group that you're doing it to impress as . . . or who you might look for out there somewhere else . . . or maybe your colleagues or . . . you know . . .	*It's all right to ask questions awkwardly as long as your concern is communicated and you don't inadvertently introduce an element that requires special attention. Here the interviewer does inadvertently supply a possible motivation for competent performance ("doing it to impress"), a motivation many respondents would want to disclaim.*
RESPONDENT: Well, obviously, uh, first I wanted to satisfy my boss, in the sense that he's—you know, I serve at his pleasure, so to speak. My annual evaluation is in his hands, so I certainly have to impress him properly and give him the level of confidence in me, you know. That's only for my benefit. About my peers within . . .	*The respondent reacts to the "doing it to impress" part of the question. He doesn't flatly reject the idea that he works to impress, but he does correct the implication that he might work only to impress. Of course he works to satisfy his boss, and in that sense to impress him, but that's his job. The respondent is starting to consider whether he works to impress his peers when the interviewer interrupts him.*
I: Which would be . . .	*The interviewer wants to know exactly who is meant. This is not necessary, and because it interrupts the respondent, is questionable.*

TRANSCRIPT EXCERPT	COMMENTS
R: . . . within the company . . .	
I: Within the company.	
R: . . . and, uh, the peers outside the company?	*The interviewer's insistence that the respondent identify his peers before saying whether he works to impress them appears to have flustered the respondent.*
I: Yeah. Like who would be your peers?	*The interviewer establishes control over the interview by requiring that the respondent provide this unessential information before going on with his story.*
R: Well, former associates . . .	*The respondent would have a right to be annoyed around here. He doesn't seem to be. He might be getting a bit cautious in his response, though; a bit concerned with whether the interviewer will understand.*
I: Oh, former associates . . .	
R: Or competitive associates. You know, people from other companies.	
I: Uh-huh. You all know each other in . . .	
R: It's . . . we may probably know *of* each other, probably more than we know each other, because we are—although it's a fairly large community in the sense of numbers, it's very small in the sense of knowledge of companies and people and, uh . . .	
I: How is that information transmitted to each other? How do they . . .	*Has the interviewer forgotten that the issue was whether the respondent worked with this audience in mind? Or is the inter-*

TRANSCRIPT EXCERPT	COMMENTS
	viewer assuming that the respondent has agreed that he wants to impress competitive associates? Actually, he hasn't agreed to this at all.
R: Usually very casually. Where we, uh, chance meetings or chance conversations. Let me say also in terms of people, of people I want to please, I want to please the people who I'm doing the project for . . .	*The respondent, God bless him, is still trying to answer the question about working to impress other people. Now he remembers his clients, whom he does want to please.*
I: The clients?	*The interviewer seems to have lost the thread of the interview and is puzzled by the respondent bringing up his clients.*
R: The clients. In the sense that it tells me that I've done a good job for them, and it tells me that my company has done a good job. And when there's an opportunity in the future, we certainly want to be considered—or even more than considered, even handed the project. Well, these are . . . I like to leave a good trail.	
I: Yeah . . .	
R: Both, again, for my own accomplishment and also for the good of the company. But we were having lunch today in a west suburb. I was there this morning. We had lunch—the client, my boss, and myself. And out from another table comes somebody I knew from a company I worked for three years ago, who I haven't seen in	*The respondent is virtually interviewing himself. He holds to a theme and looks for concrete instances. Without any help from the interviewer he here presents an incident that illustrates how people outside the company learn how you are doing.*

TRANSCRIPT EXCERPT	COMMENTS
almost—what?—three years. And through the whole chitchat . . . I introduced him and introduced the people to him and, you know, these chance meetings, chance encounters, this is how things get spread around.	
I: So what did you talk about?	*Okay, I guess. But more useful might be what went through the respondent's mind when the fellow he once worked with came up to his table to meet him, his client, and his boss.*
R: Well, just what his company was doing and what I'm doing and who these people are who were having lunch together.	*This is superficial, as well as general. A former colleague comes over to say hello and maybe check out how the respondent is doing. This would very likely elicit appraisals of relative success. It would be natural now to ask what had been the respondent's thoughts as the former colleague came up.*
I: Was it kind of the idea of impressing them with your association with the client, or was it really friendly?	*This question is at least a stab at obtaining the respondent's thoughts and feelings during the incident, but it overstructures by asking if the respondent was aiming to impress—and is a bit demeaning by making that supposition.*
R: No. Just sort of a friendly informational-type thing. Like that.	*This pretty much repeats the previous statement about what was talked about. The respondent is indicating that there's nothing more of note here.*
I: And it kind of gets spread around?	*The interviewer drops the inquiry into the meaning of the encoun-*

TRANSCRIPT EXCERPT	COMMENTS
	ter for the respondent. Instead of pursuing this, the interviewer asks a leading question about what will now happen to the information about the respondent gained by his former coworker. Sometimes leading questions are useful because they demonstrate that the interviewer is in touch or because they suggest a useful direction for development. Here the leading question only narrows the possible response.
R: Yeah. Now he'll go back and say, you know, that he saw me yesterday and who I was with.	

One of the several problems in this excerpt is the extent to which the interviewer provided wordings for the respondent. When an interviewer introduces a phrase in a question (here the phrase is "and it kind of gets spread around"), then the phrase is the interviewer's and not the respondent's, even though the respondent may accept that phrase ("Yeah, it gets spread around").

The same observation holds for this interviewer's insistence, despite the respondent's objections, on pursuing the theme of working to impress. Does this respondent really work to impress others? I would say no, not in the sense the interviewer intends. He wants recognition for his competence, but that's different from being competent in order to gain recognition. However, the interviewer kept returning to this theme, and at a couple of points elicited very qualified agreement. But it would be wrong to accept this qualified agreement as validating the interviewer's assumption.

Interview V.   Losing the Research Partnership

Despite the serious interviewing flaws in the two previous excerpts, the interviewer in each was able to maintain an interviewing partnership. When things really go badly, the research partnership is likely to be questioned by the respondent. The following example of bad interviewing is from an interview conducted by a student in a class on interviewing.

The student interviewer was concerned with identity formation among delinquents, an interesting issue for which qualitative interviewing would seem to be the appropriate data-gathering approach. The student hoped to demonstrate that criminal behavior stemmed from the development of a criminal identity and that one process leading to the development of a criminal identity was taking as a role model a figure from organized crime. The excerpt is from the student's interview with a 17-year-old who had recently been convicted of theft. The 17-year-old has just said that organized crime figures had long been heroes of his.

TRANSCRIPT EXCERPT

COMMENTS

INTERVIEWER: Did looking up to them change your behavior? Would you have gotten into crime without them?

The student makes a couple of errors here: a minor one (asking two different questions at once) and a more important one (asking the respondent for conclusions rather than observations).

The problem is that the student wants a quick confirmation of his hypothesis. He would like the respondent to say, "Yes, looking up to them made me a thief." The student interviewer would have done better to elicit his respondent's thoughts and memories and to let them *confirm or disconfirm his hypothesis.*

RESPONDENT: Yes, I tried to be an enforcer for them. I started thieving and eventually I got into trouble.

This statement in itself doesn't contribute much, but what a wonderful collection of markers it is: "tried to be an enforcer" (note the "tried"); "started thieving"; and "got into trouble." Given the research aim, I would pick up on "tried to be an enforcer" and ask "Could you tell me about trying to be an enforcer?" with the expectation of then asking "Could you go

TRANSCRIPT EXCERPT	COMMENTS
	back to where the idea came from?'' and ''How did things develop from there?'' I'd also make a mental note of the other markers and be ready to return to them when there was opportunity.
I: Why were they your role models?	*The student is determined to confirm his hypothesis; he neglects the markers.*
R: Because they were into organized crime. They had a lot of power.	*The word ''power'' strikes me as another marker. I would guess that it is an expression of something of cognitive and emotional importance to the respondent. It might be valuable to follow it up.*
I: How do you mean?	*It's going to be tough to get to the reason power is attractive, but maybe the respondent can describe the imagery associated with power. In general, it's difficult to get respondents to explore cognitive and emotional complexes. Asked for elaboration, respondents are apt to state the complex in new words rather than provide its imagistic and emotional bases. Although the question ''How do you mean?'' can be a good one if a respondent is already in a scene (if this respondent had said, ''The guy I was working for showed me he liked me''), here it's too unfocused. The respondent can't know whether the interviewer is asking for a definition (''What do you mean by power?'') or for an elaboration of the idea of power. A better question might*

TRANSCRIPT EXCERPT	COMMENTS
	have been "How did they show their power?"
R: They had the power to choose whether a person could live or die. They had the power to snap their fingers and people would do what they say.	*The respondent does provide some development of his idea of the crime bosses' power. He conceives of the crime bosses as having not only a Godlike power of life and death but also a royal power of command. It would be important to move to concrete material now. One possibility would be to ask the respondent when he first became aware of the crime bosses' power or first saw it displayed. The respondent's stories would then show what images were indexed by his words. But also the interviewer should note that the response is a bit testy. Attention to the interviewing partnership might be in order.*
I: Like how? What do you have in mind?	*This question, at this point, makes me think the interviewer was out of sync with the respondent. The respondent has just tried to answer "How do you mean?" by specifying the display of power he had in mind. Now the interviewer is again asking a kind of "How do you mean?" question.*
R: Come on, man. You know as much as I do. They don't like somebody, they get one of their people in, they say go hit him in the head. Pretty soon he's not around anymore. That's all there is to it. They had that kind of power.	*This is a rejection of "What do you have in mind?" Manifestly, the respondent rejects the interviewer's pose of naïveté. But there is also in the respondent's asperity an objection to a sense of artificiality in the interview, to*

TRANSCRIPT EXCERPT	COMMENTS
	the absence of genuine partnership.
	The level of the respondent's asperity seems mild to me. Nevertheless, the respondent is questioning the assumptions of the interviewing partnership: "Come on, man. You know as much as I do." The respondent goes on to provide an answer, but he has put the interviewer on notice that he is aware that the interviewer is playing a role and that he is made uncomfortable by it. And he refuses, at least for the moment, to provide anything more than a sketchy, if vivid, indication of what he has in mind.

There's nothing irreparable here as yet. But note how the student interviewer's failure to pick up markers, insistence on a particular line of thought, and, finally, unfocused response to the respondent's reference to crime-boss power led the respondent to challenge the research partnership. The partnership may have been fragile to begin with—and certainly the student was courageous to undertake a tape-recorded interview with a 17-year-old who had recently been convicted of theft—but closer attention to the respondent's thought and imagery and more concern for maintaining the interviewing partnership would almost surely have produced a better interview.

What is essential in interviewing is to maintain a working research partnership. You can get away with phrasing questions awkwardly and with a variety of other errors that will make you wince when you listen to the tape later. What you can't get away with is failure to work with the respondent as a partner in the production of useful material.

CHAPTER 5

ISSUES IN INTERVIEWING

THE EFFECTS OF INTERVIEWING ON RESPONDENT AND INTERVIEWER

Qualitative interviews regularly bring ·the ordinarily ˙private into view. What ˙are the effects on the respondent and on the interviewer of the respondent's sharing with the interviewer aspects of the respondent's private life?

WHAT IS IT LIKE TO BE A RESPONDENT?

Here is what two respondents, each a participant in the pilot study of people who are HIV positive, said about being interviewed. Both respondents were male and HIV positive; neither respondent had gone beyond high school.

INTERVIEWER: What was it like to be interviewed?

RESPONDENT: It was good to talk to somebody, finally. That's one thing I haven't done, is talk to many people about it. I'm getting something out of it.

I: How do you mean?

R: Well, see, there's nobody that I can talk to in my life. There's nobody whatsoever. I just don't have nobody to talk to like that. I mean, even

121

though our conversations—it's like you're like listening. I mean, you ask questions, but you're more listening. And that's all sometimes I need. See, there's nobody else that listens. I mean, you're not saying one thing or another, you're just listening. And that's to me, that's what I need sometimes. It's probably what I needed for a long, long time. Or I wouldn't be able to come in here so easily and just tell you about everything.

One interpretation of this statement is that being interviewed interrupted the respondent's oppressive isolation. It provided him with the opportunity to talk about urgent concerns to someone who listened closely and sympathetically. That the listener did nothing more—made no interpretations, offered no advice—did not matter. It was the talking and being listened to that counted.

To talk to someone who listens, and listens closely, can be valuable because one's experience, through the process of being voiced and shared, is validated. Furthermore, it is useful to be able to formulate one's experience and so to make sense of it.

The second respondent offered only a brief response to the question about what it had been like to be a respondent. But in that brief response he made evident the cathartic value of talking:

I: What has it been like, talking?

R: I haven't had no problem with it. Some days I got something on my mind maybe, and . . . well, it drains some of the pressure out of me.

I have several times been a respondent in a qualitative interview. When the interview went well, I found afterward that in the areas covered in the interview I made more sense to myself. It's not that I had been puzzled by myself before, but I hadn't given systematic attention to the issues I discussed in the interview. Furthermore, I was pleased to have had someone's uninterrupted attention for a while. I liked having a sympathetic listener. I found it confirming to have what I said treated as legitimate and valuable. I liked feeling that my accounts were useful. When the interview ended I was reminded of how rarely in my life I can talk about my experiences in something other than a condensed, allusive, or generalized fashion. Spinning out a detailed, coherent story just isn't done in conversations with friends and intimates, nor is it likely that an attempt to do so would be uninterrupted.

Although my situation is far less pressured, far less distressing, than the situation of someone who is HIV positive, the value of being interviewed seemed the same for me as for the two HIV-positive men. I believe the value of being interviewed is much the same for most respondents.

In large measure, interviewing provides respondents with an opportunity to talk about matters of emotional importance while remaining at an emotional middle distance: close enough to the emotions to experience them but distant enough to maintain self-control.[1] The alliance with the interviewer, which is an aspect of the research partnership, can provide helpful support as a respondent explores matters that had been confusing, distressing, or painful. The respondent's task—to describe in a coherent fashion what happened—requires the respondent to maintain control over the memories and feelings even as he or she experiences them anew. The result is likely to be that the respondent becomes somewhat more comfortable with matters the respondent had previously felt troubled by.[2]

The risks to respondents in qualitative interviewing are not usually significant. One risk is a consequence of the time-limited nature of the interviewing relationship. When there is a series of interviews and the respondent is socially isolated (as a single parent might be), the respondent may feel let down when the interviewing ends. But terminating a series of interviews probably doesn't leave the lonely respondent worse off than before the interviewing began, and precautions can be taken against the respondent's experiencing too severe a sense of loss. The respondent can be told in advance how many meetings are planned, and the last meeting can include a summing up to help the respondent achieve closure on the experience. And it may be possible to send the respondent a copy of a project publication.

Institutional review boards set up for the protection of human subjects sometimes worry about an interviewer shaking up a respondent's defenses and weakening his or her integration. They imagine a respondent reacting like Captain Queeg during his cross-examination, becoming all nervous tic and jittery incoherence. I suppose this is theoretically possible, but I have never known it to happen. It seems to me unlikely to happen if only because virtually all respondents will have successfully defended their character organization against severe onslaughts—such as those launched by an angry spouse—and will have little trouble dealing with the much lesser threat an interview may pose.

It is possible that interviewing may cause someone to reflect on his or her life and, in consequence, make changes. A respondent in a study of single parents, after interviews in which she described her rather barren life, decided she had become entirely too reliant on her mother. Soon thereafter, despite her mother's opposition, she embarked on a relationship with a married man. She and her mother became estranged. For a couple of months the relationship with the man was sustaining, but then the man returned to his wife and the woman became depressed. The woman thought being interviewed had contributed to her shift in life organization, but she said that she thought she would have rebelled against her mother sooner or later anyway.

On a very few occasions in my experience a respondent indicated that he or she regretted having talked too freely in the interview. Once, in an interview marked by close rapport, a woman employed in the design world talked freely about the sexual lives of her associates. She later called my office to ask that the sections of the tape containing those comments be erased. I erased the sections. In another instance a respondent withdrew from a study and demanded that his tapes be sent to him because his wife was outraged by his candor about their marriage. I sent the tapes and did not use his material in the study. In each of these cases the interview obviously had created transient discomfort.

My associates and I have found that respondents may be concerned that they will be identifiable in our publications. One man, head of a family business, was worried that we would describe him so precisely that he would lose anonymity. We reassured him that we wouldn't, and we didn't; in our report, for one thing, we omitted that his was a family business. Another man gave us an account of his marriage that contained potentially embarrassing material. He asked that if we quoted from his interview we not give any clues to his identity. We did quote from his interview, but gave no information at all about his age or occupation.

In most studies I've done, a few respondents have been dealing with a current upset, such as a recent marital separation or a recent diagnosis of serious illness, and the interviewing uncovers their distress. It isn't possible at that point to remain the unobtrusive research interviewer. Rather, you have to acknowledge the respondent's distress and, for a time, simply sit and listen and permit the person to feel whatever he or she feels. Such occasions impose on an interviewer a responsibility for providing a supportive presence, a role the interviewer may not have expected. But, as Saint-Exupéry's Little Prince pointed out, such are the risks of entering someone else's life.

Does an interviewer have the right to ask a respondent about potentially painful material? If that is what the study is about, then the answer is "of course." The respondent should have agreed in advance to the topic of the interview, and the interviewer always is responsible for being considerate in questioning and listening. If the study has another focus but the respondent has provided a marker—"Let's see, I accepted early retirement a couple of months after my divorce"—the interviewer is being invited to ask about the matter—"Your divorce?"—and probably should. If the matter is relevant to the study but the interviewer is uncertain whether the respondent wants to discuss it, the interviewer could first ask, "Is this something you would feel all right talking about?"[3]

WHAT IS IT LIKE TO SIT AND LISTEN?

There isn't any one reaction I have to listening to respondents. Sometimes I leave an interview exhilarated; at other times an interview is only an interview, an afternoon's task. To be sure, even in the latter case I am likely to feel privileged to have been admitted into someone else's private experience.

Occasionally, an interview is engaging enough for me not only to feel in tune with the other person's rhythm of speaking and thought but to see the world through the other person's eyes. At such times I feel myself to be split, with one part functioning professionally, asking questions and monitoring responses, while another part is identified with the respondent. Identification can become so strong that I feel my contact with my own core self has been loosened. I remain aware, of course, that I am with the respondent as an interviewer, but the world in which I live is replaced, temporarily, by the respondent's.

After the ending of any interview that has been engaging, I am likely to be a bit disoriented, the way someone might be on emerging from a movie. On the drive back to the office I may take a wrong turn and go in a direction I hadn't intended. But instead of being impatient and frustrated I am likely to feel as though I need the extra time to return from the respondent's world to my own.

At some point in every study in which I have done interviewing, I have found a respondent's account so evocative of developments in my own life or of my own concerns that I am flooded with thoughts or feelings. I then try as best I can to allow my thoughts and feelings to enter my awareness, while continuing to attend to the respondent, as a way of better understanding him or her. Later I try to summon the thoughts and feelings so that I can better assimilate them, or at least become accustomed to them.

My aim is to enable myself to emotionally understand someone's account without allowing my attention to be captured by my own feelings and thoughts. When we interview on an issue that is painful for respondents and when their accounts are likely to elicit sympathetic pain in us, it is almost necessary that we achieve this kind of neutralization. In a study of bereavement, for example, the interviewer should try to get to the point where he or she can hear about—and witness—the pain that follows a husband's death, or a wife's, or a child's, and understand it and respond to it while neither becoming a distanced spectator nor being flooded by personal experiences, associations, and feelings. This sort of neutralization is not callousness; rather, it is a state in which the interviewer can understand emotionally while still attending to the respondent and the interview.

Interviewing is, for me, usually tiring. I find that it takes energy to maintain an unswerving attention. It requires energy to get into sync with the respondent's way of thinking while remaining alert to what isn't being said. It requires energy for me to monitor my own reactions, to judge whether the material is vivid enough, to keep in mind the issues about which I hope to learn, to maintain a sense of how I am doing with time, and to remember to check the tape recorder's view meter to be sure the recorder is working. I can't do too many interviews in a day. Three strikes me as a lot; two would be better.

Some interviews leave me feeling washed out. Some leave me feeling perplexed, wondering if I managed them properly. I may be uncertain about the way the interview developed or feel bad about walking away from someone whose life is difficult. Whenever any of this happens, I want to talk to someone; when I have a partner on the project, I try to talk with that person about what happened. If there's no one to talk to, I can manage, but it's better to have someone to talk to.

I am always gratified if an interview has gone well. The interview will then have been a good experience in itself, and in addition I know that I have usable material on the tape. Sometimes, after an interview has gone well, I find myself believing that I am good at what I do and, in consequence, am pleased with myself. By the same token, after a bad interview I feel awful.

I have had my share of bad interviews. I think especially of interviews where I have been clumsy, a respondent has been ungiving, and my clumsiness and the respondent's obduracy each exacerbated the other. In an interview that is going badly I fumble for questions, try to remind myself of the interview's objectives, phrase badly the questions I come up with, and begin to feel acutely uncomfortable. I leave such an interview frustrated and self-doubting, sure that the interview produced little of value. I am likely to wonder whether I have not stumbled into the wrong line of work.

But even with the occasional failure, there is much I gain from the experience of interviewing. I can find myself so absorbed by the issues of the interview that I suspend awareness of myself. I am in that state that Csikszentmihalyi calls "flow": I am totally in the interview, aware of it and nothing more.[4] Or an interview can suddenly become so rich in material the study needs that it is as if I have struck the mother lode. (It is at such moments that I feel compelled to check that the tape recorder is working.) In a sizable proportion of the interviews I've done I have felt that I was being given personal instruction in some sector of living, for example, how to be a parent or how to function despite adversity. At such times I have felt doubly privileged: privileged to be permitted into the respondent's life and privileged again for the opportunity to learn.

INTERVIEWER RESPONSIBILITIES

While interviews are extremely unlikely to introduce pain or trouble in respondents' lives, they may well elicit in respondents an awareness of pain they had pushed out of their consciousness. A woman who worked for me as an interviewer was disturbed when her respondent, also a woman, suddenly began crying because she was reminded by the interview of how disappointing her life had been. But neither the interview nor the interviewer was responsible for the respondent's sadness and tears. Nor should the interviewer's relationship to the respondent have been changed by their display. It should have continued to be a partnership based on mutual respect, concerned with producing information useful to research.

Often, when a respondent is flooded by emotion, the interviewer's respect for the respondent is best expressed by just sitting quietly. When the respondent gives evidence of being back in touch, the interviewer might ask, "Is it all right to go on?" or might say something that indicates understanding, such as "It must have been hard going for you, these past weeks" or "It sounds like anniversaries are hard." The interviewer should offer such comments as a professional who is working with the respondent. It would be wrong for the interviewer to step out of role and say, as might a solicitous friend,"You just have to think of the future." Not only is this statement out of keeping with the interviewer's role, but it also suggests a reluctance to listen. And with a truly serious hurt or loss, an attempt at good advice can be felt as a minimization of how dreadful was the respondent's experience.

It would also be wrong for the interviewer to try to comfort by saying "I know how hard it can be" or, worse, "I'm sure it will be better in time." The interviewer has been granted no right to attempt to modify the respondent's feelings. Nor should the interviewer become evaluative, not even approvingly evaluative, as by saying "It's brave of you to keep going" or "I admire your ability to keep going." The interviewer is a work partner, not a therapist, not a friend, not an appraising audience.

It is appropriate for the interviewer to indicate, by his or her manner, "Yes, I understand the seriousness and painfulness of what you are reporting." The interviewer might be able to say, with sympathy, "That's too bad." Beyond this the interviewer does best to convey a middle distance in response to the respondent's feelings, in touch with them and responsive to them, but not overwhelmed by them.

There is no reason for an interviewer to feel guilty about intruding on a respondent's grief or sorrow. It's not the talking that hurts. Yes, sometimes people who are grieving want to distract their minds so that they can gain respite from their distress. But if they are aware of the interview's topic, they are likely to be prepared to talk about the loss. Still, the interviewer should bear in mind that sensitivity, tact, and respect for the respondent, always important, are essential with a respondent who displays pain.

Once, while interviewing a respondent, a lawyer who had retired from a distinguished career, I was asking about his current activities when he said, in passing, that he was dealing with some unexpected personal problems. This was, of course, a marker, and I picked it up. He then said that 5 or 6 weeks earlier his wife had left him. Then he stopped and sighed. After a moment's silence I asked how it had happened. The man then talked about his wife's long-unexpressed anger at having been his taken-for-granted spouse and how his traveling to collect an honor had been for her, unbeknownst to him, a last straw. The information was valuable for the study. It demonstrated how isolating was the double loss of work and spouse, even for a widely respected man. Talking about the loss was also, I think, helpful to the respondent.

Of course, we should not be so single-minded in pursuit of data that we encourage respondents to decompensate, to shift their defenses so that they become less capable of effective functioning. Indeed, we ought to call a halt to interviewing if it ever appears that a respondent is decompensating. I suppose an instance of this might be a respondent telephoning us, the day after the first of an intended series of interviews on bereavement, to say that as a result of the interview he had been unable to sleep and intended to stay home from work. But I have never known this to happen, and I have interviewed people who were pretty fragile.

In a study of case management I interviewed formerly hospitalized mental patients. My respondents were men and women who had been diagnosed as schizophrenic, paranoid, or brain damaged. With only a few exceptions, each had sufficient clarity to tell me how case managers had helped or had failed to help. None suffered anything more than transitory discomfort as a result of participating in the interview.

This is not to say that the interviewing never unsettled these respondents. A man in his mid-thirties, living in supervised housing, had until a few months earlier lived with his family. But when I introduced the topic of how it had happened that he had moved from his family into supervised housing, the man produced a sound like an air-raid siren, piercingly loud and unvarying in pitch, followed by a staccato burst of words whose sequence made no sense whatsoever. Then he began to sigh deep, rasping sighs. Then, again, the air-raid siren, followed by the words, followed by the sighs. The episode lasted a couple of minutes in all. Then the man was quiet. Then, in a normal voice, he returned to the interview as though nothing had happened. We talked a bit more about his current housing, and I again asked about the family events that had preceded his move into supervised housing. There was a moment's silence, and then the man went into the sequence of siren noise, word salad, and sighing. At that point I decided to ask no more direct questions about events in his family.

In another interview in that study a woman insisted, whenever the interview made her uncomfortable, that she had given birth to a child from her forehead. I'm sure her delusion had symbolic meanings, but I decided that learning what they were would not contribute to an evaluation of case management. Instead, when the woman began describing her baby's emergence from her forehead, I would try, gently, to return her to her experience with her case manager.

As these two respondents demonstrated, even formerly hospitalized mental patients who are still severely troubled have effective ways of guarding their integrity. I feel confident that being interviewed did no harm to either of these two respondents. Nor did it harm a paranoid respondent who refused to believe I was really an interviewer, several other respondents whose region of clarity was limited, nor the quite extraordinary respondent who seemed as sane as anyone but had become adapted to life as a mental patient.

I have also interviewed troubled adolescents and, again, feel confident that the interviews were not harmful to them. Most welcomed the interview. I do remember one boy who was thoroughly distrusting, but he dealt with whatever threat he believed the interview posed by limiting his responses to the most laconic. I finally said something like "You seem to be sort of uncomfortable, like you're not sure you like being interviewed." At this he brightened and said I was right. I congratulated myself on getting through to him and said, "What is it that doesn't feel comfortable? Like, is it just talking about things, or something else?" The young man hesitated, then his face set, and he said, "I don't know," and that was the end of it. He wasn't benefited by being interviewed, but I don't think he was hurt either.

Janet Malcolm suggests that interviewing is inherently duplicitous. She generalizes from a particular instance in which a writer ingratiated himself with a subject in order to obtain material that he later used to discredit the subject. (To be sure, the subject had already been discredited by a conviction for murder.) Malcolm characterizes all journalists—her argument can be extended to anyone who interviews—as confidence men, skilled at establishing relationships of apparent warmth and trust so they can obtain information that they will later use for their own purposes. The result, she says, is that respondents feel, at the very least, misled.[5]

This can be true, but I think it need not be and should not be. The relationship established with respondents should be exactly what it purports to be—a research partnership. Beyond this, I think interviewers should ensure that respondents are not hurt because of their cooperation. Unlike physicians, interviewers have no responsibility to benefit the people they talk with, but, like physicians, they do have a responsibility to do no harm.

Respondents are very unlikely to be harmed simply by participating in a research interview. Indeed, as I have noted, the chances of their being benefited by the interview are much greater than the chances of their being harmed. But they can be hurt by confrontation with a view of themselves that they feel to be injurious or by making available to others potentially discrediting information.

It is an expression of the interviewer's responsibility, quite apart from its importance as technique, to be nonjudgmental, even when that goes against the interviewer's grain. Furthermore, the interviewer has no mandate to help respondents understand themselves. This means, among other things, that the interviewer should refrain from making connections for respondents that the respondents have not made for themselves and from suggesting motivations for the respondents' behavior that the respondents have not themselves considered.

The interviewer must, of course, respect the commitment to confidentiality. Nothing a respondent says to the interviewer should be leaked to others in the respondent's world, nor should the respondent's interview materials be available to anyone outside the study. Nothing reported from the study, in print or in a lecture, should permit identification of respondents.

We have, I think, one further responsibility to our respondents. In any study we have an obligation to our sponsors (government or foundation or university or our own bank account), to our field, and to ourselves to produce the most useful report possible. We have the same obligation to our respondents. We have engaged them in a partnership in which they are expected to do their best to provide the study with observations. It is our responsibility to make their lessons known.

CONFIDENTIALITY DILEMMAS

We guarantee respondents confidentiality. Indeed, we put the guarantee into our consent forms. Furthermore, one element of the implicit research partnership we establish with a respondent is a commitment that the respondent will not be damaged because of his or her participation in the interview. Are there any circumstances in which an interviewer could nevertheless be justified in passing on interview information to whoever might be the appropriate authorities—the police, the respondent's psychiatrist, a state agency for the protection of children? Suppose the respondent confesses behavior that is criminal? Should the respondent be reported to the police? What if the respondent is homicidal? Or suicidal? What if the respondent is harming others? What if the respondent is harming children?

I have never interviewed anyone who gave me reason to believe he or she planned a homicide or suicide or was involved in child abuse. If I had, I believe I would have made an effort to contact appropriate authorities. I have interviewed people engaged in criminal behavior, including several who were engaged in illegal drug use, a few who were involved in occasional theft from retail stores, and one man who a year before our interview had committed armed robberies. (The man was a drug user who had been desperate for money.) I did not report any of these respondents to the police and would have resisted efforts to make their interview reports available as evidence against them. I hope I am not vulnerable to charges as an accessory after the fact, but I think in those cases I could responsibly honor my pledge of confidentiality.

More difficult was the problem posed by a woman respondent who was HIV positive. She said that all her life, from the time she was a child, she had been treated brutally by men. Contracting HIV from a boyfriend was only the most recent instance. Now she wanted to get even with the whole male sex. She visited barrooms every evening to pick up men with whom she could have intercourse, in the hope that she would infect them. The woman's sister had already reported her to a public health agency, mostly because she wanted the woman stopped before she was hurt by some man she had tried to infect. The public health agency did nothing.

In our final interview I learned the woman was no longer seeking revenge through sex. She had met a man who had become her steady boyfriend and who remained with her even after he was told—by that same sister—that she was HIV positive. (His first reaction was to yell at the woman and, I think, push her around.) If in our final interview the woman had reported continuing her campaign to spread HIV among men, I would have told her to stop. I can't believe that would have done much good, but I would have told her anyway. I also would have discussed her report with the head of the clinic where she was being treated, with the thought of devising some way to interrupt her behavior.

Until the woman herself resolved the issue, the problem of what to do with information that a respondent was trying to spread HIV infection to others was the most difficult dilemma I have faced in a lifetime of interviewing. But there were two other respondents in that pilot study who also raised issues of intervention. One was an HIV-positive woman, an IV drug user and an alcoholic, who blithely reported that she had passed along her hypodermic needle to an acquaintance. The respondent had known what she was doing; she had told the recipient to "wash it out good." In the interview she offered the rationalization that the acquaintance probably was already infected. I was appalled and indicated concern, but I did not tell her she should never again pass on a needle she had used. Nor did I take this information to the clinic where she was being treated. The second instance was a woman whose husband was HIV positive who was deliberately exposing herself to the risk of contracting the disease. Again I was appalled, and again indicated concern, but did not say she should stop.

These dilemmas develop at the intersection of two governing principles. We have, usually explicitly, bound ourselves to respect the confidentiality of what we are told. We have also, usually implicitly, bound ourselves to respect the integrity of our respondents, including their right to their decisions and behaviors. These commitments are on the side of inaction. On the other side are our responsibilities as citizens to prevent harm by our respondents both to themselves and to others. Generally, we respect our pledges to respondents, but there can be circumstances under which we would not. An interviewer who was convinced by a respondent that the respondent intended to kill someone, and had the gun with which to do it, would be required, under law, to do whatever might be necessary to stop the intended crime, including placing a call to the police.

It might seem that dilemmas associated with confidentiality could be avoided by noting in the consent form the conditions under which confidentiality will be breached. A statement might be made in the consent form that a serious threat to adult life or to the well-being of children would justify suspension of the investigator's commitment to confidentially. In fact, some research review boards require such statements.

Noting in the consent form that confidentiality may not be absolute can help, but it will not fully resolve the problem. If an interview produces evidence of a threat to the well-being of the respondent or others, the investigator would still be required to assess the threat's credibility. If the investigator believes the threat to be genuine and yet unlikely to be implemented, should action to forestall it nevertheless be taken, to be on the safe side? Issues of judgment remain, no matter what's in the consent form: Just how credible is the threat? Is useful action to forestall it possible? What would be the cost to the respondent and to the study of any action undertaken? What are the possible costs of inaction?

Problems of this sort are, fortunately, rare, but when they arise they are likely to have no easy solution. Nor does there seem to be any general method for their resolution. Rather, as would be true in other situations where the behavior required by one governing moral principle is contrary to the behavior required by another governing moral principle, decision can only be arrived at on a case-by-case basis.

RESEARCH INTERVIEWING AND THERAPEUTIC INTERVENTION

The techniques of qualitative interviewing may seem uncomfortably close to constituting psychotherapy unsought by the respondent. An interviewer with whom I once worked told me that she had become conscience stricken when one of her respondents said, "I'm talking to you like I would to my therapist." My colleague worried that, unknowing and unbidden, she had blundered into the realm of therapy.

There are obvious resemblances between the research interview and therapeutic interviewing. The research interviewer resembles a therapist by encouraging the respondent to develop thoughts and memories, by eliciting the respondent's underlying emotions, and by listening closely to the respondent's utterances. How different, then, is the respondent from a patient when the respondent provides what would otherwise be private observations, thoughts, and feelings? And how different from therapeutic results are the results of participation in a research interview when respondents leave the research interview more comfortable with themselves? Is qualitative interviewing really therapeutic interviewing motivated by research needs?

There are several ways in which qualitative interviewing is different from therapeutic interviewing. First, the aims and practices of research interviewing and of therapeutic interviewing are different. In therapeutic interviewing the functioning of the patient is the object of concern. Whatever the therapist does is, or should be, motivated by the aim of helping the patient. Patients understand that their talking is a means to their improvement. In order to help, therapists may do much more than simply listen closely: they may also provide interpretations of the patient's behavior, advice on the patient's choices in life, and explorations of the patient's thoughts and feelings about the therapeutic relationship. In research interviewing, on the other hand, the interviewer's questioning is motivated by the aim of eliciting information useful to a study. The respondent is a partner in developing the research information. The interviewer is without license to produce change in the respondent's functioning and has no right to give interpretations or advice. It would not be proper for a research interviewer to suggest connections between the respondent's verbalizations when the respondent has not already made them. It was improper, for example, for a student interviewer to follow a young woman's report of liking young men who were active in sports with the question "Is your father active in sports?"

Second, the material elicited during research interviewing and therapeutic interviewing is different. Therapists are likely to encourage patients not only to talk about their internal states but also to find sources in earlier life for current images and feelings. And a therapist is likely to want the patient to explore these matters until the patient has dealt with them adequately. The research interviewer is much more likely to want to hear about scenes, situations, and events the respondent has witnessed. The interviewer in a qualitative research study will want respondents to talk about their internal states only if this would be useful for the study. Once the interviewer has obtained the information needed by the study, the area of a respondent's internal state would not be revisited.

Third, the interview relationship is different for the researcher and the therapist. Therapists are responsible to patients for helping them improve in functioning. Because the patient looks to the therapist for help, the therapist will almost surely become an authoritative figure in the patient's life and thoughts. In contrast, the research interviewer is a partner in information development. The interviewing relationship is defined as one of equals, although interviewer and respondent have different responsibilities. And while therapists remain for some time important figures in the lives of patients, interviewers are ordinarily recognized by respondents as transient figures in their lives.

Finally, the patient pays the therapist for the therapist's help. The interviewer is paid not by the respondent but by the study. Indeed, the respondent may also be compensated by the study; at the very least, the respondent is likely to be thanked by the interviewer for the interview.

IF A RESPONDENT HAS NEED OF CLINICAL SERVICES

What if someone you talk with is so troubled that you feel psychiatric help is desirable? If respondents themselves indicate an interest in clinical services, there is not much of a problem. It is a good idea to have available a list of services, including therapists and social agencies, to be given to people who ask for referrals. But absent such a list, you can always tell respondents that you will check with colleagues and get back to them.

It is when a respondent doesn't indicate an interest in clinical services but you think they are needed anyway that you may have a problem. Although it is not your place to make diagnoses or judgments regarding who might be benefited by therapy or counseling or other services, if your respondent, on the way to sitting down with you for the interview, were to trip on the rug and be injured, you would of course call for emergency treatment. Similarly, if the respondent gives the kind of evidence of need that any fellow citizen would respond to, you should respond as a fellow citizen. For example, after an interview with a new widower who is baffled by his inability to manage his household, you could mention that homemaker services may be available.

But people who do a great deal of research interviewing can go through their careers without meeting more than a handful of situations in which they think it right to make an unrequested referral or offer unsolicited advice. More often they run into situations where the right thing to do isn't evident. I once interviewed a couple whose marriage was clearly troubled. They both described loud quarrels, frightening to the children and disturbing to themselves. The husband, after he and I completed our interview, asked me what I thought about his family. I said I thought all families, including his, had strengths and vulnerabilities. I waited for him to say more about what he had in mind, but he didn't. So I left.

It is not all that unusual for respondents to want to know the interviewer's reactions to them or to their situation just to be reassured that they are doing well enough. If I can offer that kind of reassurance without being false or patronizing, I will do so. If I can't, I will retreat into generalities, as I did here. Perhaps in this case nothing more was being asked for. But as I remember the ending of that interview, I suspect that the man did want something more. Maybe he wanted a referral for counseling or at least a judgment on whether he and his wife should have counseling. Maybe I should have found a way to ask if that was what he had in mind. I still wonder what I should have done.

MATCHING INTERVIEWERS TO RESPONDENTS

A few years ago it was fashionable among reviewers of proposals for the funding of qualitative interview studies to want interviewers matched to intended respondents, at least in race and possibly in sex and social background as well. There were two reasons given for the desirability of such compatibility: acceptance of the interviewer by the respondent and a greater likelihood that the interviewer would be able to understand.

One way to phrase this issue is to ask to what extent it is necessary for the interviewer to be an insider in the respondent's world in order to be effective as an interviewer. Studies of survey interviewing have shown that respondents do use observable characteristics of the interviewer, including the interviewer's skin color, dress, demeanor, age, and sex, to guess where they might find common ground. Their judgment in this respect then affects the opinions and attitudes they voice. But we can't be sure whether interviewer characteristics would also affect the sort of detailed report of witnessed events that is the more usual concern of qualitative interviewing. My guess is that even if a respondent had a tendency to slant a description of an event in order to win the interviewer's approval, the interviewer could reduce that tendency by obtaining full detail.

In any case, it is difficult to anticipate what interviewer attributes will prove important to a respondent and how the respondent will react to them. Nell Painter, a black academic woman of clearly middle-class background, found when establishing an interviewing relationship with Hosea Hudson, a radical black man of rural Southern working-class background, that the attribute that mattered to the respondent was her politics:

> When he asked about my politics I feared that would mean the end of our work together, for although I admired his long years of dedication to radical change in the face of opposition, I had to admit that I was only a Democrat. To my surprise, Hudson was greatly relieved. His worry was not that I might be a liberal, but that I might belong to one of the groups he calls "left-splinter," such as the Socialists Workers Party.[6]

There are so many different interviewer attributes to which a respondent can react that the interviewer will surely be an insider in some ways, an outsider in others. When I interviewed men who were IV drug users, I was an outsider to the drug culture but an insider to the world of men. When I interviewed a woman who was an IV drug user living in a shelter and also the mother of two children, I was an outsider to the world of women, drug users, and women's shelters, but an insider to the concerns of parents.

I have generally found it better to be an insider to the milieu in which the respondent lives, because it is easier then for me to establish a research partnership with the respondent. But some of my most instructive interviews have been good just because I was an outsider who needed instruction in the respondent's milieu. I was once instructed in the art of car stripping by a respondent who found me, as he put it, a little lame in my understanding of his hustle. For a similar reason I was told in detail about the functioning of a "shooting gallery" and the reasons for the willingness of addicts to use house needles—something an insider might not have asked about. Also, respondents sometimes talk more openly to outsiders not only because the outsiders seem to appreciate tutelage but also because outsiders don't share the values that would make them condemn those aspects of the respondents' behavior that an insider would recognize as failing insider norms.

It may well be possible to be so much of an outsider that respondents decide they cannot talk to you because you could never understand or cannot be trusted or do not know how to ask. Charles Briggs writes that different settings require that interviewing be done in different ways, and the proper way to ask questions must be mastered if there is to be an interview at all. But my experience, limited to be sure, is that learning how to be instructed is among the first things one learns in a new setting.[7] And investigators, though they may begin as thoroughgoing outsiders, are likely in time to learn from their study how to manage to interview.[8]

Robert Merton concludes after careful consideration that both insiders and outsiders can make unique and valuable contributions to an understanding of situations.[9] My own view is that a reasonably proficient qualitative interviewer can establish an effective research partnership with a very wide range of respondents.[10]

What I give in the following paragraphs is an account of my own experiences, as I am aware of them, in relation to four bases frequently considered for deciding insider or outsider status in research interviewing.

SOCIOECONOMIC STATUS

I have found that when my niche on the socioeconomic ladder was higher than that of my respondent's, because I was a college professor and the respondent was a blue-collar worker or on welfare, it was usually easy to establish a good research partnership. All it took was ordinary considerateness, together with full and respectful attention within the interview. When I was inferior in social standing to someone in a different field, as when my respondent was someone highly successful in business or medicine, our being in different fields seemed to reduce the relevance of our relative ranking.

I have found it most difficult to interview highly successful people in academic or professional fields not too different from mine. In one such interview I found myself, without consciously intending to, repeatedly making reference to my own achievements. I mentioned, for example, that I had once taught at the respondent's university; I also noted that I was the principal investigator of the study and that I had done successful work in the past. It is not unusual for men to assert their own merits in early interchanges with someone whom they respect, but it was no way for me to go about establishing an interviewing partnership; the competitive element was too obtrusive. This particular interview went badly. I suspect that similar issues, on my side and on the side of respondents, have troubled other interviews I've had with people in or near my own field.

I think it may be undesirable to be an occupational insider because issues of competition are difficult to suspend. Furthermore, confidentiality is a problem. Can you really be trusted to keep the information to yourself? Might not the interview provide material for gossip, maybe introduced by the comment, "I once interviewed him . . ."? And even if the information goes nowhere else, *you* have it and you are a potential colleague or competitor. Just as you probably should avoid interviewing people in your own family—talking with them frankly is a different matter—you probably should avoid interviewing people who are or may become colleagues. An exception to this would be if your study requires such interviews; even then I would be cautious.

RACE AND ETHNICITY

It seems like common sense that it would be better for the interviewer to be of the same race and, if possible, of the same ethnic background as the respondent. My own experience has been that here common sense is mostly wrong. Racial and ethnic differences, insofar as the respondent can infer these, may perhaps play a role in a respondent's initial reaction to the interviewer, but my experience has been that once an interview takes hold, these differences have little effect on the quality of the interviewing partnership. They become like a difference in height: there, but unimportant.

I speak as someone who is white who has interviewed people who are in other racial groups and as someone who is Jewish who has interviewed people of other religious and ethnic groups. Only on rare occasions has my religion or ethnicity seemed even relevant. Once, when I was starting out, a respondent who did not recognize me as Jewish described his own sharp negotiating as justified because his victim was Jewish. I remained an attentive interviewer. More recently, a respondent who was a retired minister quizzed me about my religion with an eye toward recruiting me to his faith. This happened after the interview had ended and seemed manageable enough. That's about it, as instances where religion or ethnicity seemed to matter.

SEX

Most often, it seems to me, men can interview women with the same success they would have in interviewing men, and women can interview men with the same success they would have in interviewing women. There is some belief in the field that women do better as interviewers with both men and women. Certainly, women are more often chosen as confidants by men as well as by other women. But among the very good interviewers with whom I have worked there have been both men and women, and good interviewers remain good interviewers irrespective of the sex of the respondent. Also, it has seemed to me, the great majority of respondents can form a good research partnership with an interviewer of either sex.

However, difficulties do sometimes appear in cross-sex interviewing that express themselves as respondent or interviewer discomfort. When interviewing women of about my age, I am often aware—and suspect that the woman is also aware—that while our relationship will under no circumstance become a sexual one, still it can be imagined that it could. This awareness, no matter how peripheral to attention, can make the research partnership more cautious. But even if it should have the effect of making the partnership more engaging, this would be no less a problem: an interviewer who feels drawn to a respondent can feel encouraged to be more present and more interactive than is entirely desirable. Similarly, a respondent can be encouraged by a relationship with an interviewer that has begun to seem intriguing to be more concerned with interaction with the interviewer than with memories and observations. But in reality any hope that might develop in an interview for a continued relationship can only lead to disappointment and confusion. If an interviewer becomes aware of a developing personal interest within an interview, an interest of the sort that is usually preliminary to a continuing relationship, it is the interviewer's responsibility to cool it. Nothing good comes from using such an interest to enliven an interview.

It is possible for women who are interviewers to be challenged by male respondents who want to test the women's sexual accessibility. My impression from women who have worked with me is that such challenges occur infrequently, but, as I noted in chapter 3, I do not think interviewers should take any risk whatsoever of assault. It seems to me only sensible for an interviewer to trust, and act on, even vague intuitions. A feeling of discomfort is reason enough to avoid an interview situation or, if one is in it, to end it.

AGE

When I began interviewing I was a young man often interviewing men and women much older than I. Now most respondents are younger than I am. Age does make a difference in the nature of the relationship that is established. When I was the younger I often took the role of someone less experienced than the respondent. Now I more often take the role of someone widely experienced, although not necessarily in the area of the interview. But in either case my stance has been that of someone who can be talked to, and, young and old, I have tried to listen attentively. The content of the interviews seems to me to be no different.

INTERVIEWING DIFFICULTIES
PROBLEM RESPONDENTS

Most respondents are cooperative and easy to work with. Some respondents present one or another sort of challenge.

The Unresponsive Respondent   kᴇy   ✓

The respondent who is unresponsive may not be convinced that candor is without risk. Or the respondent may just feel that there is no potential profit in participating in the interview and therefore no point in cooperating with it. The result is a sequence like the following, from an interview in the study of occupationally successful men:

INTERVIEWER: What's it been like for you, raising your children?

RESPONDENT: Well, I suppose you don't have to worry about running out of aggravations.

I: Could you tell me about the most recent time when you might have felt an aggravation?

R: That's just a manner of speaking. Really, things are just fine.

Maybe the interviewer should have shown more appreciation of the humor in the respondent's initial response. Maybe the interviewer's follow-up question was too abrupt. Maybe the interviewer would have been more successful with "What are the kinds of things you have in mind that might supply you with aggravations?" But there's no reason to believe the respondent would not have deflected any query. A respondent who doesn't want to respond isn't going to become cooperative because of a question's wording.

The Respondent Determined to Present a Particular Picture

A man I interviewed in the study of retirement was anxious to have me believe that he had been an outstanding success as a businessman. This may have been the case, although he was so determined to have me believe it that I was led to wonder. When I asked for incidents that would display the highs of his business career, he became evasive. Every effort I made to elicit the daily experience of running a business was misunderstood or sidestepped. A pump-priming comment I made—"It sounds like you were carrying a lot of responsibility"—elicited only annoyance. No matter how I tried, I couldn't get specifics. I gave the interview about an hour and at the end of that time felt that I had learned little. I couldn't see how a second interview would make things better and didn't try to schedule one.

I don't know if this respondent wanted to convince me of something that was counterfactual, but he acted as though he did. When a respondent wants you to believe something that is different from what actually happened, the respondent is likely to avoid providing detail and to frustrate your efforts to elicit detail. My policy in such situations is to keep plugging away for concreteness until I'm convinced further effort is pointless. If problems seem to exist primarily in one area, I will search for a study-relevant area in which the respondent is willing to be candid. If the respondent insists on remaining general, I may try saying something like "We really need stories that will show us what was happening—the more concrete and detailed, the better" or "I wonder if there's a specific incident you could describe, because then we can see what happens.'' But if the respondent doesn't have detailed stories to tell and doesn't want to admit it, this urging won't work either.

A respondent who wants to avoid an issue in an area of the research may be as difficult. I was in the early phase of an interview with a physician about his retirement when it became evident that he had been asked to resign his hospital appointment. There was some hint in what he was saying that he had become unreliable, maybe that he had botched a procedure. A colleague's vulnerability to a malpractice suit was alluded to and then dropped. As I pressed for detail about the reasons for the respondent's retirement, I could see his edginess increase. Although I then moved to an area where I thought he would be more comfortable, he wanted to be told again what the study was about and where I was from and who would know what he said. For the rest of the interview he was tense. He didn't relax until I said that I thought the questions I had brought with me had been adequately explored and that I wanted to thank him. His interview provided usable material, but it wasn't a good interview.

People Whose Feelings Are Raw

In a study of bereavement we called widows and widowers within weeks of the death of their husbands and wives to arrange for an interview. If our call was answered by a relative acting as a caretaker, we would be sent away, sometimes fiercely: what right did we have, they wanted to know, to intrude at such a time? But when it was the widow or widower who *інтєv.* answered our call, we often were welcomed. For the most part, the new widows and widowers were grateful for someone to talk to. Although their feelings were raw and their pain immediately at hand, the great majority found talking to be helpful.

When grief is new and pain intense, people need both to let their distress be known and to gain relief from the distress by pushing it away. So people want sometimes to be able to talk, sometimes not to have to talk. An interviewer—as a stranger who is understanding, indeed professional; concerned yet dispassionate; and able to listen without offering either report-limiting sympathy or a palliative formula—is exactly the right person to talk to. Usually people organize themselves so they are ready to talk during the interview. They then take other times for distraction from awareness of their loss.

If I Weren't in This Situation, You Wouldn't Want to Interview Me

Sometimes the interview is a reminder to the respondent that he or she is in a category of people who have been hurt or who are, for some other regrettable reason, special. I once interviewed a widow whose husband had been an important political figure. She felt that if her husband were still alive not only would I not be seeing her in the course of a study of bereavement but she would perhaps not even be accessible to me for an interview of any kind. And also she felt that if we were having this interview while her husband was still alive, my manner would have been deferential rather than sympathetic. The respondent was able to describe these feelings; by doing so she was instructive about the social effects of bereavement.

THE PRESENCE OF OTHERS

Having others present in an interview's setting always affects what can be asked and what will be reported. Often, the best way to deal with the situation is to include everyone present in the interview. At least then their contributions to what is said will be more nearly evident.

For example, I began an interview of a retired physician with his wife silently in the background. The physician was maintaining that he felt happily occupied despite a much-reduced work schedule. He clearly was not only reporting to me but also arguing with his wife, although I had no idea what the argument was about. When I asked the physician's wife what she thought about what her husband was saying, she said that he didn't have a reduced work schedule at all, that he was still working 10-hour days, only now he wasn't getting nearly the income he had gotten when he worked those long hours in his practice. He had given up his medical building office, to be sure, but he continued to treat patients from an office in the home. She said her husband could easily cut back his hours if he wanted to but he was determined to fill his time with work.

The joint interview provided information about the tensions that could be introduced into the marriage of retired men should the men define their retirement as bringing their work lives home. Had I been able to interview the respondent without his wife in the background, I might or might not have obtained a useful interview. But given that the respondent's wife was there, it was better to include her.

INTERVIEWING FAILURES

Sometimes respondents decide that they are being oppressed by the interview. And sometimes this is true. Being asked repeatedly for concrete instances can be experienced as badgering. Not being understood by an interviewer can be experienced as a kind of nonacceptance, and it is easy to become irritated or angry in response.

Respondents who begin being uncomfortable may ostentatiously check their watch, ask how many more questions you have, or just stop talking. In one instance in our study of occupationally successful men, a respondent fell asleep during an interview. I am grateful that I was not the interviewer, although I hope I would not have let the interview get to this pass. Going to sleep was the respondent's final move in a contest between him and the interviewer over who would control the interview.

Sooner or later every interviewer encounters a bad interview, an interview in which no matter what the interviewer does, the respondent does not provide usable material. Interviews that go badly have occurred less and less often as I have become more experienced. Nevertheless, I would guess that one interview in fifteen or twenty is a failure. When I have had an interview failure, my first reaction has been that it was my fault. Often enough, I have found much to criticize in my approach. But usually a bad interview, like a good one, is jointly produced by interviewer and respondent.

In one interview that went badly, the respondent appeared skeptical about the interview to begin with. He wanted to talk about his situation, partly to get a grip on it, but he didn't want to lose control of the discussion. I don't think he started off determined to reject the interview, although that is what he came to.

The respondent had had a distinguished career and now was retired. He lived by himself, separated from his wife. He sometimes visited his former firm when the firm had open meetings, although he then sat silently through the meetings. He had no financial problems. He presented his current life as ideal, without stress, with all the time in the world for hobbies and reading. It struck me as bleak.

The interview began with the respondent answering questions briefly, although thoughtfully. But when I tried to get him to elaborate on a response, he replied that he had already answered the question. When I said it was important for us to have a sense of the events of his retirement, he responded by wondering what I could possibly make of his words. He said that people are each unique, living unique lives, and that you can't generalize from what any one person tells you. I didn't want to get into defending the study, but not defending it may have been a kind of defensiveness too, an unwillingness to take his objections seriously. Anyway, I asked more questions. The respondent began allowing his attention to wander. I don't think he looked at his watch, but he shuffled in his chair in a way that suggested he was bored. Then, in case I had missed the body language, he told me he was bored. Then he said that he thought the kind of work I was doing was useless and that he didn't see any reason to participate further. I thanked him for his time and left.

I decided later that I should have attempted to strengthen the interviewing partnership by focusing on the respondent's former work. But when I listened to the tape of the interview, I found that I had tried doing that. The respondent had brightened briefly but then had gone silent again. That was the worst interview I have had in the last fifty or so I have done, and maybe the worst interview I've ever had.

What to Do When an Interview Is Going Badly

It isn't hard to tell when an interview is going badly. Neither the respondent nor you is relaxed. The respondent may indicate discomfort or resistance or antagonism by lapses in attention or sparse responses or outright challenges. Even without this, you are likely to be uncomfortable. You can't get engaged by the interview. You find it hard to listen closely to the respondent. You aren't in touch with the respondent's account, limited as it is. Your questions are awkward. You fail to ask the respondent to extend a description or give detail for an incident, although usually you would do this almost automatically. You flounder. The interview takes on a survey research quality: you ask a question, and then the respondent gives a brief response and waits for the next question. You are painfully aware of how little the interview is producing and yet feel unable to rescue it.

What can you do? If it is the first few minutes of the interview, you might simply continue in the hope that you and the respondent will become more at ease. But if the interview has been going as long as 5 minutes, and the respondent indicates discomfort, you ought to try to strengthen the research partnership. You might check that the respondent understands and accepts the study's assumptions. A pause in questioning to discuss the study's aims can make it easier for the respondent to ask for further information. You might search for an area of easy rapport; the area of the respondent's work will often do. You should make every effort to follow the respondent's lead in deciding what to talk about, so long as it is within hailing distance of the study's substantive frame (as the interviewer did in the second interview in chapter 4). More than anything else, you should attend closely to both text and subtext of the respondent's statements.

A way of dealing with ungiving respondents that I haven't tried, but have been told by other investigators is effective, is to say, "It is important for us that the people we talk with give us complete accounts of their observations or experiences in the area of the study. Is this something you feel you can do?" If this can be said so that it isn't confrontational, it might make it easier to obtain useful materials.

My own practice, if an interview is going badly and nothing seems to be working and yet I do not want to give up entirely, is to end the interview before the respondent begins to think about ending it, and set another appointment. To justify returning, I name some topics still to be discussed. Back at the office I talk to a colleague about the problems in the interview or at least think about how to approach the next interview.

With some respondents, nothing can be done. It may be that the particular match of interviewer and respondent is wrong. Or it may be that the respondent will always refuse to provide usable information, or is unable to. Some people play their lives close to their chests and will never show their hand, no matter the circumstance. Chalk it up to experience. Everyone has some bad interviews. It is not essential for a study that every interview be illuminating. If this respondent does not provide information about some phenomenon, then another will. It's a shame to lose the opportunity to learn from a respondent, and a bad interview is a loss for the study. But the loss is virtually never fatal.

ISSUES OF VALIDITY: DO RESPONDENTS TELL THE TRUTH, THE WHOLE TRUTH, AND NOTHING BUT THE TRUTH?

How much of what a respondent tells you can you believe? And how much is left out?

A while ago I was a respondent being interviewed by a skillful and sympathetic interviewer about the history of a research training program I had helped organize. I wanted the interviewer's project to succeed and wanted to provide her with whatever information I had. And yet as I described the early days of the program, I observed myself slide over incidents that had been important at the time, because describing them would have made evident the frictions that had developed among the program's staff. Here I was, determined to be a good respondent and to describe exactly how it had all happened, and I was being less than candid. My justification to myself was that I didn't want to compromise other people's privacy nor to rehash old quarrels. Nor was I entirely happy with my own part in the conflicts of those long ago days. I dropped one or two markers to indicate that the program had had its problems, and had the interviewer asked me to say more about them, I would have. She didn't, and so I let them be. But what an incomplete report I provided!

I was also struck by the gaps in my memory. These, for all I know, may have been more significant. I could not remember how a critically important proposal had gotten written, although almost certainly I had done most of the writing. I vividly remembered going to Washington to seek further funding after the program had completed its first years, and my unsatisfactory encounter there with a representative of a granting agency. Perhaps defending a program that had become emotionally important to me was a more memorable event than writing a proposal for a program that did not yet exist. But it was surprising to me that I could provide detailed information about the one event and no information about the other.

Cooperative respondents asked about a past no longer much thought about will probably display, as I did, oases of vivid memories within a desert of uncertainty. They are likely also to display, as I did, unwillingness to make all their memories accessible. On the other hand, they may, again as I did, provide markers to the elided material that an attentive interviewer can recognize.

There was one thing I did not do in my responses to that interview: I did not invent events that had not occurred. Indeed, I felt no temptation to invent anything—not a role for myself I hadn't played nor a success for the program it hadn't had. I think this too is likely to be the case for most respondents in most studies: what is reported may be spotty, but little will be invented. The lying respondent happens less often than people who don't do interviewing may imagine. For one thing, it's difficult to maintain a counterfactual reality when being pressed to provide detailed descriptions of events. And why should anyone want to do it?

But while we as interviewers can anticipate that we will be told the truth, we cannot assume that we will be told the whole truth nor the precise truth. If respondents want to keep from us events or behaviors or a sector of their lives, there is every reason to believe that they can succeed. While it would be difficult for respondents to produce the circumstantial detail and corroborating incident necessary to make an invented reality seem plausible, it is very easy for them not to report something—and to give no indication that there is something not being reported.

There are some kinds of events that we are unlikely to hear about unless we have established an interviewing relationship in which there is extraordinary trust. People will not endanger themselves to contribute to social research. In our interviewing of occupationally successful men we were told of no incidents in which our respondents embezzled from their employers, although we heard of incidents in which others had embezzled. It seems to me unlikely that we had in our sample only men who were aware of others' dishonesty and none who were dishonest themselves.

Nor can we be sure we will be told the precise truth. The vagaries of respondent memory make for reports in which some observations are crystal clear while others are obscured or distorted or blocked. Respondents also may shade their responses to present a positive picture of themselves. This seems to me most likely in a first interview; in later interviews a respondent, more confident of acceptance, may provide corrective information. One respondent, an HIV-positive IV drug user, in a first interview described breaking a syringe against the wall when importuned by a friend to share it; in a subsequent interview he described another occasion when he agreed to share his needle. He wasn't lying in his first story. It really happened—or maybe came close to happening. But it wasn't until the later interview that he presented the more mixed picture.

Shading responses to present a positive picture of the self is especially likely when respondents are asked about opinions, attitudes, appraisals, evaluations, values, or beliefs. These can express an identity appropriate to the situation of the interview as much as something more stable. Asked by a friend to comment on the future of an institution the respondent is involved in—for example, a company or university—the respondent might express his mood of the moment; with an interviewer, the respondent might be more thoughtful and analytic.

Information is context dependent—that is, shaped in part by the interview situation—when it is free of anchors in observations of events.

Generalizations from experiences also tend to be context dependent because they depend on weightings of what may be discordant observations. A question like "Is your relationship with your sister good or not so good?" can have many true responses, including those indicating that the two get on well enough, that the two have a barely submerged rivalry, and that the two stopped talking for a year after the sister disputed a will. If we are seen as a friendly stranger, we may be told that the relationship is amicable, which is true. If we are seen as a sympathetic listener, interested in the respondent's disappointments, we may hear that the sister is not to be fully trusted, also a true response.

While questions about concrete incidents—such as "What happened when you and your sister were last together?"—may be answered from more than one perspective, they are less likely to be modifiable by the interviewing context. Thus, we will obtain more reliable information and information easier to interpret if we ask about concrete incidents than we will if we ask about general states or about opinions.

Despite all the ways in which interview material can be problematic, richly detailed accounts of vividly remembered events are likely to be trustworthy. Nor does apparent inconsistency always demonstrate invalidity. After all, people can act in inconsistent ways or maintain inconsistent feelings. Business partners, for example, can be both grateful and resentful. A respondent who in a second interview describes an attitude toward a partner contradictory to an attitude described in a first interview may in both interviews have been telling the truth.[11]

Sometimes we can check on the validity of a respondent's account by interviewing other respondents. Occasionally, there are records we can look to for corroboration.[12] But for the most part we must rely on the quality of our interviewing for the validity of our material. Ultimately, our best guarantee of the validity of interview material is careful, concrete level, interviewing within the context of a good interviewing partnership.

CHAPTER 6

ANALYSIS OF DATA

Most investigators let analysis slide until the advent of an "analysis phase." Anselm Strauss, in *Qualitative Analysis for Social Scientists,* his manual on analysis in the style of "grounded theory,"[1] and Miles and Huberman, in their more eclectic *Qualitative Data Analysis,* consider this bad practice. They urge that analysis begin as soon as there is data collection. Miles and Huberman observe that the more investigators have developed understandings during data collection, the surer they can be of the adequacy of the data collection and the less daunting will be the task of fully analyzing the data.[2]

Despite the unquestionable merits of this view, a conspiracy of forces regularly impedes early analysis. During the interviewing phase the investigator must deal with all the demands of obtaining the data: recruiting the respondents, conducting the interviews, getting them transcribed, deciding whether the right information is being collected, and returning to conduct more interviews. Nor can the investigator escape awareness that when the interviewing is finally over, not only will all the data be at hand but there will be uninterrupted weeks or months available for their analysis. Undoubtedly the investigator will develop insights, speculations, and small-scale theories beginning with the first pilot interview or before. But it is likely to be only after interviewing has ended that the investigator can give full attention to analysis and writing.

Although analysis and writing can be separated from data gathering, they cannot be separated from each other. The kind of report that will be written and the kind of analysis that will be done must be decided jointly. Each implies the other. If the report is to be a set of case studies of respondents, then each respondent's material must be organized and interpreted separately; conversely, if each respondent's materials are organized and interpreted separately, the only report possible is a set of case studies.

We can identify four different approaches to analysis and reporting. The four approaches represent the different combinations of decisions regarding, first, whether the report will focus on issues or on cases and, second, what is to be the report's intended level of generalization.

Analysis and reporting can deal either with issues as they are learned about from respondents or with the respondents themselves: they can, for example, deal with the effect being forced to retire has on feelings of worth, using relevant materials from all respondents; or with particular respondents and how they happened to retire, and what were their subsequent experiences, perhaps including their feelings of worth. We can call the first approach "issue-focused" and the second "case-focused."[3]

Analysis and reporting can also either remain on the level of respondents' reports or be generalized from their reports: they can, for example, deal with the effects of retirement on the particular administrators and professionals who were respondents in the study, or they can use what was learned in the study to consider the effects of retirement on all or most former administrators and professionals. We can call the first the "level of the concrete," the second the "level of the generalized."

When the report is issue focused and generalized, we have the usual sociological account. When the report is issue focused and concrete, we have the usual historical or journalistic account. When the report is case focused and concrete, we have the usual case studies of individuals. When the report is case focused and generalized, we have typological description. Later in this chapter I give descriptions of reports in each of these modes.

No matter the level or focus of the final report, there is no single tried-and-true method of analysis or strategy for presentation of findings. Investigators have different styles, studies different requirements, audiences different needs. Consider only the extent to which the investigator's voice is present. Studs Terkel's books present respondent's voices, one after the other, without editorial interruption,[4] Daniel Levinson's *Seasons of a Man's Life* presents theory and generalized observation interrupted by heavily interpreted case materials.[5] In some chapters of Elliot Liebow's *Talley's Corner* the only voice presented is the author's; in others, passages of interview, of dialogue, and of group conversation provide a sense of the reality that underlies Liebow's observations.[6] Any of these might serve as a model, but they would be different models.[7]

In one respect all good reports, despite wide variation in style, are similar: they tell a coherent story. They provide a line of argument, or an image of how it all works, such that material presented early in the report prepares the reader for material that will appear later and later material draws on the earlier. The reader, at the end, can grasp the report entire.

The kind of story the investigator can tell must be consistent with the kind of data that has been collected. As I noted in chapter 3, a coherent story may be achieved either by the diachronic strategy of describing movement through time or by the synchronic strategy of describing the integration of elements at a moment in time. A report whose subject is single parents might begin with the way in which people become single parents, go on to describe how they manage to meet the problems they encounter, and then assess the benefits and stresses of single-parent life. Alternatively, it might move from sector to sector within single-parent life, describing first the way single parents organize their households and then their relationships with their children and so on. One of these strategies of presentation will almost surely have been anticipated when the interview guide was developed, and it would be difficult now to move to the other. In other respects, however, the investigator is likely to be able to choose how the data should be presented, and so how it should be analyzed.

In the following pages I shall discuss first what might be involved in issue-focused analyses and then what might be involved in case-focused analyses. In my discussion of issue-focused analyses I will begin with the generalized level, because the analytic issues are clearer there; in my discussion of case-focused analyses I will begin with concrete description, because this provides an introduction to the problems of generalizing from individual cases.

ISSUE-FOCUSED ANALYSIS

What I believe is the most frequent social science approach to presenting the findings of a qualitative interview study is to describe what has been learned from all respondents about people in their situation. An analysis whose aim is issue focussed would concern itself with what could be learned about specific issues—or events or processes—from any and all respondents. Some respondents might contribute more to the analysis, others less. The analyst would become like the medical specialist who is interested in livers, not in particular patients, except that the analyst would be concerned with more than a single set of issues.

An issue-focused description is likely to move from discussion of issues within one area to discussion of issues within another, with each area logically connected to the others. A report about people who retired might begin with a discussion of how the retirement occurred (an area). In the discussion it might consider the different impacts of being pushed out of one's job, retiring to gain freedom from the job, and retiring for reasons of health (specific issues). The next area to be discussed might be early reactions to retirement. This area would, of course, have its own issues. Then would follow still other areas, again each with its own issues. The whole would together describe the retirement experience in a number of areas for the group the respondents represented.

There are four distinct analytic processes involved in producing an issue-focused analysis of interview material. These are coding, sorting, local integration, and inclusive integration. Early in the analysis, coding is likely to predominate; later, local and inclusive integration may absorb the most energy and attention. But all analytic processes occur throughout the analysis. Coding is intended to provide the materials for sorting and integration, but sorting and integration can also raise questions for further coding.

CODING

The idea in coding is to link what the respondent says in his or her interview to the concepts and categories that will appear in the report.

Suppose that in analyzing data on retirement we read in the transcript of an interview with a retired surgeon the following comment: "I started the process of retiring several years ago when I began winding down my practice and cut out the major surgery and went just to doing minor surgery." We could code this—that is, link it to concepts and categories—by noting that it is an instance of (1) preparation for retirement in which there is movement to the periphery of the occupation; (2) withdrawal from tasks of high responsibility, tension, skill, and visibility;

(3) unclear regarding the source of the pressure to retire; and (4) more a change in work routine than a change in identity as a physician. How we code it depends on our theoretical assumptions and the research interests we bring to the project.

Some coding categories we bring to our studies before ever knowing what the interviews will produce. We plan to use them because they are related to the problem we hope to study, as an aspect of the problem or an explanation for it or a consequence of it. Others we bring with us as readinesses to interpret respondents' comments in one way or another. The readinesses come from our training, our reading, our life experiences, and our general understandings. When I code a respondent's description of night sweats as an expression of stress, my coding comes from my having learned to attribute a particular meaning to this particular symptom. Many codings seem to be immediately plausible abstractions from respondents' statements. For example, the respondent statement "We don't agree on the children's bedtimes, but I'm the one who has to deal with them" might be coded "conflict over children resolved by reference to domain responsibility."

I find myself coding automatically as I read interview transcripts. The code categories I use, at least initially, are efforts to capture the interview material. I don't try to make sense of every "meaning unit"—every utterance that provides a complete thought—nor of every sentence or paragraph. But as I go through the material I do ask myself what I am seeing instances of, what I am learning about, and what questions the material raises.

I generally write my codings, along with formulations or speculations, in the margins of the transcripts I am working with. Later, I go back over my marginal notes. If they still make sense, I dictate them into a tape recorder, together with the interview excerpts on which they are based, to be transcribed as background notes. I am likely to use the formulations in these notes as I develop chapter drafts, but I may not. However, once I have dictated the notes, I remember their formulations at least in outline and can carry them in my mind and review them and think about how to test them or develop them. I am likely, too, to return again to the interview excerpts in the notes to reconsider whether they truly support the codings I have made.

Fairly early in a study, if I am doing issue-focused analysis, I shift from reading and coding transcripts of interviews to reading and coding "excerpt files.'' These are collections from many interviews of excerpts dealing with the same issue. I say more about excerpt files in the next section.

As I make decisions regarding whether instances fit my coding categories, I find it necessary to further specify what I mean by the categories. Thus, the coding category is developed and defined through interaction with the data. Take the category ''shares responsibility for home maintenance,'' which was one of the categories in my study of occupationally successful men. One man said that he fully shared household responsibility and performed many of the household tasks, except at those times when his professional work load became heavy. When his professional work load became heavy, he would ask his wife to take over the entire responsibility of the home, and he believed it was her place to do so. I then realized that I meant by ''shared responsibility'' a responsibility for home maintenance that was understood by the couple to be shared not just when other responsibilities permitted it but always.

Coding of this sort cannot be delegated to a research assistant. Coding is thinking about the material, and the thinking should be that of whoever will be responsible for the report. This is not to say that others cannot help. It is almost always useful to be able to talk about codes, and having others code the same material can be a good basis for such talk.

When do you stop coding? Only when you stop reading transcripts— and that may not be until the final report is completed. But there is a change in the character of coding as a study progresses. By the end of the analysis phase the investigator should more and more see the data fitting into already established codes. While the point is never reached where new material can no longer enrich codings, toward the end of the analysis there should be few important phenomena that significantly extend or deepen or qualify codings.

SORTING

Before the advent of computers and word-processing programs there was a standard approach to the analysis of interview transcripts and other qualitative data: Make second copies of transcripts and notes. Put the first copies away, to serve as an archive. Label file folders with the titles of the sections of the report, the chapters, or chapter sections. Cut up the second copies of the material into topical units corresponding to the labels on the file folders. File each excerpted topical unit in its proper folder. If folders become too full, divide the materials by subtopics and sort into new folders.

The result is a set of folders containing excerpts from cases, each folder holding a category of material. What happens next with the material is, first, "local integration," in which the material of the file folder is interpreted, and, second, "inclusive integration," in which the collection of file folders is organized into a coherent sequence.

The cutting and sorting into file folders, which is the traditional approach to qualitative analysis, can now be done by computer word-processing programs. Instead of literally cutting up interviews and putting the snippets into appropriate file folders, the analyst at a computer electronically moves material from an interview file or a file of notes into an appropriate excerpt file. Then the excerpt file can be printed out as needed.

As I noted, in doing issue focused analysis I find it more satisfactory to code from excerpt files than from full interviews. If an initial excerpt file becomes too bulky, I can break it into smaller excerpt files dealing with narrower topics. If it is too narrow to start with—this doesn't often happen—I can amalgamate it with other excerpt files.

In analyzing material from the study of occupationally successful men for one section of a chapter on fathering, I began with an except file of expressions of paternal investment in children. That turned out to be too thick to deal with. So I divided it into several more narrowly focused excerpt files: one dealt with indications of pride in the children, another with instances of dealing with crises, another with instances of acting in a paternal role in sports or discipline or character formation, and so on. I then coded each of these files (by writing in the margins of transcript pages) and dictated the codes and exemplary excerpts for later transcription.

I find it most efficient to produce excerpt files only as I need them. If the interviews provide a great deal of material regarding an issue, I will not require that the excerpt file contain it all. An excerpt file that runs to 80 pages of single-spaced text, with wide enough sampling from the interviews to make me confident the interview materials are adequately represented, strikes me as good enough and about all I will want to work through.

While I haven't found it possible to have others help me in coding, I have found that others can help in making up an excerpt file. Sometimes the decisions they make about what belongs in a file aren't exactly the decisions I would make, but ordinarily they are good enough. I can always add to or subtract from the file if I want to.

The use of a computer in making up excerpt files makes for greater flexibility in managing data. It is easier with a computer file than with sheets of paper in an actual file folder to break a too inclusive file into narrower files or to amalgamate too thin files. Furthermore, the computer excerpt file can be printed out to provide a set of passages from interviews to be read and coded, formatted in any way you like. Computer programs exist whose aim is to facilitate the coding and sorting of interview material. While their use is not without problems—including the need to invest time in mastering them and the risk that, once mastered, they will dictate the direction of the analysis—they can further facilitate analytic work.[8]

LOCAL INTEGRATION

The codings of the material in an excerpt file constitute a statement of what we believe the material tells us. We now need to find a way of organizing and integrating our observations and understandings in each section of the report. This I call local integration. I find myself beginning to do this as soon as any interview materials show up and continuing it all the way through the study, although it becomes a focus of my effort only when I am involved in producing the final report.

One way to achieve local integration is simply to summarize the excerpt file and its codings: Here is what is said in this area, and this is what I believe it to mean. We might first summarize the main line of the material: what most respondents say. Then we could turn to the material that does not fit in the main line, the variants, and summarize them. If there are too many variants, our definition of what constitutes the main line is unsatisfactory and we need to move to a more inclusive formulation.

An example of summarizing the main line and its variants might be taken from bereavement project material dealing with widowers who were parents of small children. Here we could summarize material dealing with the fathers' reliance on their mothers or their sisters or on female housekeepers or, in a few instances, their mothers-in-law. We could then summarize as cases that did not fit the main line the stories of fathers who did not at all rely on women to help them care for their children. We would try to provide enough material about the main line so that our summary made sense to the reader, and it also made sense that this should be the most frequent development. We would also try to explain why cases that did not fit the main line were different. We might note, for example, that the fathers who did not rely on women to help them care for their children had older children or had decided to stay home from work for a time.

A theory that makes sense of the materials is preferable to a descriptive summary of main lines and variations. I find myself developing, from the very beginning of the study, "minitheories," hypotheses whose aim is to make sense of material dealing with specific issues or material within a particular sector. As the study progresses I retain those that are supported by the data and drop those that are not, almost without noticing that I am doing so.

Early in my study of occupationally successful men I found myself developing a minitheory about the meaning for the men of challenge at work. The theory was attractive to me because it made a connection that I thought valid between two things that weren't obviously connected: the men's zest for challenge and their frequent stress at work. The minitheory was that the men viewed challenge at work as a test of their worth and responded by mobilization of their energy and attention. They relaxed their energy and attention if they met the challenge successfully—indeed, they then felt good about themselves. If they didn't meet the challenge successfully, however, they remained mobilized. This persisting mobilization was exactly work stress. Further, the men's jobs consisted of meeting challenges, one after another. This was what the men wanted. Such a job gave them maximum opportunity to test themselves and gain the pleasure of self-approbation. But it also made it likely that sooner or later they would run into a challenge they could not meet, and so experience work stress.

I liked this minitheory because it explained a lot, fit with the interview material, and had an aesthetically pleasing neatness. Almost all the excerpted materials corroborated it. A few men did seem to have nonchallenging work, but they didn't like it or didn't respect it. So even material off the main line could be assimilated to the minitheory. I began extending the minitheory, adding to it ideas such as that successfully met challenge could augment self-confidence and so make the next challenge less daunting.

But while this minitheory offered one basis for the integration of a good deal of material in the area of work, it didn't deal with other material adequately, or at all. This included, for example, material on the importance of teamwork, on work as a kind of play, and on the importance of recognition. In these other sectors I had to develop other minitheories about men's investments in work.

When I turned to still other sectors of men's lives, including their marriages and their relationships with their children, I had to develop new bases for local integration. This meant working with new excerpt files and new codings, from which I could develop new summaries and try to develop new minitheories. When I came to write chapters for the book that was the eventual project report the summaries and minitheories became the armatures of the chapters.

If a minitheory seems both plausible and potentially useful, I try to verify it. If there is interview material I haven't included in the excerpt file, I might now consult it. If I know of relevant literature, I without fail examine it. But if, after having done this, the truth value of a particular minitheory seems to me high, that is, if it is well supported by the interview material and in addition makes sense, then I go on to the next excerpt file. My anticipation is that as minitheories become organized into more embracing theories, the truth value of the minitheories will be enhanced.

INCLUSIVE INTEGRATION

Local integration brings coherence and meaning to excerpt file materials and their codings. Inclusive integration knits into a single coherent story the otherwise isolated areas of analysis that result from local integration.

The problem in inclusive integration is to develop a framework that will include all the analyses the investigator wants to report, moves logically from one area to the next, and leads to some general conclusion. An initial framework for the report is likely already to have been outlined in the course of developing the interview guide. But that first framework will probably now require further development, or even fundamental revision, given the need to incorporate within it the understandings realized by the interviewing and analysis.

It may be useful for me to review how I came to the framework I used in a report on single parents.[9] My aim in that study was to describe the life experience of custodial parents after the turmoil of separation and divorce had subsided. I anticipated a report in which I would describe the structure and functioning of the single-parent household, with the idea that this would help make sense of the problems single parents encountered. The interview guide, in consequence, focused on the tasks of daily life in single-parent households and how single parents managed them, the single parents' relationships with their children and with others, what the single parents saw as the problems of their lives, and how they coped with those problems.

In analyzing the interview material, I focused first on what seemed to me the two core areas of my intended report. One was the parent's relationships with the children, which provided the "structure" of the single-parent household. Here I noted, among other things, that in single-parent households children were likely to be treated as junior partners in household management. My other core area of analysis was how things got done in the single-parent household—how the household functioned. I described here, among other things, how employed parents might have even quite young children do some household chores.

At this point it seemed to me that the report in which I presented these analyses should begin with how single-parent households developed. I now did further analysis, comparing the experiences with marital dissolution of my largely divorced sample with the experiences of bereavement of a small number of widowed respondents. I hadn't initially intended to include widowed single parents, but had interviewed a few anyway, and now I found I could use the materials of their interviews. It also seemed to me that I needed to follow descriptions of my core areas with material describing the personal life of the single parent, including relationships with other adults and issues of loneliness and of sexuality. The interviews had collected information on these issues, and I now proceeded with their analysis.

It was only when I had produced about half the report that I worked out how the report should conclude, although that was something I had worried about as soon as I began to write. What seemed an appropriate conclusion was to identify what were the problems faced by single parents and how they coped with them. I found that the interviews had collected the needed information, and again I was able to proceed with analysis in the area.

As I look back, it seems to me that much of the work developing the report's story line took place away from my desk, as I repeatedly considered what would constitute a satisfactory report. This strikes me as the way I have customarily developed the framework for a report. Very early in the study I had a general idea of what issues I would eventually discuss.

This sense of the issues to be discussed gave shape to the interview guide and later suggested the core areas for analysis. On achieving local integration in the core areas, I could then think further about what might be the shape of the final report and what materials should precede and follow the core areas. But the final framework wasn't entirely in place until I had finished the report.

Other investigators with whom I have worked seem to have proceeded in roughly the same way I did. They, too, began with a rather sketchy framework, developing it further as they went along, but did not have everything in place until they had their report nearly done.

VISUAL DISPLAY

Many researchers find visual display of the elements of their story a valuable means of achieving both local integration and inclusive integration. Miles and Huberman recommend diagrams on paper, with lines linking related issues, to display graphically the conceptual framework of the final report.[10] Becker suggests putting data and memos about the data on file cards that can then be spread on a large flat surface and arranged and rearranged until they achieve a logical sequence.[11] Agar suggests finding an empty classroom full of blackboards on which can be drawn maps of concepts and their interrelations.[12]

I don't much use visual display myself, although I do often make tentative lists of chapters or chapter sections in what I believe to be logical order. But visual display as a way of achieving local or inclusive integration is so often recommended that researchers who are just beginning to work with qualitative interview material might want to see whether this approach works for them.

A GENERALIZED ISSUE-FOCUSED REPORT

Most studies of family life have been based on interviews. Other methods don't work nearly as well in capturing family life: adequate observation of families is intrusive and time consuming, and family records such as letters, diaries, and photographs tend to be sparse and to emphasize the ceremonial. Interviews, however, can obtain information not only about family events but also about the ordinarily unvoiced perceptions and emotions that underlie family dynamics. Mirra Komarovsky's *Blue-Collar Marriage*[13] is among the earliest of the studies to ask how a type of family or type of marriage worked, although still earlier interview-based studies of families had examined how families dealt with the Great Depression and how men and women responded to divorce.[14]

Komarovsky interviewed husbands and wives in 58 blue-collar marriages. Her aim was to learn how blue-collar marriages were different from other marriages and thus how social class affects marriage. Her eligibility criteria for respondents required that, in addition to being married, they be white native-born Protestants, without any college education, and with the husband in a blue-collar occupation. She also wanted respondents to be currently raising children. She obtained the names of her couples from a city directory, from membership lists of Protestant churches, and, in two instances, from recommendations by other respondents.

Two 2-hour interviews were held with wives, and a third 2-hour interview with the husband. The interviews were for the most part qualitative, "within a carefully worked out guide," but also included questions and checklists to be asked of everyone. Komarovsky did not do much tape-recording: her study was conducted before tape recorders were common household equipment, and she thought that her respondents would be made uncomfortable by them. Instead, her interviewers were required to take detailed notes.

Some of the codings of responses appear to be immediately plausible categorizations of respondents' comments. For example, husbands were asked "How does marriage change a man's life?" and wives were asked the parallel question "How does marriage change a woman's life?" Komarovsky used the coding "escape from home" to characterize responses like these:

> He's got his own place and he's boss. With my mother, I had to come home when she said or I wouldn't get anything to eat. Now I can come and go whenever I like. [*A husband's comment*]

> One reason I got married at sixteen was to get away from home. . . . They would tell us kids that they stayed together for our sakes—that made us feel real good. [*A wife's comment*][15]

Other codings seem to be expressions of interest Komarovsky brought to the study. Thus, couples were assessed on the extent to which their marriage was close or distant and on the extent to which the spouse was a friend, even when closeness and distance weren't directly discussed by the spouses. In addition to "closeness," codes dealing with adequacy of marital communication and with level of marital happiness appear to have been brought to the study by Komarovsky.

Still other codings seem to be neither *a priori* categories nor immediate inferences from responses. These are possibly the most interesting. They include "the pull of the male clique," which in Komarovsky's view "retarded the domestication or the marital socialization of the husband." This coding, and others like it, must have come from a good deal of thought about the meaning of responses.

The sequence of material presented in Komarovsky's book begins with a description of the respondents and proceeds to the respondents' motivations for marriage, the division of labor in their marriages, their marital communication, and the relative power of the two spouses in the marriage. It then proceeds to kin ties, economic and occupational issues, the couples' use of leisure, and, finally, the implications of the findings. Sorting of materials was undoubtedly done within this structure and probably was straightforward.

Local integration may well have absorbed most analytic time and energy. Each chapter seems to have been treated almost as a separate study. Chapter 5, "The Marriage Dialogue: Expectations," begins by setting out the problem to which it will attend: Do working-class husbands and wives share the desire and expectation of middle-class husbands and wives that their marriages will be relationships of communicative intimacy? The data used to answer this question came primarily from respondents' reactions to vignettes describing problems in marital communication and answers to questions about the qualities of a good husband and wife.

The chapter reports that couples who shared middle-class ideals regarding intimacy were likely to be better educated. If not, the wives were better educated and the husbands aspired to upward social mobility. Other blue-collar couples, however, are presented as happy despite little talk that could be called intimate. To show how such a marriage might work, Komarovsky presents a case study of a husband and wife who were happy although noncommunicative. Komarovsky's conclusion is that while working-class marriages of a certain sort display the communicative ideals of middle-class marriages, other working-class marriages do not—and they aren't necessarily unhappy.

Komarovsky achieves local integration in this chapter by posing and then resolving the question of intimacy in working-class marriages. She first proposes a minitheory about which of her respondent couples would display communicative intimacy and then presents material that illustrates and supports the minitheory. She then presents further material that suggests necessary qualifications in the minitheory. Other chapters display the same movement from problem statement to minitheory, to supporting data, to qualifications, and finally, to conclusions. Most chapters could stand alone as sector reports.

Komarovsky accomplishes inclusive integration by leading the reader from the early days of a couple's marriage and the couple's division of marital labor to what appears to be her primary concern, the closeness of the present marriage. That occupies the bulk of the book. At the end, chapters are added on economic and occupational issues as they may affect a couple's marriage and on how couples use leisure. A final chapter, "Theoretical and Methodological Conclusions," is intended to wrap up the whole thing.

How good was Komarovsky's analysis? It was certainly good enough to enable her to influence thinking about working-class marriage and about the problems, as well as benefits, of presumably supportive relationships with friends and kin. (Komarovsky calls the wife's continued closeness to her mother "the working-class marriage triangle.")

Maybe more could have been learned about the lives of the husbands and wives had there been less focus on marital communication and less reliance on checklists. There is almost nothing on courtship. Sex is discussed, but there is little discussion of love and affection. There is surprisingly little about children and the problems of parenting: about all there is appears in a section where Komarovsky notes that parents sometimes quarreled over how the children should be raised.

More than the most authors of qualitative studies, Komarovsky is concerned with quantification. She regularly reports the proportion of cases that had particular characteristics: that, for example, exhibited communicative distance. Because the sample was not representative of any meaningful universe, the proportions cannot be taken as estimates of anything; they are only descriptive of Komarovsky's sample. Still, reporting proportions does suggest the strength with which the sample supports generalizations, and it gives the reader reason for confidence in the probity of the analysis.

In a few respects, the study's methods place the study in an earlier era of qualitative work. Quotations have the choppy quality that comes from being based on notes rather than tape recordings. There is a pervasive concern with demonstrating that there is legitimacy in qualitative work even though it may appear less scientific than large-scale surveys. And the data gathered included, at least for my taste, too much material regarding expectations and reactions to hypothetical vignettes and not enough regarding ongoing life. But the analysis is thoughtful and thorough, and if the resulting picture is not as vivid as it might be, it is thoroughly credible.

AN ISSUE-FOCUSED REPORT AT THE LEVEL OF CONCRETE MATERIAL

An example of how concrete excerpts can be organized to tell a story is provided by Ronald Fraser's *Blood of Spain*. Fraser's aim was to weave a history of the Spanish Civil War not from the perspective of its leaders but, rather, from the perspective of the ordinary people swept up in it. He conducted more than three hundred interviews in order to, in his words, "describe the major contours of the war through eye-witness narration."[16]

Although Fraser does not tell us his analytic methods, he must have coded his interview responses for the time in the war they referred to, the particular region they gave information on, and whether their perspective was Republican or Nationalist. His sorting would then have been straightforward: collect materials by time and, within time, by event. Local integration would require that he work out what descriptions he would give of the historical context and how he would introduce the interview materials; how much space he would give particular perspectives; which interview excerpts he would quote and which he would paraphrase; and when he would enter the report in his own voice and when he would have respondents speak. Inclusive integration would have been a matter of organizing events temporally.

Fraser begins his book with interview excerpts describing the years before the war, when Spain was governed by the Left. He sketches the opposition to the government by business leaders, the military, and the church and shows the hatred and fear that existed between the classes. Then he tells us how the war started, through interviews with those who had participated in the uprising of army units in Morocco in July, 1936. He uses further interview excerpts to display the reaction in mainland Spain to the news of the uprising.

Throughout the book Fraser places his interview excerpts and paraphrasings within their historical context. The historical context, in turn, is illuminated by the interview excerpts. His style may be suggested by the following paragraph from the book, in which he describes the resignation of one leftist government and the formation of another:

> In the evening the government resigned. A new government . . . was formed. To a Left Republican school teacher, Regulo Martinez, the new government seemed a prudent move. . . . But the people took the news badly. "Even members of my own party—Azana's party—began tearing up their membership cards. The masses wanted revenge, revolution. They threw caution to the wind; courage and resolution were the order of the day . . ."

Fraser's style provides a "you are there" sense of the disorganization that accompanied the early days of the war, the breakdown in civil order, the excitement and hope of participating in heroic action, and the pervasive blindness on both sides to the misery the war would bring.

Fraser goes on to describe, in the same way, the early days of the war, in which battles sprang up between isolated units distant from the larger forces and everywhere people acted on thin information and often mistaken surmise. As his story moves on to the full-scale war, Fraser presents excerpts from respondents that describe the callousness of leaders, the advent of atrocity and counteratrocity, the many casually ordered deaths, and the fewer narrow escapes. In passing, Fraser reproduces published materials of the time, including a full-page announcement from a right-wing newspaper pleading for the confidence of readers. Finally, Fraser describes the end of the war and the advent of the Franco government.

The book does wonderfully well in providing a sense of the experience of the Spanish Civil War for a reader removed from it in time and space. It may, perhaps, give disproportionate space to the vivid. This bias is understandable; the ordinary does not hold our attention. Nevertheless, there is enough in the book to make evident the torn texture of daily life and the numbed reality of a daily round carried on against a backdrop of catastrophe.

CASE-FOCUSED ANALYSIS

CONCRETE CASES

Feature stories in newspapers and magazines regularly begin with an account of a particular case. Our interest is much more likely to be attracted by the concrete and particular than by the abstract and general.

And we understand the concrete more easily: we can identify with actual people and immediately grasp real situations whereas the abstract and general requires us to understand in a more secondary way.

What concrete case studies of individuals do superbly is make the reader aware of the respondents' experience within the context of their lives: this is what it is like to be this person in this situation. Case studies take readers into respondents' lives.

In addition, case studies regularly imply generalizations, although without assurance of their validity. Readers take from case studies a sense of the case as exemplary, with general lessons to teach. They believe themselves to be learning not just about particular people but about people who are like them, not just about particular situations but about a class of situations.

Because investigators, as well as readers, grasp concrete cases more easily than abstract models, constructing case studies can be useful even in an issue-focused analysis. I have found that when I am unable to work out a persuasive conceptual scheme or unsure of what to emphasize in achieving local integration or inclusive integration, I am helped by putting together the materials of an individual case. I gain from the experience of case construction a more immediate understanding of the situation of respondents, and I can then more easily imagine how that situation might be presented and explained. For example, my first step in the analysis of data dealing with single parents' lives was to construct two extensive case studies. With them at hand, I could see how central was the issue of vulnerability to overload.

Producing a case study begins with sorting. Material that deals with the same issue must be brought together no matter where the material originally appeared in the interview transcripts. The material is then organized into a story of that issue. In the single-parent study, "fights with children" was one grouping of material. Integrating is likely to be done in two stages: a first stage of bringing together material into coherent scenes—the case-study parallel to the local integration of an issue-focused analysis—and a second stage of inclusive integration, in which scenes are linked into a coherent story. The investigator may also want occasionally or regularly to introduce a "voice-over," that is, a paragraph or page of commentary in which the reader is told what the case materials mean or what general processes they illustrate.

It takes me several drafts to arrive at an organization of interview material I feel presents a case properly. In my first drafts of a case study

I include too much; I want to preserve respondents' words, as if I were a curator of language. Only as I read and reread the material can I see where points are being made, what is superfluous, and where the argument has begun to veer off the track. New drafts are likely to suggest additional voice-overs, or better ones. At the end I will have to do a final editing to eliminate redundancies, straighten out the story line, and ensure that the case reads as well as it can. A good case study may make a reader believe that putting it together was easily done, but I have not found this to be true.

An interesting question is the extent to which the investigator who constructs a case study intends from the beginning of the analysis to illustrate a particular conception or provide support for a particular theory. My guess is that most often the investigator's understanding and the developing organization of the case material interact. The investigator's preconceptions help to decide the initial organization of the material, but then the material forces modification of the investigator's thinking, which then leads the investigator to revise the organization of materials, and so on for several iterations.

In the two examples given here of the case-study approach, the investigators make different choices regarding explicit generalization. Oscar Lewis, in an introduction to his cases, proposes that from them one can infer the grand, inclusive hypothesis that the lives described in the book were shaped by a "culture of poverty." Ronald Blythe is more circumspect in his treatment of case material. But he too seems to have a more general story in mind for which he intends his study to provide an instance: that the organization of society structures and constrains individual lives, but the human spirit, given the least opportunity, will break through the limitations that social organization imposes.

TWO CASE-FOCUSED REPORTS AT THE LEVEL OF CONCRETE MATERIAL

In *Children of Sanchez: Autobiography of A Mexican Family,* Oscar Lewis presents the autobiographies of the four children of Jesus Sanchez, a restaurant worker in Mexico City.[17] Lewis edited and rearranged segments of his interview transcripts so that the lives of his respondents are told by the respondents themselves. He begins the book by having Jesus Sanchez describe coming to Mexico City to make a life for himself. He ends the book with Jesus Sanchez speaking of his present life as an older man who has succeeded, finally, in obtaining title to a dwelling of his own. Between this beginning and end, Lewis has the children describe their lives—in the first section, their childhoods; in the second, their early adulthoods; in the third, their current lives.

Lewis's editing is intentionally novelistic. The first of the children to be presented is Manuel, the oldest. The excerpt from Manuel's interviews that Lewis chooses as Manuel's introduction has the quality of an early memory, like the beginning of Joyce's *Portrait of the Artist As a Young Man*. But it also sets the stage for what follows.

> I was eight years old when my mother died. I was asleep on a mat on the floor next to my brother Roberto. My little sisters, Consuela and Marta, slept on the bed with my Mama and Papa.

Here we are introduced all at once, in the space of three sentences, to the main characters, to the poverty that defines them, and to the mother's death that was the tragic beginning of their lives with a father we later see to be brusque and resentful. We are also introduced to what will be the dominant tone of all the narratives: a flat, matter-of-fact description of intensely emotional events.

The last sentence of this first section of Manuel's account is a statement of the event that ended his childhood: "That's how we got married: I had just turned fifteen and she was nineteen." By his marriage, Manuel established himself as an adult despite his age. Consider how much control of his material Lewis needed to be able to find just the right quotations with which to begin and end this section.

Lewis next introduces Roberto, the younger brother, who will describe recurrent problems with the law. The quotation with which Lewis has him introduce himself is "I started stealing things from my own house when I was small." The theme of thieving is presented at once.

The end-of-childhood statement that Lewis gives Roberto, with which Lewis ends the first section of Roberto's narrative, is "Then I joined the army, first because I wanted to be a soldier, but most of all, because it was getting impossible for me at home." And so we learn of another way of establishing adulthood.

While maintaining the autobiographical form, Lewis was able to introduce descriptions of the social institutions that structured low-income Mexican life. Here, for example, is Manuel on seeking admission to the United States to work as a migrant laborer:

We got in line [in front of the U.S. Customs House] and waited. There were people from all ends of the Republic, all dirty, in rags, and starving. . . . Everybody was anxious to get through; I understood their desperation because I felt the same way.

Then the squeezing and pushing began. . . . The shoving got worse. I was standing between two big guys, and when I was being smothered and felt myself walled in, I grabbed the two of them around their necks and pulled myself up. . . . The Immigration Office was at the height of a flight of stairs. Well, these guys began going up the stairs with me hanging from them; otherwise I wouldn't have made it . . .

When I reached the office, I got nervous. We were all convinced that the Immigration Officer knew who was lying and who wasn't. . . . Then, "Thank God and the Holy Mother," I said to myself, "I think they are going to let me in." . . .

Always, in reading autobiographical accounts, we give some attention to the credibility of the narrator. Especially do we do this when narrators talk about themselves. Because Lewis presents the views of four siblings, we hear not only the self-appraisals of each but the appraisals made of them by their siblings. After hearing Roberto deprecate himself, it is instructive to have his brother, Manuel, tell us, "Roberto was really very noble, the most noble in the family."

The last words of the book are the ruminations of Jesus Sanchez about the meaning of his life. Lewis proposes in his introduction that the message of his book is the way the culture of poverty works to prevent people from rising. But the final statement of Jesus Sanchez suggests that his story may have a different message. Here are the words with which *Children of Sanchez* ends:

I struggled and worked day and night to establish my home, a poor home, as you can see, but I have my happy moments with my grandchildren. It is first for God and then for my grandchildren that I'm on my feet, plugging away. . . . I hope God will allow me to be with them until they can earn their own living. . . . I want to leave them a room, that's my ambition; to build that little house, one or two rooms or three so that each child will have a home and so they can live there together. . . . It will be a protection for them when I fall down and don't get up again.

This final speech of Jesus Sanchez suggests that the book is not about poverty as much as it is about fathers and children. The book's title—*The*

Children of Sanchez, not *The Lives of Members of a Poor Family*—suggests that Lewis may have recognized this. Although many stories may be found in the book, the one that is for me the most compelling is Sanchez's story of how he came to Mexico City as a young man in search of a better life, rapidly became the father to four children by his wife and to other children by another woman, provided for his children and raised them—while bitterly resenting having to do so—and discovered at the end that his children's lives, filled with troubles about which he knew little and yet in some fundamental way shaped by him, and the lives of his children's children, had become the ultimate justification for all his struggles.

Ronald Blythe, in his *Akenfield: Portrait of an English Village,* presents many more voices than does Lewis, none of them extensively and some only briefly. He is concerned less with the events that made up the lives of his respondents than with their personalities and their place in the life of his village.[18] In a long excerpt, for example, one of the village's bell ringers talks about his obsession with ringing: "You have to be bitten by the bug. You have to be smitten. If you are a real ringer you think about bells morning, noon and night, and you only live for the next time you can have a go at them."

Early in the book, a man, aged 71, remembers leaving the village for the battles of World War I: Gallipoli and the battles in France. Another man, aged 80, talks about the Armistice. Both had been underpaid farm workers before they enlisted, and both returned to find conditions no better. There was a strike, bitter and inconclusive. A bit later in the book, retired officers and gentlemen are introduced to give their different views, and the class structure emerges. This is the way Blythe shows us how the personal and the social intermesh.

Blythe frequently introduces other material in addition to the interviews: he offers his own observations of a pub evening; he gives excerpts from the log book of the village school, beginning in 1875; he gives the local version of the Rumpelstiltskin legend, transcribing it in the local dialect; and he offers brief essays as introductions to interviews. He is willing to include anything—whatever scenes caught his eye, whatever thoughts came to his mind—that might deepen the picture of the village.

The result, one reviewer said, is "sociology written by a poet." Blythe offers a few generalizations about English life, but these are context for the lives he presents rather than the point of his work. His aim is to tell his readers what life is like in the small and, by extension, in the large.

The impulse seems to be like that underlying Thornton Wilder's *Our Town:* to capture the tragedy of the ordinary. At the very end, after having considered the many rhythms of the village, Blythe allows its grave digger to muse:

> I have no family, none at all. No one in all the world is my relation. I never did read a lot. I never could give my mind to it. I talk too much, that is my failing. I come into contact with many people at a serious time, so I have picked up serious conversation. What most folk have once or twice in a lifetime, I have every day. I want to be cremated and my ashes thrown in the air. Straight from the flames to the winds, and let that be that.

These final words of the grave digger are also Blythe's final words: "Straight from the flames to the winds, and let that be that." So very many things can be done with a concrete case study—even the composition of a long prose poem.

Because Blythe says nothing about his analytic methods, we must guess how he put this case study together. My guess is that he sorted, arranged, and rearranged his case materials, probably several times, until he found a sequence that made a compelling story. He may have done this in his mind, but I think it more likely he shuffled pages on a table. Levi-Strauss is reputed to have said that if he had a card table big enough he could figure out all of France.[19] There's much to be said for a large flat surface when trying to generate a coherent story from case material.

TYPOLOGIES AS GENERALIZATIONS FROM CONCRETE CASES

A way of generalizing from concrete cases while yet retaining their holistic character is to introduce types. Description of a type suggests that a common core has been identified within a set of particular cases and now is being named. The investigator, in presenting the type, is saying to the reader, "Here is the underlying structure, the skeleton of the case, unencrusted by the idiosyncrasies of specific instances, and here is a model of the dynamic that sets its parts in motion."

The type embraces many cases in a single framework. By invoking a type, the investigator need not describe first this particular case of, say, a young upwardly mobile couple of middle income and then that particular case of a young upwardly mobile couple of middle income and then the next, but can instead describe, all at once, "The young upwardly mobile couple of middle income."

Investigators often tell readers what they think is essential in a type by the name they give it. Suppose we believed that what was essential about young upwardly mobile couples of middle income was that they were doing everything in their power to achieve social success. We might communicate this by naming them "young strivers." We could then propose that this essential characteristic was responsible for much of the behavior of our respondents. We could therefore call on it to explain, among other things, the frequency with which they maintained dual careers and their determination to send their children to the best schools.

This view of types is close to the biological idea of species. One type is different from another in the same way an oak is different from an elm; there is a difference in kind. If it is a single type that is being described—the suburban family or the American housewife—the underlying idea is of a single inclusive species. But often a typology made up of several types is identified. Cuber and Harroff, for example, identified five types of marriage among the affluent: "conflict-habituated," "devitalized," "passive-congenial," "vital," and "total." Each of these is equivalent to a subspecies within the inclusive species of marriage of affluent couples.[20]

We can use our model of the type to report, in a fashion similar to the local integration of issue-focused data analysis, the main line of our interview material and the variations from the main line. We would first describe what we believe to be true of the group as a whole and then turn to its usual expression and variations from that. For example: "While all young strivers are limited in the time they can give to being with friends, their responses differ. Most accept that they will see friends less often than they would like. But one couple arranged with two other couples to have potluck dinner together, children included, every other weekend, with each couple serving as hosts in turn. And a second couple each summer arranged to take a vacation home with another couple, not always the same one."

Types can be constructed of anything that could serve as the subject for case studies—not just individuals but also relationships, families, organizations, and more. Gerhardt, in a study of dialysis patients, found it useful to construct two idealized "patient careers," one leading to invalidism and the other to a return to normal or near-normal life.[21]

Types are effective ways of communicating images that then are easily incorporated into thinking. Indeed, types can be seductive in their capacity to simplify thought. It is easier to picture in one's mind *the* single parent than the range of family arrangements and living situations that would be found by a survey of single parents—although it is the range of family arrangements that is the reality.

The Epistemological Status of Types

Where do types come from? Are they inferences from observations or are they conceptual inventions? Arguments can be made for each view.

When most people invoke a type, they imply that the type captures essentials shared by all the instances it embraces. People who talk about "deadbeat dads," for example, have in mind a way of acting toward a family left behind that they believe is common to a group of irresponsible divorced fathers. The essentials that are believed to mark the type presumably have been inferred from examination of instances. To the extent this is the case, types are anchored in reality.

What is often unclear, however, when a type is thought of as a classification based on essentials, is how one is to know in any particular instance whether the essentials are there. Is Madame Bovary an instance of the neurotic type or just a victim of romantic novels? How can we judge whether Madame Bovary's behavior is essentially neurotic or not? The difficulties of deciding in any given case on the presence of inferred essentials may suggest that types would be better defined by the observables themselves rather than inferences from the observables. Then we could decide whether Madame Bovary was or was not an instance of the neurotic type by considering whether she displayed such observables as nervous tics or unjustified fears.

A second approach to typing, then, would be to define a member of a type by a conjunction of one or more significant characteristics. For example, a "young striver" would be someone in the right part of the age range (between 25 and 35), with the right marital status (married), the right occupation (middle-class), and a high score on a rating scale of desire for upward mobility. We could leave open the question of whether the observables (between 25 and 35, married, middle-class occupation, rating scale score) are causes or expressions of some underlying essential. Some might hold that the conjunction of observable characteristics locates an unobservable essential (such as conformist striving) with more or less success. But others might hold that the conjunction *is* the type, period.

Defining a type in terms of observables can be helpful for the work of classification. (It is the approach taken by the American Psychiatric Association's *Diagnostic and Statistical Manual of Mental Disorders.*) Insofar as it is unsatisfactory, it is because there is something odd about proposing a special name and implying a special set of dynamics for individuals who differ only slightly from others. Could someone be almost neurotic but not quite? Once we admit that, yes, this is a possibility, we suggest that we are imposing typological thinking on what are actually continua.

This brings us to the third meaning of types, in addition to their identifying essentials and their representing a conjunction of characteristics: types, no matter their source, are conceptualizations, mental constructs. Whether they have been inferred from real instances or not, they are themselves only imagery, theories in the form of models of people or families or institutions.

This is the construction Weber would have us make of types. He proposed that we treat types as pure conceptualizations, with no necessary match in any real instance. Their purpose is to help us grasp our empirical cases by providing us with coherent models of what would exist if essential elements of the cases were in pure, idealized, form. We can then understand actual cases by comparing them with the conceptual template provided by the type. We note where the cases match the type and where they do not. And we can understand the dynamics of an individual case by understanding those of the ideal type and then considering how much the individual case is a modification of the ideal type.[22]

The Weberian approach is appealing. And, yes, we do use types in our thinking and in that sense all types are conceptualizations. But beyond this the Weberian view has limited application. The types we use in the reports of our studies are almost always intended to be descriptive of our data. Even when they are presented as idealizations, they are idealizations of a state real instances are thought to approach. Consider the typology of the "other-directed" character type and the "inner-directed" character type in *The Lonely Crowd*.[23] Although the types were idealized, they were used descriptively to suggest how the America of its time had changed, and readers certainly interpreted them as descriptive of the characters of real people.

My own view of the matter is that types are almost always generalizations from observed instances or at least purport to be. If the instances have been well observed and the types capture important dynamics, they can be a powerful device for explaining how things happen. They also can offer vivid imagery even when there is no evidence for the theories they imply. A commonly used typology of personal functioning classifies people, on the basis of their birth dates, as Libras or Geminis or any of ten other types. This classification is believed by many to make individual behavior understandable and to an extent predictable. There is, of course, no evidence whatsoever to support the theory. In general, types and typologies are a valuable resource in data analysis, but they should be treated with caution.

An Example of Generalized Case-Focused Analysis

In *The Gamesman: Winning and Losing the Career Game*,[24] Michael Maccoby attempted to present portraits of the managerial types who direct large American businesses. Working from structured and unstructured interviews with 250 managers from 12 major companies, Maccoby identified four character types: "gamesmen," "craftsmen," "jungle fighters," and "company men." The types differed in motivations, goals, resources, and ways of treating others, but what was most important for Maccoby was that they approached their managerial jobs in different ways. The gamesman treated work as a gamelike challenge, the craftsman as a set of technical problems, the jungle fighter as a conflict to be won, and the company man as an opportunity for service.

Maccoby describes in detail how each of his four types of business leader functioned in the business environment. He also provides case studies to suggest the kinds of people he classified into each of his types and the kinds of business environments in which each type might do well. Because he thought gamesmen would be the managerial style of the future, he gave a good deal of space to describing a respondent whom he characterized as a "creative gamesman."

Where did Maccoby's types come from? Maccoby reports that he based the typology on his study of the managers' self-descriptions, augmented by their responses to Rorschach ink blots and descriptions of them provided by their colleagues. Maccoby describes his approach in this way:

> Once we had scored [the respondents] in terms of dynamic character traits, different types began to emerge as distinct from one another in terms of the individual member's overall orientation to work, values, and self-identity. We eventually came to name four main psychological types in the corporate techno-structure: the craftsman, the jungle fighter, the company man, and the gamesman. These are "ideal types" in the sense that few people fit the type

exactly and most are a mixture of types. But in practically every case, we were able to agree on which type best described a person, and the individual and his colleagues almost always agreed with our typing. (p. 37).

Maccoby alludes to three analytic processes in this paragraph. The first process was perceiving a typology among the different groupings of scores respondents had been given on such traits as aggression and intellectuality. Theories of personality may have played a role in the interpretation of the observed clusterings, but chances are a certain amount of inspiration also entered in. We have to guess, because we aren't told exactly how the typology was developed.

The second analytic process was the naming of the emergent types. Here Maccoby clearly sought words that would accurately communicate each type's essential nature. Implicit is a theory of individual functioning in which some single self–other outlook determines social behavior. Actually, the types proved too broad for many analyses, and at several points Maccoby had to introduce subtypes. Craftsmen were divided into the "dutiful," who were driven and hierarchical, and the "receptive," who were more life-loving and democratic. Jungle fighters were subspeciated into "lions," who terrorized, and "foxes," who manipulated. As I noted, one gamesman was a "creative" gamesman; presumably, others were not.

The third analytic process to which Maccoby refers in the quoted section was the assignment of individuals to one of the four types. Although Maccoby first notes that few people precisely fit a single type, he then says that there was agreement by respondents and their colleagues regarding the type to which respondents were closest. It seems to me that Maccoby is waffling a bit on the epistemological status of his types. On the one hand he describes the types as inferential, developed from a study of diagnostic material. He asserts that in practically every case managers could be fit into one type or another and that there was agreement regarding the typing. But in introducing the types, Maccoby described them as ideal types, which real instances might approach but should not be expected to match.

One test that Maccoby's typology passed with flying colors was acceptance by its readers. *The Gamesman* made the best-seller list. Most reviews were positive. Those that were not were critical of Maccoby's view of the managers rather than of the methods he used in his study. One reviewer, for example, speculated that, given the time they were able to take from their work to participate in the study, Maccoby's managers were second-stringers rather than real leaders. Another reviewer thought the managers banal and uninteresting. But all reviewers accepted Maccoby's typology as valid. For a time, at least, the book was influential in business circles.

THE DEMONSTRATION OF CAUSATION

In qualitative interview studies the demonstration of causation rests heavily on the description of a visualizable sequence of events, each event flowing into the next. In *Children of Sanchez* we can see how the tensions in the Sanchez home, together with the values of the society in which he lived, pushed Manuel into independent adulthood at age 15. In *Blood of Spain* we can follow the widening impact of garrison revolts into first skirmishes and then war. In *Blue-Collar Marriage* we can see the ways that mutual trust and respect, plus a secure marital partnership, can produce contentment in a marriage in which there is little apparent companionship. And in *The Gamesman* we can see how managerial styles affect organizational cultures.

The description of a visualizable sequence of events differs from the approach of quantitative studies as a way of demonstrating causation. Quantitative studies support an assertion of causation by showing a correlation between an earlier event and a subsequent event. An analysis of data collected in a large-scale sample survey might, for example, show that there is a correlation between the level of the wife's education and the presence of a companionable marriage. In qualitative interview studies we would look for the process through which the wife's education or factors associated with her education express themselves in marital interaction.

A search for the visualizable process that led from one event to the next can be one of the directing forces in an interview. At the end of many interviews the investigator can offer, with some confidence, a description of how some aspect of the respondent's life or situation came to be. If the same sort of description fits a series of respondents, the investigator can feel justified in proposing a more general statement as a hypothesized minitheory. Each new interview can then be a test, the results of which will support the minitheory, discredit it, or, most likely, require that it be augmented or qualified.

One idea of how to establish causal connections using qualitative interview material no longer has much currency. This was the idea that an invariable sequence must be found in the material, that is, that determinant A must always be followed by consequent B and consequent B must always be preceded by determinant A. Robert Cooley Angell, in *The Family Encounters the Depression,* and Donald Ray Cressey, in *Other People's Money,* were among those in the social sciences who tried to find a process in their materials that was present each and every time. Angell hoped to show that income loss in families that were initially poorly integrated would always end in familial disintegration whereas in better-integrated families income loss could be taken in stride. He ultimately gave up on this hypothesis; some families that looked bad to begin with were nevertheless able to pull themselves together. Cressey did find an invariant association between certain potentially causal elements, including the embezzler's ability to find some way of justifying what he was doing, and ultimate embezzlement. But, by and large, invariable associations aren't to be found, not in interview data any more than in survey research.

However, a process does not have to be invariable in order to be causal. There are always extraneous factors that can modify the direction of a particular process. All that is necessary to show that a process may be causal is to make evident how it moves from cause to consequence. *Blood of Spain* shows that news of the garrison revolts in Morocco led to battles elsewhere in Spain, although such battles did not happen everywhere. It is a distinct problem—albeit a most important one—to identify the factors that can impede, redirect, or facilitate a causal process.

In chapter 2 I pointed out that qualitative interview studies regularly lack comparison groups; it's hard enough to study the group of interest without taking on the study of another group. I also suggested that it is often desirable nevertheless to do some limited interviewing of comparison respondents. Here let me note that we quite often can make comparisons within the sample we are studying. Komarovsky had within her study the comparison groups of couples who had completed high school and couples who had not. And although she had limited her study to people who were raising children, she could ask her respondents to tell her about their preparental lives. Her respondents could, in a way, serve as their own comparisons. On the other hand, if Komarovsky had wanted to consider the possible effects of the working-class status that all her respondents shared, she would have needed at least a few comparison cases from the middle class.

Respondents often have beliefs regarding causal processes, but they must be treated cautiously. The returned veterans of Blythe's *Akenfield* blamed the landowners for the hard times they experienced on their return from war, but the landowners too were caught in an economic downturn that affected them all. Potential causal factors outside respondents' observational fields cannot be referred to by them.[25]

Caution in the treatment of respondents' causal explanations should be extended to respondents' explanations of their own behavior. People tend not to be fully aware of their emotions and their motivations. This does not mean that their self-reports have to be disregarded. Rather, they should be treated as likely to be incomplete.

Nevertheless, we do well to attend to respondents' descriptions of causation in social developments as well as in themselves. Often, they have identified at least part of the dynamics that have produced events. Some respondents may be especially worth attending to because they were close to the decision-making process or to some other development that set events in motion, or are especially perceptive or thoughtful. We will, of course, have to treat what these respondents tell us as suggestions to be investigated further, but they may point us in the right direction.

I think we ultimately have to judge the validity of our identification of a causal process by considering all of our evidence together. We have to weigh the nature and density of the interview information supporting the identification; consider whether we have negative cases and, if we do, whether we have plausible explanations for them; and determine whether there are other bases for support or, on the other side, reasons for doubt.

SUMMARY

Certain analytic processes show up in every analysis of the data of qualitative interview studies: sorting the data, achieving local integration, achieving inclusive integration. In analyses intended to generalize regarding issues, coding is also important. In a typological analysis, the characterization of types is crucial.

Each analytic approach has strengths and drawbacks. The generalized approaches, both issue-focused and case-focused, contribute to our understanding on the level of theory. The approaches that provide us with concrete materials, again both issue-focused and case-focused, enlarge our experience and provide us with a basis for developing our own inferences.

Causal explanation can be found in the products of every analytic approach, issue-focused and case-focused, concrete and generalized. Its demonstration rests on empirical and logical grounds that are different from those of a survey or an experimental study, but it need be no less a contribution to our understanding for that.

CHAPTER 7

WRITING THE REPORT

GETTING STARTED

By the time a study has reached the phase in which writing is its investigator's primary concern, it will have amassed a great deal of material. The study's file cabinets are likely to contain—in addition to the interview transcripts and excerpt files—codings of transcripts, descriptions of minitheories, data supporting the minitheories, summaries of the literature, and lists of questions to be answered, together with some answers to the questions. There may also be outlines and drafts of chapters or papers. Despite all this—maybe because of all this—it can be hard for the investigator to know where to start the report.

A first effort might be to reconsider the questions that motivated the study and how they have been answered. This may in itself provide an outline for a brief report. But it may be that answering the study's initial questions will use only a small part of the information that has been gathered. Or the study's initial questions may no longer seem of central importance, after all that has been learned.

If the investigator has already given a good deal of effort to analysis, the results of the analysis should provide the material for a report. All that may be necessary is their organization, development, and presentation. On the other hand, the investigator may have postponed full scale analysis until a decision was made on what was to be reported. In either event, but espe-

183

cially in the latter, the investigator may be uncertain about where to begin.

Here are some exercises that may be useful preparation for beginning a report. None are necessary, but one or two of them may help the investigator make a start.

BEGINNING WITH THE CONCRETE

What stories do you have to tell? Write down all the stories you can think of that strike you as interesting enough to hold an audience's attention. Now sort the stories so they achieve a sequence. (It could help, if you're not using a word processor, to put each story on its own index card.) If you now tell a reader your stories in the sequence you have developed, augmenting them with appropriate introductions and lesson drawing, you'll have a report. If there are gaps, you should now be able to see what has to be added.

A variant of this is to identify exemplary respondents, develop their interviews into case studies, and then put the case studies in logical sequence. You might now note what can be learned from each case study. Having done this, you might think about the best way of communicating these lessons. Do you want to leave your case materials as is? Or do you want to retain the "caseness" of your material but generalize to a typological report? Or do you want to emphasize the issues the cases display by developing an issues-focused report?

A third possibility is that you might write about your own experience in doing the study. (Although this could be hard if you haven't been keeping a diary.) You might start with your preconceptions, describe how you went about learning, and end with what you now know.

BEGINNING WITH THE GENERAL

In developing your interview guide you almost surely thought about how you might present findings. This would especially be the case if you relied on an accounting scheme to develop the guide. Return to the guide now and imagine a generalized respondent. For every issue raised in the guide, sketch how this generalized respondent would deal with it. If you now develop your sketch and add supporting materials, you have the skeleton of a report. Now go back to the interview data so that you can decide where you will introduce real instances, including those that exemplify the main line of your findings and those that are variants of it.

Another approach would be to list your findings—all of them. Imagine you are to present them to an audience. Which do you start with? How do you connect them? What would make them into a coherent story rather than a listing of items?

You might compare your actual findings with those you anticipated when you began the study. After all, when you began your study you were in the position of the ordinary well-informed person. What do you know, now that the study is done, that you didn't know then? This should tell you where your study will be instructive to its likely reader. Now think about how to organize what you have to report and how to back it up with evidence. The result should be an outline of your report.

BEGINNING WITH THE MIX OF MATERIAL

You might take printouts of all the analytic material you have developed in your study, including memoranda, notes, and especially instructive interview excerpts, and sort them by topic. Now try to summarize the sortings. For each sorting, attempt to integrate what you have by finding an underlying dynamic, or some way in which everything expresses a common theme. Or search for a way in which everything adds to the understanding of an important outcome. This done, search for a way of integrating the themes or stories you developed for each sorting.

Or you might review the literature on your topic. What is it that other investigators are interested in? Can your study speak to their interests? What is it that people believe? Does your study provide corroboration? Or does it require that some general belief be revised? Work out how you will develop your argument, the order in which you will make your points, and how you will bring in your evidence.

FIRST DRAFTS

My own experience is that I begin to write the report before I get to the end of any of these preparatory exercises. And almost always I begin with chapter 1, even if the really important material won't show up for another 50 pages. It may be that I need the sense of pushing the manuscript ever forward. However, I generally leave the introduction, where I tell the reader what the report is about, to the very last—when I know myself.

I try to do my first draft quickly, to assure myself that I have all the parts. And then, as I note later in this chapter, I rewrite. In the course of writing and rewriting, a number of issues may arise having to do with the way in which material is presented. The remainder of this chapter deals with what I think are the more important of these issues.

TO WHAT AUDIENCE IS THE REPORT DIRECTED?

How you present your material may depend on the audience you want to reach. Here are some thoughts about audiences.

ACADEMIC AUDIENCES

Academic audiences are likely to want first to be told how the report will add to their knowledge or understanding. The report must justify its demand on their time. You may have to argue that the report will teach them something new and important.

Academic readers are likely to accept as valid the material of the interviews. Case studies, if they contribute to an understanding of an important area, are likely to be accepted with no further scrutiny. Inferences, generalizations, interpretations, and theory, on the other hand, are likely to be examined closely.

Academic readers have high standards for credibility. They are likely to think about comparison groups. Some of them will be skilled in devising alternative interpretations. Generalizations beyond your sample may make them uncomfortable. They will want to know your justification for generalizing.

Should you advance an argument about the way things are, based on your interview material, your task is not only explication but advocacy. The analysis of your data led you to a conclusion; now you have to convince your readers. You must play fair with your evidence, but you also must develop your reasons for coming to your conclusion. If you think something is likely to be true, but you're not sure, all of that is worth saying. Try to get to the heart of the matter; academic audiences will not quite join with Diaghilev in demanding that they be astonished, but they do want to go beyond superficials.

Quantitative support for key points is helpful. One of the strengths of *Recovery from Bereavement,* my book with Colin Parkes, was that key points were supported by counts and correlations. We were able to report, for example, what proportion of our sample who early on displayed strong pining later failed to recover from grief. Although we didn't have many tables in the book, the fact that we had tables for key points helped the entire report gain acceptance.

PROFESSIONAL AUDIENCES

Professional audiences are likely to be concerned with the applicability of your report. Professionals must stay informed of current understandings in their fields and be able to implement what is currently endorsed as good practice. They will want a report that contributes to their competence.

Professionals are a bit less likely than academics to ask for conclusive evidence. Although they will want to be assured that credible evidence supports the conclusions of the report, they are ordinarily less concerned than academics that it all be displayed or at least be obtainable. They will care most about whether the report helps them do their work.

CLIENTS WHO HAVE COMMISSIONED THE STUDY

Client groups tend to want diagnoses and recommendations. They have come to you, ordinarily, with a problem in their organization or in their program. They want to know what is going wrong and, even more, how to make it right.

Vividness is valuable, as is completeness. The arguments for recommendations should be spelled out, as should be the possible costs of implementing them. The client group ordinarily will not demand extensive evidence for assertions, although they will want to know that sound evidence exists and, in general terms, what it is. A methods section describing how the study was done may be essential, even if it is unlikely to be read closely.

Controversy produced by the conclusions of a report is not infrequent. Indeed, you should assume that a report that is in any way critical of any sector of a client organization or of any program that has loyal backers within the client organization will become controversial. The credibility of the findings and conclusions of the report are then likely to be attacked, and you should be sure that good evidence is available and should present it fully and clearly. And if you suspect that your report is likely to stir controversy within the client group, you should give serious thought to strategies for presenting the report. You might also discuss such strategies with figures within the client group who might help in the report's presentation.

THE GENERAL READER

Interview-based studies can be of genuine interest to a general audience if they offer enough opportunity for insight into the lives of others to involve and instruct a casual reader.

A general audience is likely to be more interested in being informed than in being presented with support for one hypothesis or another. Although a general audience may be concerned with issues of credibility, it will not be as critical as an academic audience. Members of a general audience are more apt to respond positively than would an academic audience to a succession of anecdotes and interview excerpts. Indeed, the loosely attributed anecdote about "a person I know" would be acceptable as evidence only by a general audience.

One image of the typical member of a general audience is someone you meet at a party who is at first only mildly interested in your topic. Your listener is intelligent enough but with no special need for the information you can provide. You can assume that your listener's attention will stray if you become boring.

General readers, like other readers, require the best thought and the clearest writing of which the investigator is capable. They should not be written down to. It may be inadvisable to use specialized language, but it is important to make available all that you know. What you write should be as full and rich as you can make it.

CAN YOU WRITE FOR MORE THAN ONE AUDIENCE?

The density of information, careful review of findings, and systematic citation of literature that would satisfy an academic audience might make a report too heavy and slow-moving for a general reader. A client report, as well as a report intended for a professional audience, would almost surely focus on questions specific to its audience's concerns. It's hard to write a report for more than one audience.

Yet occasionally a report does succeed in reaching both a general audience and a more specialized one; *Children of Sanchez, Blood of Spain,* and *The Gamesman* are examples. An investigator hoping to achieve the like might be best advised to try for a report so interesting and so valuable that it will attract a general audience, while members of other audiences will make allowances for its not being directed solely to them. Thus, if you write for the intelligent layman and the report is important enough, others will read it too.

TO WHAT EXTENT DO YOU ENTER AS A FIGURE IN THE REPORT?

To what extent do you introduce your own experience in the report? Do you remove yourself entirely, except as someone presenting and interpreting the reports of respondents? Or do you describe for the reader your problems in data collection, your encounters with respondents, and your understanding of their responses as they were made? The first approach provides the reader with the information you obtained, but neglects the issue of how you obtained it. John Van Maanen calls this the "realist" style, in his discussion of rhetorical styles in the social sciences. The second approach shares with the reader the experiences you had in producing the report. Van Maanen calls this the "confessional" style.[1]

The realist style is generally written in what Van Maanen calls "didactic deadpan," that is, an even-voiced, self-confident presentation of fact. The investigator may describe his or her own experience in an introduction but after that the investigator appears only to set a scene or comment on a statement, like the stage manager in *Our Town*. Should the investigator take over to tell the respondents' stories, paraphrasing and summarizing respondents' interviews, it is still the respondents who are the only actors.

In the realist style the investigator remains an invisible, dispassionate observer, even when the report deals with material of great emotional intensity. Here is how Glaser and Strauss describe what they learned from interviews with nurses about working with the families of patients dying at home:

> In the typical lingering death at home, the closer to the end, the more difficult the care becomes for the family members. The amount of deterioration and the work it entails are not easy for them to imagine unless they have experienced such deaths previously. Consequently, the nurse almost inevitably finds herself stepping up the number of her visits during this phase of dying: "Toward the end you generally have to start going in more frequently, and this gives you an idea the end is near."[2]

This is the traditional style of report writing, and the approach most like that used in the physical sciences. A chemist would hardly interrupt a description of a chemical reaction to describe how he had gone about obtaining test tubes. Nor do Glaser and Strauss interrupt their narrative to tell the reader how they presented themselves to the nurses they interviewed, what their problems were in eliciting descriptions of disturbing experiences, or what their own reactions were.

But with increasing frequency investigators in the social sciences are including in their reports their experiences in conducting the studies. They present not only the story of one or more respondents but also the story of the investigation—if not the problems it encountered, then how it felt to conduct it and what decided them on the research choices they made. They may describe their reactions when they met their respondents and how further acquaintance with respondents affected their feelings about them.

Writing in this confessional style makes it possible for investigators to introduce novelistic devices. They can, for example, describe their response to a setting as a way of suggesting the emotional tensions within it. Here is how Arlie Hochschild, in her study of two-job marriages, introduces a couple for whom overload had led to marital strain: "When I entered the Livingstons' home, I noticed a half-empty trellis standing ready to support a frail, outreaching bougainvillea with leaves of brilliant crimson. A window was cracked. The paint was peeling."[3]

This confessional style of presentation permits investigators to confide in the reader their developing understanding of a respondent's character or circumstance. They can engage the reader's interest by introducing story elements such as witnessing a tense interchange between a husband and wife. The confessional style permits the investigator to include in the report anecdotes that would otherwise be restricted to dinner table conversation. It can help make the report a good read. Beyond that, it can make the report more useful.

Here is an example of how the confessional mode provides an additional dimension to observations. It is from Maren Carden's qualitative interview study of feminist movements of the late 1960s and early 1970s. By describing her concerns with her own dress she illuminates the ways dress signaled identity in the groups she was learning about.

> In my manner, dress, and general behavior I tried to fit into my surroundings without violating my own integrity. For example, I wore informal sweaters and skirts for Women's Liberation meetings but did not wear the near-universal jeans or slacks because I feel uncomfortable in them. When interviewing several people on one day I would often wear the same knitted dress to meet someone from WEAL [Women's Equity Action League] and someone from Women's Liberation. For the WEAL interview, I would add a gold pin and slightly dressy shoes—the sort of outfit in which I might

lecture; for the Women's Liberation interview, I would add a sweater and change to plain shoes—the sort of outfit I might wear to go to a movie.[4]

Issues of credibility are for the most part the same in a consistently realist presentation and in one that now and again adopts the confessional mode. But the report in the confessional mode makes an additional argument for credibility through its inclusion of first-person material. The reader is encouraged to adopt an identification with the author that, in turn, fosters suspension of disbelief.

USING EXCERPTS AS ILLUSTRATION AND AS EVIDENCE

Excerpts from interviews can do more than simply enliven a report, though this alone might be enough to justify their use. Excerpts also provide evidence for our assertions: "What I said is true; here it is in this quotation." They provide examples of the words and images respondents use and a sense of the lives that underlie our findings. They foster identification with respondents and facilitate understanding of their points of view. They show the particular forms of general phenomena. But presenting excerpts is hardly problem free. We always select from our files of materials a small part to present. And we almost always edit. Each of these processes deserves examination.

SELECTION OF RESPONDENTS TO QUOTE

It is a matter of common sense to select the quotation that makes the point in as strong a fashion as possible. It is, however, important to check that the quotation is representative in the sense that a member of Congress is supposed to be representative, that is, that it forcefully presents what is widely shared. Respondents whose material makes a different point should then be given their own representatives.

Some report writers provide a string of quotations from different respondents, each saying about the same thing, as a way of demonstrating to the reader that they are playing fair. I don't see the point in this strategy. If the reader doesn't trust you, providing half a dozen quotes instead of one isn't going to make a difference. When I come to these pages of snippets, I read one or two and skip the rest. It would be better to provide a couple of quotations and then indicate the proportion of respondents who say something similar.

Most of the quotations I eventually use come from the notes I developed reading interview transcripts or excerpt files. Occasionally, I will give a good deal of time to developing at length a particularly instructive story in the respondent's words, and will then actually quote only a part of the story in my report. Occasionally, too, I will realize only in the writing of the report the need for an illustrative quotation, and then if I do not remember a respondent who said something appropriate, I will check the nearest transcript in a drawer full of them or scan the excerpt files in my computer. If I find an illustrative quotation easily, I am reassured that what I am reporting is generally true.

While quotations are useful, the report writer should be aware that they require the reader to shift attention from the writer's voice to a new voice. Doing this several times in a few pages can be fatiguing for the reader. A high ratio of text to interview excerpt can help.

A few long excerpts are preferable to listings of snippets. However, if longer excerpts are used in an issue-oriented report, readers are likely to want them interrupted now and again by text that tells them the point being made. Excerpts should forward an argument. If they don't, they should be dropped. An excerpt whose contribution to the text is mysterious risks losing the reader.

HOW SHOULD QUOTATIONS BE EDITED?

Blauner distinguishes between two philosophies in the treatment of interview excerpts: the "preservationist" and the "standardized." The first would present the original speech in such a way as to reproduce the sounds on the tape as accurately as possible. The second would remain true to the words and meanings of the original but would accept editing that made the excerpt easier for a reader to grasp.[5]

The Preservationist Approach

There are two arguments for the preservationist approach. The first is that speech communicates not only the dictionary meanings of its words but also the speaker's feelings, including the speaker's passions and uncertainties.[6] The thought here is that every element in a respondent's expression—including the respondent's hesitancies, nonstandard grammatical constructions and pronunciations, and circuitous rather than straightforward narrative—has value as communication. As Catherine

Riessman has put it, "Speech that has been 'cleaned up' to be more readable loses important information."[7]

The second argument for the preservationist approach is that speech is a presentation of self and that changing speech misrepresents both the respondent's personality and the respondent's place in society. As Van Maanan says, standardizing respondents' speech turns all respondents into "mannerly, pleasant, rational, and down-to-earth chaps who speak the King's English remarkably well."[8]

Both these arguments hold that only the original speech, pristine and without any editorial change, can adequately represent the respondent's meanings and self. Anything else distorts. In the preservationist view it would be best if the reader could hear the original speech, with its pitch and sounds. Next best is to render these into words on a page with as much fidelity as possible. Anything less is playing with the evidence, no matter how benign the intent.

The Standardized Approach

The argument for standardizing respondent quotations is that nonstandardized speech distracts from content. A too faithful rendering of respondent dialect, instead of enriching a quotation, may strike the reader as mannered and annoying. Almost surely the reader will have to puzzle out the respondent's meaning instead of being able to understand it immediately. According to this view, speech needs to be cleaned up to be readable. Furthermore, nonstandard speech suggests an uneducated respondent. Such speech may therefore encourage the reader to disregard or disparage what the respondent says.

The Usual Compromise

Generally, investigators in the social sciences make those modifications in the quotation excerpts they present that they believe make the excerpts easier to grasp but that they are certain have no effect on the respondent's meaning. They are likely to permit themselves to eliminate words, sentences, and paragraphs—and also, most of the time, their own questions—in order to achieve a more compact statement. They will bring together in one place material dealing with the same issue that originally appeared in different sections of the interview transcript. They will standardize the slurrings of colloquial speech: "I was gonna" would be rendered as "I was going to." But never is a word changed, never is a word supplied.

In a book on how journalistic aims intersect with ordinary understandings, Janet Malcolm describes a more liberal practice in editing taped statements. Her editing takes revision for coherence and grace far beyond anything anyone in the social sciences would have the wish or the skill to do. She introduces her own connectives ("and this, too," "since"), regularly straightens out her respondent's grammar and syntax, and not only condenses but sharpens her respondent's argument. Her defense is that we are always translating speech into English: "Our ear takes it in as English, and only if we see it transcribed verbatim do we realize it is a kind of foreign tongue." According to Malcolm, a written quotation should be just such a translation, now produced by the report writer rather than by a listener. It is only necessary for the report writer to be sure that the translation is faithful to the subject's thought and characteristic mode of expression.[9]

So much assumption of editorial prerogative strikes me as going much too far. Quotation marks do not indicate that this is what the respondent *meant,* they indicate that this is what the respondent *said.* The reader is being misled when an investigator rephrases a respondent's statements and then attributes the rephrasing to the respondent. It is one thing to standardize word use and drop out repetitions, but it is quite another to provide as the respondent's statement a much more literate and pointed and effective translation. Not only is the character of the respondent changed—the respondent made into someone whose competent use of language implies a more general competence—but the respondent's thoughts become less clouded than they were in reality, less blurred by other thoughts. Incidents are described more starkly.

Perhaps the much milder sort of editing that seems to me customary in social science could also be attacked as changing the respondent's presentation of self. But I think the rule that words should never be supplied is one defense against this, and the effort to retain the respondent's phrasings is another. And there is much to be said for making the respondent's statements accessible to the reader. While I strongly believe that if the words aren't the respondent's, they shouldn't be attributed to the respondent, I also believe that absolutely literal transcription of a respondent's words can interfere with understanding them.

In my book on occupationally successful men, as part of my discussion of how they managed stress, I present the story of a crisis in the business life of a respondent whom I named Mr. Daniels. Mr. Daniels had agreed to arrange a loan for a contractor. Collateral for the loan would be equipment the contractor said that he owned. In reality, the contractor was only renting the equipment. Only after Mr. Daniels had gotten others involved in the arrangement did he learn that the contractor had lied to him. As soon as he learned this, he called the contractor to tell him the deal was off. The contractor then threatened him with violence.

The evening after the blowup with the contractor, Mr. Daniels met with an old friend. Mr. Daniels told us that before meeting with the friend he had hardly been able to think of anything other than the failed business deal. He was chagrined at having blindly accepted the contractor's assurance and embarrassed at having involved others. He was also a bit worried by the contractor's threat, although he preferred not to admit that, not even to himself. But when he met with his friend, Mr. Daniels said not a word about what had happened.

I wanted to make a couple of points with the following quotation. The first was that Mr. Daniels maintained his functioning by compartmentalizing his distress, keeping it away from the forefront of his consciousness. The second was that to maintain his friend's respect for him he said his business was going just fine, when in fact he was fending off awareness of a business reversal. What I wanted to show was how Mr. Daniels's style of stress management—and, by extension, the style adopted by most successful men—implied that when he was troubled he would *not* confide in a close friend.

In the left column is the transcript excerpt; in the right, the material that ended up in the book.

INTERVIEW EXCERPT AS TRANSCRIBED	PUBLISHED INTERVIEW EXCERPT
RESPONDENT: I didn't even mention that, this whole thing. I remember at dinner, at one point, toward the end of dinner, we're having a cup of coffee and he just asked me, "How's business?" and you know, I was having a nice time and I really didn't want to, just didn't want to even bring it up, and go through it all, because	*I didn't even mention this whole thing. At one point, toward the end of dinner, we were having a cup of coffee and he asked me, "How's business?" I was having a nice time and I really didn't want to even bring it up and go through it all. Because there's no point in it. It wasn't going to do any good. I really wanted*

INTERVIEW EXCERPT AS TRANSCRIBED	PUBLISHED INTERVIEW EXCERPT
there's no point in it. It wasn't going to do any good. INTERVIEWER: Sounds like you needed something else . . . R: Yeah, I really wanted that really to go away, and to be gone, and so, I just said," Oh, it's okay. We're doing all right."	*that to go away, to be gone. So I just said, "Oh, it's okay. We're doing all right."*

Immediately preceding the material I used for the quotation was the following material, which I dropped:

R: Wells knows what's going on in my life, but he doesn't as far as the business thing goes, and I don't know if you want to hang on to that or what, but as far as that goes, he plays a very small role in that. He could tell you generally that things look good, terrible, crisis time or not, but I would never weigh him down with any of the details because there wouldn't be any benefit in it. He would not . . . advise me, I wouldn't want him to. That's not what Wells is.

I: It sounds like that relationship is for other things.

R: Yeah, but it's a very good relationship. It's one I'm quite fond of . . . most fond of, really.

This material makes the point that Mr. Daniels, like many men, thinks of friendships as having purposes, with one friendship quite possibly having a different purpose from another. This is an important point to make, and I do make it elsewhere in the book. At this moment, however, the book is dealing with the issue of stress management. The general principle is that the issue to be illustrated should decide where an excerpt begins and ends.

OTHER PROBLEMS IN HANDLING EXCERPTS

Here are some other problems that may emerge in dealing with quotations from interviews.

Suppressing Interviewer Contributions

Note that in preparing the excerpt from the interview with Mr. Daniels for publication I omitted the interviewer's questions and comments. In consequence, Mr. Daniels's response to the interviewer saying, "Sounds like you needed something else..." appears as a continuation of Mr. Daniels's previous statement. Does this distort? My judgment was that although Mr. Daniels might not have said "Yeah, I really wanted that really to go away" had it not been for the question, running his response into his previous response in no way changed its meaning.

Occasionally, including an interviewer's question in the published text is necessary in order to make clear the meaning of a response. Then I would include it. But for the most part, I find interviewers' questions and comments to be distracting.

In this interview, as in any, the interviewer repeatedly made encouraging or sympathetic noises: "Uh-huh" or "Mmm". The transcriptionist frequently indicated these, but I dropped the indications from the published excerpt. Here again it seemed to me that the interjections were unnecessary distractions in the text, however valuable they may have been in the interview.

Dropping Out Conversational Spacers and False Starts

Most respondents use conversational spacers—"you know" or "uh"—to cover a pause while they search for a word or a continuation of a thought. Or they find a start to a sentence unsatisfactory and begin again. Or they repeat a phrase as though weighing its meaning: "I think that he must have gone, he must have gone..." I almost always edit these out unless the spacer or false start or repeat communicates uncertainty or serves some similar purpose. So when Mr. Daniels said, "And you know, I was having a nice time," I edited out the "And you know" and rendered the statement as "I was having a nice time."

I am not sure I was right, in this instance, to have regularized Mr. Daniels's speech as much as I did. His hesitancies, spacers, and repeats do communicate a certain informality in speaking style. I did not, however, in any instance add a word Mr. Daniels did not use or substitute a word of mine for one of his or change a sentence except to drop a spacer or a redundancy.

Good transcriptionists will accurately represent common condensations of speech, such as "He's gotta say what he wants." I find this useful in reading the transcript, but in reporting I would almost certainly change the "gotta" to "got to." I see no value in retaining what is a kind of personal dialect. On the other hand, I never correct grammatical errors. If someone says, as Mr. Daniels did at another point, "I think of he and I as close," I'll let that stand.

In general, I try to be faithful to the respondent's word choice and sentence structure. In the unusual circumstance that it is necessary to introduce a word to make clear a respondent's meaning, I put the introduced word in brackets: "I called her [R's sister] on the telephone."

Reorganizing for Coherence

I sometimes do a fair amount of reorganizing of a respondent's report in the interests of coherence. If a respondent developed a theme, went off to something else, and then returned to the original theme, I will bring together all the materials dealing with the theme. It's asking a lot of a reader to sort out scattered thematic material. It's possible, of course, to use ellipsis points to indicate that material has been removed, but this rarely seems to me useful.

Disguising People, Places, and Institutions

In telling Mr. Daniels's story I changed the nature of the deal he was involved in while retaining its structure. I cannot say here what was actually going on, but it did involve collateral and a client who lied about the collateral. The changes I made were enough to provide disguise without changing the human elements that were the essential part of the story.

I want to ensure that respondents are not recognizable to others in any quotations I give. I would also like it if they were not recognizable to themselves, but that seems more than I can always achieve. Still, I was once told by a respondent whom I had quoted extensively that he had looked in the book for himself without success.

I change names, getting new names from the telephone book. I look for one-syllable or two-syllable names, sometimes with an ethnic flavor not too different from that of the respondent's name. If I do choose a name of similar ethnicity, I want the code name to be not so strongly ethnic as to constitute a comment; I might turn O'Brien into Conley but not into O'Malley.

If it doesn't matter, I will try to drop a reference to a place rather than invent a substitute. If a respondent refers to a daughter who lives in California, I might put her in Oregon or "out West," but I would prefer to drop the place reference entirely. Another possibility is to put a generalized reference in brackets: [in another state].

I change occupations, trying to find substitute occupations that involve the same general kind of work. Mr. Daniels did indeed arrange business deals involving clients and collateral—I had to keep this for his story to make sense—but the rest of what I described as his work was invention.

I try not to distort the character of a respondent's life situation, but where it doesn't matter much I will make whatever changes seem useful for disguise. Occasionally I have changed the number of children a respondent had, and once I changed a child's gender. When material strikes me as truly sensitive—capable of bringing embarrassment or injury if the respondent were identified with it—I give no information, not even false information, about occupation or place. In addition, I may give a new false name to the respondent, different from the false name I used for the respondent elsewhere in the report.

Checking the Transcript

Good transcriptionists, in my experience, will get a respondent's words almost right but never entirely right. When preparing this chapter I listened again to Mr. Daniels's tapes. The transcriptionist had been conscientious and was generally accurate. Nevertheless, he had rendered Mr. Daniels's remark "There'd be no real point in it" as "There's no point in it." That's only a small change in meaning—certainly not as much of a change as would be produced by omitting a "not"—but still a change.

For the most part, I am sure, the transcription was good enough so that I had been right to work from transcripts when writing that project's report rather than returning to listen to the tapes. And yet, for excerpts that will be used in a project's report it might be worthwhile to return to the tape if the respondent's exact wording and indications of the respondent's intonation and hesitancies could turn out to be important.

JUSTIFICATIONS FOR USING QUASI-QUANTITATIVE TERMS RATHER THAN COUNTS AND PROPORTIONS

A problem often encountered in reports of qualitative studies is how to communicate the proportion of cases that have particular characteristics. We tend to use terms that have quantitative implications but that specify no particular number or proportion: terms like ''a few'' or ''some'' or ''many.'' Should we not report instead the actual numbers or proportions of instances we have found? Why do we not report the correlation coefficient rather than saying that people who have one characteristic ''seem likely'' to have another?

One reason is that many issues do not require that we code and count. An impression is good enough. ''Most respondents found the interview to be interesting'' is a statement of this sort. We would not make the study more valuable by the more precise statement ''Seventy-three percent of respondents gave evidence that they found the interview to be interesting.'' And the more precise statement would suggest either that the proportion was an important finding or that the investigator had no sense of what was important and what was not.

A further reason for using ''most'' rather than a percent or proportion can be that the sample is so very nonrepresentative, so different from any population to which there might be generalization, that to be more precise would be misleading. Suppose that some members of a sample of retirees were volunteers and others were referred by the personnel directors of the firms they had worked for and still others were obtained from a community sample. It would be more in keeping with this sample of convenience to say ''The great majority of the sample have adult children'' than to say ''Eighty-five percent of the sample have adult children.''

Notwithstanding these concerns, sample numbers or proportions should probably be reported when an issue is central to a study. In a paper on the processes by which people move into retirement, I told readers how many in our sample had retired for reasons of health, how many had retired because they wanted to, and how many had been pushed out. I thought it important for readers to know how many cases we drew on for our appraisals of the effects of different processes of retirement.

HOW YOU WRITE ABOUT YOUR INFORMANTS AND RESPONDENTS

Any report on people conveys an attitude toward them: sympathetic, indulgent, critical, dispassionate. The attitude may not be made explicit but will in any event be expressed in the way the people are presented to the report's readers. (Readers will then have their own reactions to the respondents, the author, and the author's attitudes.) Let us consider three attitudes investigators might display toward their respondents in the report of their study.

THE INVESTIGATOR AS ADVOCATE, SYMPATHETIC REPRESENTATIVE, OR VIEWPOINT PRESENTER

One test of the adequacy of a report is whether it can convince its readers that had they been in the situation of the respondents, with the respondent's histories and understandings of their options, they would have behaved just as did the respondents. The rationale for this position is that most people, respondents included, behave reasonably; a fully adequate report, therefore, will make evident to readers that respondents behaved reasonably, given their understanding of their situations.

But the attempt to demonstrate the reasonableness of respondents' behavior, if adopted by an investigator of crime or vice, tends to turn the investigator into a defender of that crime or vice. The report appears to demonstrate that the criminal or sinner is not at fault, that crime or vice just happen, that the reader has no right to judge because in the situation of respondents the reader would do no better. To escape this trap the investigator must be able to communicate awareness that the behavior is wrong, even while demonstrating that it is understandable.

Sometimes investigators, as a consequence of their research relationships with respondents, find themselves acting as their respondents' representatives to the society at large. The time and emotion and thought investigators have invested in understanding their respondents have fostered a sense of responsibility for their welfare. The investigators feel themselves responsible not only for making their respondents' situations understandable but also for speaking for their respondents.

Occasionally, investigators "go native." They incorporate the respondents' behaviors and worldview. They may then find it difficult to retain the perspective of their field. Yet representing respondents is different both from identifying with them and from endorsing everything about them. A sense of obligation to a group the investigator has studied seems to me at least defensible, whereas identification with the group and endorsement of their values seem to me developments ordinarily to be avoided.

THE INVESTIGATOR AS CRITIC

Quite the opposite position from that of identification with respondents is also possible in the writing of a qualitative interview report. A colleague of mine once offered as a general rule that if your report on a group you have studied has truly gotten to the inner dynamics of the group, you can never again visit that group with safety. His idea was that every group has secrets kept from outsiders that the group would be loath to have revealed and still other secrets, even more fundamental, kept from itself, whose surfacing would enrage it. He gave as an instance a study he had conducted of men in a working-class social group whose aggressively masculine displays in drinking, athletics, and quarreling he believed both expressed homosexual impulses and hid their existence.

Some interviewers seem to subscribe to a milder form of this position, which is that any portrait that has integrity will display unflattering elements as well as flattering ones. The investigator may not be hostile, but balance will require warts along with dimples. Other investigators, however, fully anticipate that their work will damage some respondents or damage groups in which their respondents have membership. Indeed, this may be the investigators' ultimate aim. Investigative reporters are often out to "get the goods" on people they interview.

Insofar as investigators are confrontative in their interviewing style, the respondents whom they hope to damage are on notice. This is as far as an investigative reporter is likely to go in obtaining informed consent. No investigative reporter carries consent forms. When investigative reporters have been friendly, understanding, and sympathetic and then use what they were told to damage, respondents may with justification claim they were misled. Investigative reporters can offer as defenses that the respondents were themselves operating in such bad faith that they had no right to expect better from others, and that a higher good was achieved by the investigator's work. Sometimes these defenses seem good enough.

THE INVESTIGATOR AS DISPASSIONATE LISTENER AND REPORTER

A third position is to be neither sympathetic nor unsympathetic, nor to attempt to balance the two, but to be concerned only with accurate rendition. The investigator takes the position of telling the facts, just the facts, with no responsibility for the light in which disclosure puts respondents.

There is much that is attractive in the notion of the dispassionate investigator. Worth attention, however, is the discordance between the dispassion in the written report and the sense of partnership the investigator is likely to have sought during the interview. The investigator may not be overtly critical, but as Janet Malcolm argues, even a dispassionate report can distress the respondent who provided its material. She sees the problem in the discrepancy between the sense of sympathy that develops in the research interview—and that is an important element in the interviewing partnership—and the more distant stance likely to be displayed in the report:

> What rankles and sometimes drives [the subject] to extremes of vengefulness, is the deception that has been practiced on him. On reading the article or book in question, he has to face the fact that the journalist—who seemed so friendly and sympathetic, so keen to understand him fully, so remarkably attuned to his vision of things—never had the slightest intention of collaborating with him on his story but always intended to write a story of his own.[10]

Investigators, at least when they are starting out, may not always recognize how much printed depictions of respondents can matter to them. I once participated in a class for nonfiction writers. One of the class members was about to publish a story in which the owner of a hairdressing salon was gently ridiculed. A passage in the story pictured the owner delicately eating a chicken wing while talking soothingly to a client on the phone. The class member had sent the owner a prepublication copy of the story, and the owner had responded with an irate phone call threatening legal action. The class, when told this story, couldn't understand what upset the owner.

Whether respondents are named or not, investigators have the ability in their reports to present to public view portraits of respondents that are too detailed, authoritative, and permanent for the respondents easily to shrug off.

AN EFFORT AT RESOLUTION

There is no simple solution to the issue of the stance to be taken toward respondents when writing the report. There may, however, be a variant of the Hippocratic oath that could be adopted by people—investigative reporters excepted—writing up interview materials: at least do no harm.

I like to feel that I can guarantee respondents that although they may not gain by entering into a research relationship with me, they will at least not lose. I may not make this commitment explicit, but I feel it to be necessary for my own moral comfort when engaging a respondent in an interviewing partnership. This does not mean that in writing the report I will necessarily present a sympathetic portrait, although I think it likely that a full portrait will make readers sympathize. It does mean that I will make every effort to make respondents' own perspective understandable even as I meet my commitment to tell the whole truth.

But what of the investigative reporter? As I have noted, the investigative reporter can argue that the harm suffered by one or more respondents is outweighed by gain for the larger society. And many efforts in this mode have without question made things better for many people, though not for absolutely everyone.[11] Moreover, in investigative reporting the need always to be protective of respondents may need qualification. Some respondents are less vulnerable than others; the rich and powerful, presumably, can take care of themselves. And members of a criminal conspiracy might deserve no concern at all.

But it is a problem for investigative reporting that the harm its reports produce is relatively sure and the gain often less so. So I would worry about a piece strongly critical of the teaching staff of a local high school that would appear in a publication read locally: I would want at least to be sure in my own mind that the piece was as balanced as possible, that it had a chance of producing desirable results, and that there was no better route to encouraging improvement.

It may be that there is no single rule to cover an investigator's responsibilities to respondents, and that every case must be evaluated separately. But before engaging in investigative reporting I think I would want to be convinced that the justification of the greater good was valid.

GETTING IT OUT THE DOOR

Howard S. Becker calls it "getting it out the door."[12] Lots of research people have trouble getting their report out the door. Yet, as Becker says, that's what it's all about.

As I noted earlier, I try to produce a first draft as rapidly as I can. My practice is to dictate a very rough draft of a particular section of the report into a tape recorder, including with it summaries of supporting literature and supporting material from interview transcripts. I rewrite the resulting typescript once or twice and then go on to the next section of the report. I continue in this way until I have a draft of the entire report. Then I rewrite the report, this time spending as much time on a section as it needs. Then I edit.

Becker observes that most of writing is rewriting, editing, changing, adding and subtracting. He says: "Few people can write long papers making complex arguments based on complicated data in their heads and get it right on the first try."[13] It's necessary to accept that writing is a process of development, and you have to start somewhere. The first draft, if you've thought hard about your material, should be partway there. The next draft will be better, and the next better yet. And so on, until you hit diminishing returns or are up against a deadline or can't stand to work on the material any more.

If the first problem in writing is getting the material down on paper, the second is the oppressive presence of standards. No one wants to produce slipshod work. You are likely to want your report to be absolutely first-rate, to meet your own standards and everybody else's. And you are likely to fear the criticism and loss of people's respect that would result from work that is flawed. Writing is exposure.[14] Loss of standing as a result of faulty work may indeed occur. But the greater danger, for many investigators, is that fear of producing flawed work will prevent the work from appearing at all.

Furthermore, our hopes for our work can set such high standards that it must inevitably fail to meet them. I would like my work to be accurate, precise, absolutely clear, fully inclusive—and besides all that, interesting, even entertaining. But it never is, certainly not the first time through—but not the second or third or fourth time through either. The phrasing isn't quite right or is repetitious, or the argument isn't neatly sequential but instead jumps and circles and doubles back. Chapter beginnings are abrupt or else long-winded, chapter sections aren't in the right order, and chapters don't end properly. There is too little quotation, or a quotation doesn't work in context, or there is so much quotation that it overwhelms the narrative. And so on. As I recognize shortcomings, I edit and revise.

It is good practice to ask for comments from colleagues. At the least, you will remind yourself that you are writing for readers. Colleagues can tell you where your argument is unconvincing or your discussion perplexing, where you have failed to consider existing literature or have misinterpreted the literature you have considered. Some people have established understandings with certain colleagues that enable each to respond reliably to the style and substance of the other's work. A professional writer I know speaks of "writing buddies" who do this for each other. But colleagues tend to be busy with their own work. Ordinarily they cannot be counted on for close readings. How, then, do you obtain close readings? If you have someone you can call on, whose judgment you respect, you are fortunate. If you do not, you might consider paying for an editorial review from a professional editor in your field.

Use reactions from others, together with your own assessments, to guide further revisions. But accept that at some point before achievement of the perfect report, the process must end. Getting it out the door, to quote Becker once again, is what it's all about.

APPENDIX A

OTHER NAMES FOR QUALITATIVE INTERVIEWING

The term *qualitative interviewing* is only one among several terms for the style of interviewing described in this book. Other terms for it include *intensive interviewing, in-depth interviewing,* and *depth interviewing.* Each of these characterizations identifies an aspect of the approach. *Intensive interviewing* emphasizes its concern for detail and completeness in accounts, as does *in-depth interviewing. Depth interviewing* suggests an effort to obtain the psychological underpinnings of beliefs or opinions.

Still other terms for qualitative interviewing are *unstructured interviewing* and *free interviewing.* Here what is emphasized is that questions are developed in the course of the interview and flow naturally from what preceded. Related terms are *conversational interviewing* and *narrative interviewing.* All these terms draw attention to the relaxed, conversation-like appearance of qualitative interviewing, in contrast to the more formal and distanced appearance of survey interviewing. Actually, none of these terms is entirely accurate. Qualitative interviewing is always constrained by the goals of a study; it is never free to veer off into any area at all. And the structure of qualitative interviewing is unlike that of an ordinary conversation; for one thing, one participant takes responsibility for providing direction, the other for providing content.

Another term that emphasizes the style of the interviewing is *nondirective research interview.* Here what is focused on is the attentive, nonjudgmental, and receptive stance of the interviewer and the interviewer's willingness, like that of a nondirective therapist, simply to listen. Actually, the interviewer in a qualitative interview is not nondirective in the Rogerian manner, that is, reflecting and clarifying but otherwise passive; rather, the interviewer guides the interview through a definite research agenda. And whereas the Rogerian therapist is concerned with helping clients come to terms with themselves, the interviewer must obtain information for a report.

Social workers, in particular, seem to use the term *clinical research interview* to refer to qualitative interviewing. The term captures the importance of sensitivity and awareness in this style of interviewing. But it may foster confusion between the aims and approaches of therapeutic work and research interviewing. As I argued in Chapter 5, these are quite different.

Merton, Fiske, and Kendall have described a particular form of qualitative interview as a *focused interview.* This is a style of qualitative interviewing aimed at eliciting the cognitive and emotional sources of respondents' reactions to some event. It treats respondents as subjects whose response to the event is the material to be understood, rather than as reporters from whom we will learn about the event itself.[1]

Still other terms for the approach are regularly being invented. Daniel Levinson referred to his use of qualitative interviewing to learn about respondents' lives as *biographical interviewing.*[2] The method of qualitative interviewing, although a natural approach to learning from others, is not yet so well established in the world of social science research that it has a single name.

APPENDIX B

FIELDS THAT USE
QUALITATIVE INTERVIEWING

Qualitative interviewing is important in a number of fields: the social sciences, of course, but also in journalism, advertising research, history, biography, and criminal justice. Different fields have different concerns and use the approach differently. In criminal justice interviewing the goal is highly specific, namely, to learn what happened and who was involved. In the social sciences and in advertising and marketing research, it is important to be able to generalize, to report not just about particular individuals or particular institutions but to make credible assertions about a larger class of individuals or institutions.

In the social sciences, respondents tend to be treated, as is recommended in this book, as fellow members of the research team, field observers who will report their observations. But in advertising research respondents are more often treated as subjects, guinea pigs in a search for advertising approaches that work. Respondents are led to display in the interview the extent of their knowledge or the nature of their concerns. Investigators can then make assessments of respondents' cognitive styles, knowledge, intelligence, motivations, or personalities. This use of interviewing treats respondents as psychological subjects rather than as reporters on realities, internal or external, and treats respondents' reports as test materials.

In journalism, respondents are sometimes treated as partners in the

209

production of a profile or a story, very much as they might be in a social science effort. But they may also be treated as contestants in a game in which the interviewer seeks factual detail while expecting the respondent to retouch reality to make his or her cause more appealing. Or the respondent may be treated as an antagonist from whom significant material is to be elicited by guile or wrested by confrontation.[1]

In criminal justice, respondents who are believed to have information that may incriminate them or people to whom they feel loyal are treated as adversaries to be disarmed, cajoled, confronted, and intimidated into telling their stories. The interviewer tries to establish not partnership with the respondent but moral dominance.[2] This approach, although rare in the social sciences, is not unknown; Kinsey's original interviewing team sometimes acted as friendly cops, assuming the worst of respondents, in the belief that only by taking it for granted that the respondent had engaged in discrediting behavior could they combat attempts to cover up.[3]

There is also a difference across fields in the kind of information that is sought. In the social sciences, investigators may hope to provide readers with insight into processes or mechanisms that may explain a range of behaviors or experiences. Historians and journalists are likely to want accurate, vivid, and complete descriptions of particular events and to have relatively less concern for identifying the dynamics of situations. Psychologists and psychiatrists are, like social scientists, concerned with theory, but they are more likely to want either to develop a theory about a particular case or to be able to describe the processes that produce a particular type of case.

And yet even though every field that uses qualitative interviews does so differently, there is a common core to the approach across fields. In every field the qualitative interview is an effort to elicit from respondents detailed, dense, and coherent reports of external or internal experiences from which descriptions, inferences, and conclusions can be drawn.

APPENDIX C

SOURCES OF BIAS
AND THEIR CONTROL

Experimenters try to guard against "experimenter effects," that is, effects not due to the experimental treatment but, rather, to the experimenters' acting, unbeknownst to themselves, to produce the results they expect and want. As a protection against experimenter effects, studies of drug effectiveness use a double-blind procedure in which the experimenter who administers the drug does not know which subjects are in the experimental group and which are controls. We cannot avail ourselves of double-blind procedures when we do qualitative interview studies. How then can we protect ourselves, and our studies, from experimenter effects?

A beginning is made if we recognize how vulnerable to experimenter effects the qualitative interview study is. As investigators, we are ourselves present in the study in every phase, from selection of respondents to report writing. In the sampling phase, we can slant the sample toward fellow believers. While interviewing, we can ask leading questions and be friendly toward responses that support our preconceptions. In our analysis of material we can, instead of getting to the heart of the matter, try to find support for a position we brought with us to the study. And in our reporting we can easily give that position the best of the argument. We can do all this without full awareness of what we are doing.

On the other hand, most investigators, I believe, select reasonably adequate samples; conduct interviews whose aim is to learn rather than to demonstrate; perform dispassionate, responsible, and careful analysis; and are faithful to their findings in their presentations. Here, briefly, is how pitfalls might present themselves in the different stages of qualitative interview studies and how they can be avoided.

SAMPLING

Biased sampling occurs when we take respondents who have particular points of view as a representative sample of a more inclusive group. A study of political ideas based on interviews at the Republican National Convention would not necessarily be a biased sample of elite Republican belief but would be misleading as a basis for learning about American belief.

A random sample is always an unbiased representation of the population from which it is drawn. When, as is most often the case, we must make do with a convenience sample, we should try to ensure that it contains adequate range on critically important dimensions. For example, in a study of the experience of shared parenthood, this might mean finding instances in settings that are supportive of such efforts, such as a suburb favored by academic couples, and instances in settings that are not supportive of such efforts, such as a working-class ethnic neighborhood. Failing this, we have to make clear the limits of the population to which we can generalize.

INTERVIEWING

Biased interviewing occurs when we encourage respondents to provide material supportive of our thesis. This can be done in the way we present ourselves and the study to respondents, by the kinds of questions we ask, and by the way we treat responses. We can guard against bias in the interview by establishing a research partnership in which the respondent understands that what we need is a full and accurate report, by obtaining detailed, concrete material rather than context-dependent generalizations, and by fashioning a substantive frame for our study that effectively captures the complexities of whatever it is we are studying.

We can reassure readers of our report about the quality of our material by providing a copy of our interview guide. Even though every interview is likely to depart from the guide in some respect, the guide will suggest the concerns of the study and the issues it explored. The presentation of interview excerpts can then suggest the adequacy of our interviewing.

INTERPRETATION AND REPORTING

The interpretation and reporting of our material are procedures especially vunerable to the introduction of bias. We can easily make an argument come out our way by treating comments that support our view as gospel and subjecting to skeptical scrutiny those that don't, by reporting material we like and disdaining the rest, and in general by behaving like a lawyer with a brief to advance. Our only defense against this happening is to discipline ourselves to deal fully and fairly with all the evidence and to report everything we've learned about an issue, absolutely everything, including cases that don't fit our theories as well as cases that do.

INTELLECTUAL HONESTY

A former head of a department of government who, while in government, had been determined that a program he was sponsoring be the one adopted, once said to me that he had often sponsored research whose results he thought would support the program. If the results came out the way he wanted them to, he would publicize them for all they were worth. If they did not, he would bury them.

I suppose it is all right for people in or out of government to choose the research they will honor. It is not all right, though, for the people doing the research to be determined that their findings should come out the way they want them to. Yet people convinced of the social value of a cause sometimes do feel justified in selecting and stretching research results so that their report supports their cause. They treat research as a form of rhetoric rather than a method of learning.

People who do research should have only one concern in their work, and that is to capture, with scrupulous honesty, the way things are. Then, after the work has been completed, they can think about its implications for social action. As for work done by others that has been slanted to shore up an outlook or program, we can trust that it will ultimately lose value in the marketplace of ideas. Although the validity of a research report is only one among many determinants of its credibility, we can reasonably hope that it will prove decisive in the end.

APPENDIX D

CONSENT FORMS

Consent forms are required for most studies that are federally funded or that are conducted under the auspices of universities or medical institutions. Exceptions may be made by an institution's review board for some studies where the forms would be inappropriate, so long as the process of interviewing poses minimal risk to respondents: for example, a study in which visitors to a museum are asked for brief appraisals of exhibits. Studies based on telephone interviews would be required to obtain consent to a verbal statement of the contents of a consent form.

Consent forms are not universally required. Journalists are for the most part unaware of consent forms, although they do inform respondents that they are journalists. Consent forms are likely to be waived for political scientists who are interviewing important government figures, perhaps on the assumption that people so well placed can take care of themselves. And anthropologists studying another society may be excused on grounds of the likely unfamiliarity to their respondents of the very idea of a consent form.

My own view is that, in the sort of interviewing exemplified in this book, consent forms are usually a good thing. They can help establish that the interviewing relationship is a working partnership, and they can provide the respondent with a clear statement of the aims, auspices, and methods of the study.

A consent form that covers the following issues would be consistent with federal guidelines for the conduct of social research.[1]

1. *A statement of the study's objectives and methods.*
   When I draft a consent form I begin by saying what will be the focus of the study in a way that will suggest the topics that might be included within the study's frame. I also try to make the study seem interesting and potentially valuable.
2. *How it happened that the respondent was chosen.*
   This isn't actually required by federal guidelines, but respondents almost always want to know. Federal guidelines do suggest that respondents be told the approximate size of the sample.
3. *What will be asked of the respondent.*
   Here I tell respondents that we are asking them to participate in one or more interviews, and that the interviews will be taped and transcribed.
4. *Who will have access to the respondent's materials.*
   The name of the responsible person and institution is probably enough, but when I am the study director I generally list not only my own name but also the names of the other members of the study's staff.
5. *A description of reasonably foreseeable risks or discomforts and of reasonably expectable benefits.*
   This statement can be weighted toward the negative, because every potential risk in the study should be listed, but only the likely benefits.
   In most interview studies the primary risk is a breach of confidentiality. Federal guidelines require that there be "a statement describing the extent, if any, to which confidentiality of records identifying the subject will be maintained." On the benefit side, there is almost always some possible benefit in talking, although it can't be guaranteed.
6. *A statement that participation is voluntary and that respondents' questions will be answered fully.*
   This is required by federal guidelines.
7. *What will be published.*
   This is not required by federal guidelines, but is likely to be among the questions respondents will have.

8. *To whom questions should be directed.*
Federal guidelines require that the respondent be told whom to contact with questions about the study. I think the respondent should be given the telephone numbers both of the institutional review board and of the study's director.

Consent forms should be kept concise, one page if possible. It seems to me that it takes long enough for a respondent to grasp a single-page form. A longer form strikes me as forbidding. But I have seen consent forms that fill two pages and I can imagine forms in medical settings that are even longer.

My practice is to bring two copies of a consent form to a first interview, both of them signed by me as director of the study. I give both of them to the respondent, and ask the respondent to read the form, sign one copy and give it to me, and keep the other.

Here is an example of a consent form.

CONSENT FORM

Work and Family Research Unit
University of Massachusetts

Study of Individuals in the Retirement Years

1. *What is the aim of the study?* The aim of the study is to learn about different ways of organizing life in the retirement years. We hope to learn how different people decide what they will do in their retirement years, what experiences they have in the different sectors of their lives, and what adds to their well-being or reduces it. Our ultimate aim is to make others in our society better able to deal with retirement.

2. *How was I chosen?* We will interview about 80 retired people. Some of those we are interviewing were chosen randomly from street lists of residents. Some were chosen because they are retiring from firms that are helping us do the study. We are also interviewing some respondents who volunteered for the study.

3. *What will be involved in participating?* We will schedule one or more interviews with you, depending on what seems most useful. Ordinarily the interviews will last between an hour and two hours. We will tape the interviews and make transcriptions from the tapes.

4. *Who will know what I say?* Only the staff of the study will have access to your tapes and transcripts. The staff includes: Dr. Robert S. Weiss, a sociologist at the University of Massachusetts, Boston, and the study's director; Anna Sant'Anna, also a sociologist at the university; John Drabik, office manager for the study; Mary Coffey, transcriptionist; and Jane Doe and Robert Roe, interviewers.

5. *What risks and benefits are associated with participation?* We do not foresee any risks to you other than a possible breach of confidentiality. To protect against that risk we will ensure that your tapes and transcripts are held in the offices of the Work and Family Research Unit and that access to them is limited to study staff. Your name will not appear in the transcripts. In any publication or public statement based on the study, all names, occupations, or other potentially identifying information will be omitted or changed. Two years after the end of the study the tapes will be destroyed.

   Sometimes people find participating in an interview to be beneficial insofar as it gives them a chance to talk about things that matter to them.

6. *What are my rights as a respondent?* You may ask any questions regarding the research, and they will be answered fully. You may withdraw from the study at any time. Your participation is voluntary.

217

7. *What will be published?* We make our findings known through lectures and publication. We anticipate publishing two or three article-length reports that will appear in professional journals or as book chapters. We hope eventually to publish our findings in a book.

8. *If I want more information, whom can I contact about the study?* This study has been approved by the University of Massachusetts Institutional Review Board for the Protection of Human Subjects. This board continues to have standing in relation to the study. The board can be contacted through the Office of Grants and Contracts at the University of Massachusetts, Boston, at (617) 287-5000. Dr. Weiss, the study's director, can be contacted at (617) 287-7275.

Robert S. Weiss, Project Director   Respondent,   date

APPENDIX E

QUANTITATIVE CODING OF QUALITATIVE INTERVIEW MATERIAL

THE CODING OF QUALITATIVE DATA

If a set of qualitative interviews has covered more or less the same areas, it is possible to code within those areas in the same way that open-ended items in surveys are coded. That is, it is possible to make up codes for specific issues so that respondents who would be rated as having the same positions on the issue are given the same code.

Depending on the number of issues to be coded and on the ambition and the funding level of the study, coding can be anything from a major undertaking involving several people over the course of months to a single evening's work. Coding would be a major undertaking if dozens of issues were to be considered and the reliability and validity of the coding were to be assessed. It would be a much simpler enterprise if the investigator wanted only to judge respondents on one issue, such as the quality of their adaptation to their situation. In the simplest case a single code might be worked out, with the investigator applying it. In the most ambitious case many codes might be worked out, tested and retested for reliability and validity, and then used as a basis for assessment of respondents by several coders.

What follows is a page of a code book used in a coding effort that was part of the analysis of material from my study of occupationally successful men. The code book contained almost two hundred codes dealing with material in the areas of work, family, friendship, and well-being. Each code was devised from a reading of early interviews and then revised after being used for new interviews by several staff members. When the codes seemed both stable (no need for new categories) and reliable (different staff members made the same coding decisions), they were used by a team of five coders. Two to four hours were required to code the three interviews we had with most respondents; where we had four or five interviews with a respondent, more than four hours might be required for coding.

SEGMENT OF A CODE BOOK:

11. Does R bring work home?

    R does not bring work home..1

    R brings work home occasionally, when tasks demand................2

    R brings work home regularly, routinely....................................3

    Other (explain)..8

    Not enough material to judge...9

Basis for coding:_____

_____ page nos. _____

12. How regularly is R absorbed by work when at work? (Coder judgment)

    R is always absorbed by work when working...........................1

    R is sometimes not absorbed by work when working.................2

    Other (explain)..8

    Not enough material to judge...9

Basis for coding:_____

_____ page nos. _____

13. Is R absorbed by work when away from work? (Coder judgment)

    R is not absorbed by work when away from work......................1

    R is sometimes absorbed by work when away from work............2

    R is generally absorbed by work when away from work..............3

Other (Explain)..8

Not enough material to judge..9

Basis for coding:_____

_____ page nos. _____

14. Does R experience internal conflict between his commitment to work or the time he believes required by work and his commitment to family or the time he believes required by family? (Coder judgment)

R experiences such a conflict.....................................1

R does not experience such a conflict..........................2

Not enough material to judge....................................9

Basis for coding:_____

_____ page nos. _____

The material for each of these codes could appear anywhere in the interview transcript. It was necessary for coders to be ready, as they read through the transcript, to use any of the codes in the code book. Thus, a coder might have found that the passage being read provided material for code item 25 and that the next passage provided material for code item 14. Generally, however, material dealing with a particular topic showed up in most transcripts at about the same place: material on experience at work in the first interview, on fathering toward the end of the second, and so on.

So that coder judgments could be appraised, it was necessary for coders to note in their code books the material on which they based their coding decisions. The "basis for coding" lines were used by the coders for brief quotations or summaries of the respondent's statements, and coders also indicated the page of the transcript on which such material appeared.

To understand the material of this study we found it invaluable to have not only the actual counts of how many respondents reported what but also the quotation and page references. The procedure was expensive but, at least in this particular study, worthwhile.

It might happen in another study that there is only one issue important to code: adaptation to retirement, for example. The code building procedure would be the same as if there were many such issues: Read the interviews to identify potential indicators for codings; specify the potential indicators; have several people attempt to use the potential indicators to code new interviews; work together to identify problems with the codings and resolve them; repeat the procedure until the code stabilizes and appears both reliable and valid.

In qualitative interviewing it will almost certainly be the case that not every issue will be explored with every respondent. This means that in most codes a number of respondents will be coded as "Not enough material to judge" or something like this. It may nevertheless be useful to be able to report, "Of the fifty respondents who provided enough material to judge, 56% reported that . . ."

We found a database program to be useful as a way of dealing with the mixture of numbers and text that our coding approach produced. Such a program can also provide simple statistics, including both the proportions of responses associated with particular coding categories and cross-classifications.

NOTES

Preface

1. For a description of his approach, see Ernest Dichter, *Handbook of Consumer Motivations*, New York: McGraw-Hill, 1964.

Chapter 1 Introduction

1. When the interviewing conducted for survey studies is subjected to close scrutiny, questions regarding the interpretability of responses arise. Careful empirical study has demonstrated that survey studies involve a good deal of miscommunication; see Lucy Suchman and Brigitte Jordan, "Interactional Troubles in Face-to-Face Survey Interviews," *Journal of the American Statistical Association*, 85, no. 409 (March 1990): 232–41. The journal followed the paper with comments by informed discussants. Most agreed that the validity of data from survey studies would be enhanced if the interviewers were permitted more freedom in phrasing and interpreting questions. Another position, however, was that the cure for the ills of survey studies lies in improvement in the crafting of questions, after which the survey approach should be adhered to unchanged. See also Jean Peneff, "The Observers Observed: French Survey Researchers at Work," *Social Problems*, 35, no. 5 (1988): 520. See also Charles L. Briggs, *Learning How to Ask* (New York: Cambridge University Press, 1986). Survey studies ordinarily do not recognize problems of miscommunication. As Elliot Mishler writes, the more controlled approach of survey research, compared with qualitative interview studies, does not make for lesser involvement with language and intersubjectivity but only obscures the involvement; see his *Research Interviewing: Context and Narrative* (Cambridge, Mass.: Harvard University Press, 1986).
2. Lisa Peattie has demonstrated in a number of studies the contribution qualitative interview studies can make to understanding economic processes. For a general discussion, see Lisa Peattie, "Economic Anthropology and An-

thropological Economics,'' in *Currents in Anthropology: Essays in Honor of Sol Tax*, ed. Robert Hinshaw (The Hague, Netherlands: Mouton, 1979).

3. See Robert K. Merton and Patricia L. Kendall, "The Focused Interview," *American Journal of Sociology*, 51, no. 6 (1946): 541–57.

4. See Catherine K. Riessman, *Divorce Talk: Women and Men Make Sense of Personal Relationships* (New Brunswick, N.J.: Rutgers University Press, 1990).

5. See Howard Schwartz and Jerry Jacobs, *Qualitative Sociology: A Method to the Madness* (New York: Free Press, 1979). These authors believe that the aim of making the outlook of respondents understandable implies qualitative method and especially qualitative interview studies: "Qualitative methods, which use natural language, are best at gaining access to the life-world of other individuals in a short time. . . . Without knowledge of chess as a game, together with the strategies, reasons, and 'moves' that might go with it, one might describe the actions of chess players as two people moving pieces of wood around a board'' (p. 5).

6. Other authors have offered other lists of reasons for doing qualitative interview studies. David Silverman lists, as justification for qualitative approaches in general, a need for observational or narrative information, for convincing stories, and for corroboration of information collected in another manner; see his "Telling Convincing Stories: A Plea for Cautious Positivism in Case Studies," in *The Qualitative–Quantitative Distinction in the Social Sciences*, ed. Barry Glassner and Jonathan D. Moreno (Dordrecht: Kluwer Academic Publishers, 1989), pp. 57–77. For a valuable presentation of an economist's uses of qualitative interview studies, see Michael J. Piore, "Qualitative Research Techniques in Economics," *Administrative Science Quarterly*, 24 (December 1979): 560–69. Lisa Peattie has used qualitative interviews to demonstrate as mistaken the assumptions economists make about the economic behavior of low-income people in underdeveloped countries; see her "Economic Anthropology and Anthropological Economics."

7. As Robert Emerson says, the investigator's "intimate familiarity" with the topic of study, a familiarity that makes possible the "thick" description of good qualitative work, could not be gained without the investment of the investigator's time and energy. See Robert M. Emerson, "Four Ways to Improve the Craft of Field Work," *Journal of Contemporary Ethnography*, 16, no. 1 (April 1987): 69–89.

8. For one description of such disparagement, along with evidence that it is mistaken, see Piore, "Qualitative Research Techniques."

9. Kai T. Erikson, *Everything in Its Path: Destruction of Community in the Buffalo Creek Flood* (New York: Simon & Schuster, 1976).

10. Maren Lockwood Carden, *The New Feminist Movement* (New York: Russell Sage Foundation, 1974).

11. I include here my own work on marital separation and my work with Colin M. Parkes on bereavement. For the former, see my *Marital Separation* (New York: Basic Books, 1975) and *Going It Alone: The Family Life and Social Situation of the Single Parent* (New York: Basic Books, 1979). For the latter, see Colin M. Parkes and Robert S. Weiss, *Recovery from Bereavement* (New York: Basic Books, 1983).

12. See the material drawn on by Judith Lewis Herman in her *Trauma and Recovery* (New York: Basic Books, 1992).

Chapter 2 Respondents: Choosing Them and Recruiting Them

1. William F. Whyte, *Streetcorner Society* (Chicago: University of Chicago Press, 1943).

2. See Dean Hammer and Aaron Wildavsky, "The Open-Ended, Semi-Structured Interview: An (Almost) Operational Guide," in *Craftways: On the Organization of Scholarly Work,* ed. Aaron Wildavsky (New Brunswick, N.J.: Transaction, 1989), pp. 57–101. See also Marc-Adlard Tremblay, "The Key Informant Technique: A Non-Ethnographic Application," *American Anthropologist,* 57, no. 4 (1957): 688–701.

3. Sampling statisticians are ordinarily more focused on another characteristic of probability samples, the likelihood that a sample characteristic is within a given range of the population characteristic: for example, that the average age of subjects in a sample is within a year of the average age of those in the population. This seems a less important concern for qualitative interview studies than the likelihood that a characteristic that appears infrequently in the population will nevertheless have at least one representative in the sample.

4. The discussion in the following paragraphs draws on Barney G. Glaser and Anselm L. Strauss, *The Discovery of Grounded Theory: Strategies for Qualitative Research* (Chicago: Aldine, 1967), pp. 23–26. For an application of their approach, see Eloise Dunlap, Bruce Johnson, and Harry Sanabria, "Studying Crack Users and Their Criminal Careers," *Contemporary Drug Problems,* 17 (Spring 1990): 121–44.

5. See Jan E. Trost, "Statistically Nonrepresentative Stratified Sampling: A Sampling Technique for Qualitative Studies," *Qualitative Sociology,* 9, no. 1 (Spring 1986): 54–57. Trost suggests the approach of a formal quota sample.

6. In a fine article, Howard Becker has considered the issue of locating a sample of groups for whom there is no listing: "Studying Practitioners of Vice and Crime," in *Pathways to Data,* ed. Robert W. Habenstein (Chicago: Aldine, 1970). pp. 30–49.

7. Diane Ehrensaft, *Parenting Together: Men and Women Sharing the Care of Their Children* (New York: Free Press, 1987).

8. Donald Ray Cressey, *Other People's Money* (Montclair, N.J.: Patterson Smith, 1973).

9. See, for example, Robert L. Rubinstein, Janet C. Kilbride, and Sharon Nagy, *Elders Living Alone: Frailty and the Perception of Choice* (New York: Aldine De Gruyter, 1992).

10. Our proposal for a larger study wasn't funded. If I had to find newcomers now, I would try real estate agents, newcomer clubs, and neighborhood associations. But since I haven't actually tried any of these sources, I can't say which, if any, would work.

11. Ralph Waldo Emerson, "The American Scholar," in *The Collected Works of Ralph Waldo Emerson* (Cambridge, Mass.: Belknap Press, 1971), vol. 1, pp. 49–70.

12. Cressey, *Other People's Money.*

13. Judith S. Wallerstein and Sandra Blakeslee, *Second Chances: Men, Women, and Children a Decade After Divorce* (New York: Ticknor and Fields, 1989).

14. Ehrensaft, *Parenting Together.*

15. I don't know of any good estimates of the proportion of families in which the husbands might be considered house husbands. My estimate that house husbands might be found in 2% or 3% of families is based on Pruett's discussion of his case-finding experience; see Kyle D. Pruett, *The Nurturing Father* (New York: Warner Books, 1987). Pruett's experience was with middle-class families. I would guess that the proportion in working-class families is no higher than that in middle-class families.

16. Helen MacGill Hughes, ed., *The Fantastic Lodge: The Autobiography of a Girl Drug Addict* (Boston: Houghton Mifflin, 1961).

17. Ken Plummer, *Documents of Life: An Introduction to the Problems and Literature of a Humanistic Method* (London: George Allen and Unwin, 1983).

18. This checklist is similar to the list provided by R. L. Gorden, *Interviewing: Strategy, Techniques, and Tactics* (Homewood, Ill.: Dorsey Press, 1969), pp. 165–73.

Chapter 3 Preparation for Interviewing

1. The term *accounting scheme* was, I think, first used by Paul Lazarsfeld and Morris Rosenberg. It appears in their book *The Language of Social Research: A Reader in the Methodology of Social Research* (New York: Free Press, 1955), pp. 387–491. An example of an accounting scheme is provided by J. Stannard Baker's study of accidents, "A Framework for Assessment of Causes of Automobile Accidents," in Lazarsfeld and Rosenberg, pp. 438–48. Baker's accounting scheme considers early or remote causes that provided conditions for the accident, such as poor highway design; contributing causes that led directly to the accident, such as speeding to get home for dinner; key events, such as sliding off the road; responses to key events (or

failures to respond) that made the accident happen in just the way it did, such as trying to steer the car back on the road; the accident event itself, such as coming to rest in a ditch or hitting another car; and the ultimate result in property damage and human hurt. This is not a theory of how accidents happen that can be said to be true or false, but rather a framework for telling the story of particular accidents that, when applied, will prove useful or not useful.

2. There are all sorts of functional approaches, including Malinowski functionalism, with its emphasis on individual need; Radcliffe-Brown functionalism, with its emphasis on the needs of the collectivity; and the structure–function Parsonian approach modeled on biological description. I offer here a version of Radcliffe-Brown functionalism that seems to me often useful in synchronic studies. Robert Merton provides a justly celebrated exposition of functional analysis in the chapter "Manifest and Latent Functions" in his *Social Theory and Social Structure* (New York: Free Press, 1968 Enlarged Edition), pp. 73–138.

3. Matthew B. Miles and A. Michael Huberman believe that conceptual frameworks may largely be implicit in the preconceptions of the investigator. They write that "terms such as 'social climate,' 'stress,' or 'role conflict' are typically labels we put on bins containing a lot of discrete events and behaviors. When we assign a label to a bin, we may or may not know how all the contents of the bin fit together, or how this bin relates to another one. But any researcher, no matter how inductive in approach, knows which bins to start with and what their general contents are likely to be." Bins come from the investigator's theory and experience, as well as from the general objectives of the study envisioned. "Laying out those bins, giving each a descriptive or inferential name, and getting some clarity about their interrelationships is what a conceptual framework is all about." See their *Qualitative Data Analysis: A Sourcebook of New Methods* (Beverly Hills, Calif.: Sage Publications, 1984), p. 28.

4. Dean Hammer and Aaron Wildavsky, writing about guides to be used with a panel of informants, recommend keeping guide questions to a minimum. However, they think that it might be useful to anticipate awkward areas and work out wordings for appropriate questions beforehand; see their "Open-Ended, Semi-Structured Interview," pp. 57–101.

5. It might be noted how strongly synchronic is the treatment here. I may, in part, have been influenced in this decision by awareness that Daniel Levinson and his colleagues had already produced a diachronic discussion of men's careers in their *Seasons of a Man's Life* (New York: Random House, 1978). The material gathered through use of this guide has been published in my *Staying the Course: The Emotional Life and Social Situation of Men Who Do Well at Work* (New York: Free Press, 1990).

6. Starting out with clear research aims is, for some investigators, an unusual

experience. See the discussion in Barbara Katz Rothman, "Reflections: On Hard Work," *Qualitative Sociology,* 9, no. 1 (Spring 1986): 48–53.

7. Marjorie L. DeVault. "Talking and Listening from Women's Standpoint: Feminist Strategies for Interviewing and Analysis," *Social Problems,* 37, no. 1 (February 1990): 96–120. DeVault says that Howard Becker makes this claim.

8. I use a tape recorder with a unidirectional external microphone, which I can direct away from background noise, such as an air-conditioner.

9. Notes, too, get cold. I find them harder to fill out if I let even a day go by before transcribing them. Hammer and Wildavsky ("The Open-Ended, Semi-Structured Interview," p. 79) recommend expanding and developing notes at the first opportunity: "Coffee shops are ideal for this purpose, but parked cars, bathrooms, window ledges, or anything handy can be used. Remember: with every moment that passes, a nuance of the interview may be lost."

10. Timothy T. Johnson, James G. Hougland, Jr., and Richard R. Clayton, "Obtaining Reports of Sensitive Behavior: A Comparison of Substance Use Reports from Telephone and Face-to-Face Interviews," *Social Science Quarterly,* 70, no. 1 (March 1989): pp. 173–83.

11. Jane E. Tausig and Ellen W. Freeman, "The Next Best Thing to Being There: Conducting the Clinical Research Interview by Telephone," *American Journal of Orthopsychiatry,* 58, no. 3 (July 1988): 418–27. They warn that the success of the approach depends in good part on the confidence of the respondent in the identity of the interviewer and in the confidentiality of the process.

Chapter 4 Interviewing

1. The generalized past can also have a rhetorical use. Catherine K. Riessman, in discussing differences in narratives, writes about a respondent conveying "the feeling of blurred time" by use of the generalized past. See her "When Gender Is Not Enough: Women Interviewing Women," *Gender and Society,* 1, no. 2 (June 1987): 172–207.

2. Dean Hammer and Aaron Wildavsky advise: "Always remember that you, the researcher, are the theorist, not the person you are interviewing." "The Open-Ended, Semi-Structured Interview," p. 61.

Chapter 5 Issues in Interviewing

1. The concept of talking at a middle distance is Tom Scheff's. He discusses it in *Catharsis in Healing, Ritual, and Drama* (Berkeley: University of California Press, 1979).

2. For an extended discussion of the usefulness of talk, see James W. Pennebaker, *Opening Up* (New York: William Morrow, 1990).

3. Barbara Laslett and Rhona Rapoport describe handling a situation in which an interviewer asked questions a respondent resented: "During the first interview with both parents, there appeared to be an openness and willingness to discuss events in the family's early history. At the second interview (which was scheduled for the father separately) the mother, in a side conversation with the interviewer, voiced her feelings of resentment that the first interview covered material that was, in her mind, an illegitimate subject of inquiry. Following the supervision in which this reaction was discussed, the interviewer dealt directly with the issue. . . . On the telephone . . . the interviewer apologized for having moved into areas of inquiry which the mother did not feel were 'proper' without first working through with her what her attitudes were. Once the legitimacy of the mother's feelings were acknowledged, the mother became more receptive." See Laslett and Rapoport, "Collaborative Interviewing and Interactive Research," *Journal of Marriage and the Family*, 37 (November 1975): 968–77.

4. Mihaly Csikszentmihalyi, *Flow: The Psychology of Optimal Experience* (New York: Harper Collins, 1990).

5. Janet Malcolm, *The Journalist and the Murderer* (New York: Knopf, 1990).

6. Nell Irvin Painter, *The Narrative of Hosea Hudson: His Life as a Negro Communist in the South* (Cambridge, Mass.: Harvard University Press, 1979).

7. However, see Charles L. Briggs, "Questions for the Ethnographer: A Critical Examination of the Role of the Interview in Field Work," *Semiotica* 46–2/4 (1983): 233–61.

8. See the discussion of obtaining acceptance in a most difficult situation in Arlene Daniels, "The Low-Caste Stranger in Social Research," in *Ethics, Politics, and Social Research,* ed. Gideon Sjoberg (Cambridge, Mass.: Schenkman, 1967), pp. 267–96.

9. Robert K. Merton, "Insiders and Outsiders: A Chapter in the Sociology of Knowledge," *American Journal of Sociology,* 78 (1972): 9–42.

10. It may be the case that a particular interviewer doesn't hit it off with a particular respondent for no identifiable reason and that another interviewer would do better. Efforts to achieve good interviewer–respondent matches are described by Laslett and Rapoport, "Collaborative Interviewing and Interactive Research," and by Aaron V. Cicourel, "Fertility, Family Planning, and the Social Organization of Family Life: Some Methodological Issues," *Journal of Social Issues,* 23, no. 4 (1967): 57–81. Cicourel's approach was to have interviewers end the first interview early if they felt they couldn't get along with the subject or felt uncomfortable within the household or with the subject's spouse. Cicourel would then send in another interviewer.

11. See also John P. Dean and William Foote Whyte, "How Do You Know If the Informer Is Telling the Truth?" *Human Organization,* 17, no. 2 (1958): 34–38.

12. Tamara Hareven has suggested that in interview-based historical research only the corroborated statement should be accepted as fact. See her *Family Time and Industrial Time: The Relationship Between the Family and Work in a New England Industrial Community* (New York: Cambridge University Press, 1982). Hareven tells the story of a former worker in the textile factory whose history she studied who reported that her employment at the factory ended at the time of a strike. The company's ledger book, however, showed that the respondent had continued to be employed. Told of the discrepancy, the respondent said that the strike had so changed the factory's culture that it became a different place. However, if the respondent's employment history had been a central concern of the study, she could have been asked "Could you walk me through how it happened that you left the factory?" and her perception of the situation, in which it was the factory that had left her, would have surfaced.

Chapter 6 Analysis of Data

1. Anselm L. Strauss, *Qualitative Analysis for Social Scientists* (New York: Cambridge University Press, 1987).
2. Miles and Huberman, *Qualitative Data Analysis*, p. 49.
3. Bob Blauner names the first analytic focus the "thematic" and the second the "first person." He distinguishes between the two by saying the thematic is concerned with illustrating or elaborating a conceptual theme, while the first person is concerned with acquainting the reader with a particular individual's life or ideas. See his "Problems of Editing 'First Person' Sociology," *Qualitative Sociology*, 10, no. 1 (Spring 1987): 46–64.
4. Studs Terkel's work includes *American Dreams, Lost and Found* (New York: Pantheon Books, 1980); *Hard Times: An Oral History of the Great Depression* (New York: Pantheon Books, 1970); and *Working: People Talk About What They Do All Day and How They Feel About What They Do* (New York: Pantheon Books, 1974).
5. Levinson et al., *The Seasons of a Man's Life*.
6. Elliott Liebow, *Tally's Corner: A Study of Negro Streetcorner Men* (Boston: Little, Brown, 1967).
7. See also John Van Maanen's discussion of styles of ethnographic writing in his *Tales of the Field: On Writing Ethnography* (Chicago: University of Chicago Press, 1988).
8. For a listing of computer programs developed, as of 1991, to facilitate the analysis of qualitative data, see the appendix on resources in Nigel G. Fielding and Raymond M. Lee, eds., *Using Computers in Qualitative Research* (Newbury Park, Calif.: Sage, 1991), pp. 195–199. For cautions regarding overreliance on computer programs in qualitative analysis, see Michael Agar,

"The Right Brain Strikes Back," in *Using Computers in Qualitative Research,* pp. 181–94, and John Seidel, "Method and Madness in the Application of Computer Technology to Qualitative Data Analysis," in *Using Computers in Qualitative Research,* pp. 107–18.

9. Weiss, *Going It Alone: The Family Life and Social Situation of the Single Parent.*
10. Miles and Huberman, *Qualitative Data Analysis.*
11. Howard S. Becker, with a chapter by Pamela Richards, *Writing for Social Scientists: How to Start and Finish Your Thesis, Book or Article* (Chicago: University of Chicago Press, 1986).
12. Agar, "The Right Brain Strikes Back."
13. Mirra Komarovsky, with Jane H. Philips, *Blue-Collar Marriage* (New York: Random House, 1962).
14. Interview-based studies of family life completed before World War II include Robert Cooley Angell, *The Family Encounters the Depression* (New York: Scribner's, 1938) and Mirra Komarovsky, *The Unemployed Man and His Family* (New York: Dryden Press, 1940). An interview-based study of divorce was Willard W. Waller, *The Old Love and the New: Divorce and Readjustment* (New York: H. Liveright, 1930).
15. Komarovsky, *Blue-Collar Marriage,* pp. 24–25.
16. Ronald Fraser, *Blood of Spain: An Oral History of the Spanish Civil War* (New York: Pantheon Books, 1979), pp. 31–32.
17. Oscar Lewis, *The Children of Sanchez: Autobiography of a Mexican Family* (New York: Random House, 1961).
18. Ronald Blythe, *Akenfield: Portrait of an English Village* (New York: Dell, 1969).
19. Reported in Agar, "The Right Brain Strikes Back."
20. John F. Cuber and Peggy B. Harroff, *The Significant Americans: A Study of Sexual Behavior Among the Affluent* (New York: Appleton, 1965).
21. Uta Gerhardt, "Patient Careers in End-Stage Renal Failure," *Social Science and Medicine,* 30, no. 11 (1990): 1211–24.
22. I am grateful to Uta Gerhardt for discussing with me the use of ideal types in qualitative research and for sharing with me her unpublished paper, "The Use of Weberian Ideal-Type Methodology in Qualitative Data Analysis."
23. David Riesman, with Reuel Denney and Nathan Glazer, *The Lonely Crowd: A Study of the Changing American Character* (New Haven, Conn.: Yale University Press, 1950).
24. Michael Maccoby, *The Gamesman: Winning and Losing the Career Game* (New York: Simon & Shuster, 1976).
25. See George W. Brown, "Some thoughts on Grounded Theory," *Sociology,* 7 (1973): 1–16.

Chapter 7 Writing the Report

1. See Van Maanen, *Tales of the Field.*
2. Barney G. Glaser and Anselm L. Strauss, *Time for Dying* (Chicago: Aldine, 1968), p. 79.
3. Arlie Hochschild, with Anne Machung, *The Second Shift: Working Parents and the Revolution at Home* (New York: Viking, 1989). This work has successfully bridged an academic and a general audience.
4. Carden, *The New Feminist Movement,* p. 107.
5. Blauner, "Problems of Editing 'First Person' Sociology."
6. DeVault, "Talking and Listening from Women's Standpoint," especially pp. 105–10.
7. Riessman, "When Gender Is Not Enough," p. 189.
8. Van Maanan, *Tales of the Field,* p. 70.
9. Malcolm, *The Journalist and the Murderer,* pp. 155–57.
10. Malcolm, *The Journalist and the Murderer,* p. 3.
11. See Jessica Mitford, *Poison Penmanship: The Gentle Art of Muckraking* (New York: Knopf, 1979). One example among many might be the same author's *The American Way of Death* (New York: Simon & Schuster, 1963).
12. Becker, *Writing for Social Scientists,* p. 124. Tracy Kidder reported the phrase as one used by computer designers to refer to moving a new design from workbench to marketplace. See Tracy Kidder in *The Soul of a New Machine* (Boston: Little, Brown, 1981).
13. Becker, *Writing for Social Scientists,* p. 19.
14. Pamela Richards develops this theme in her chapter on the risks of writing in Becker, *Writing for Social Scientists,* pp. 108–20.

Appendix B Fields That Use Qualitative Interviewing

1. Robert K. Merton, Marjorie Fiske and Patricia L. Kendall. *The Focused Interview: A Manual of Problems and Procedures.* Second Edition. New York: The Free Press, 1990.
2. Levinson et al., *The Seasons of a Man's Life.*

Appendix C Sources of Bias and Their Control

1. Mark Kramer brought to my attention "The Art of the Confrontational Interview," by Chris Ison and Lou Kilzer, reporters for the *Star Tribune* in Minneapolis. Their article appeared in the 1991 volume of *Writing Coach,* a newsletter for journalists published in Milwaukee. Ison and Kilzer won the 1990 Pulitzer Prize for investigative journalism for a series on people who profited from fires. The interviewing techniques they describe include confronting respondents with evidence that they were lying, as a way of pressing

them to be more truthful; indicating to respondents that they, the reporters, were already fully informed even when they weren't; and returning to respondents again and again, whenever new information could justify new questions.

2. The following excerpts are from a text by Arthur S. Aubry, Jr., *Criminal Interrogation*, 3rd ed. (Springfield, Ill.: Charles C. Thomas, 1980), chaps. 16 and 17:

"The interrogator seeks the defeat and final surrender of the subject—the securing of the confession being the final objective. . . . The interrogator crumbles the defenses of the subject. . . . He knocks out strong points. He demonstrates that the subject is lying. He destroys alibis by pointing out their absurdity or impossibility."

"Another specific technique that works well with a wide variety of subjects is the relatively simple procedure of inviting the subject to tell the story, or tell his side of the story, and let him ramble on without interruption. . . . The interrogator may also ask the subject to repeat his story, perhaps on the pretext that he didn't understand it; the idea is to tangle the subject in discrepancies."

"The interrogator wants to maintain the psychological advantage over the subject and so refuses to address the subject as Mr. but insists on being called Mr.—or Officer—in response: "Good afternoon, Tom, I'm Mr. Caputo.""

3. See the discussion of interviewing techniques in Alfred Kinsey, Wardell B. Pomeroy, and Clyde E. Martin, *Sexual Behavior in the Human Male* (Philadelphia: W. B. Saunders, 1948).

Appendix D Consent Forms

1. See "Federal Policy for the Protection of Human Subjects: Notices and Rules," *Federal Register,* 56, no. 117 (June 18, 1991): 28001–28018, especially pp. 28016–28017. Some states have additional regulations governing health-related research.

REFERENCES

Agar, Michael. "The Right Brain Strikes Back." In Nigel G. Fielding and Raymond M. Lee, eds., *Using Computers in Qualitative Research* (pp. 195–99). Beverly Hills, Calif.: Sage, 1991.

Angell, Robert Cooley. *The Family Encounters the Depression*. New York: Scribner's, 1938.

Aubry, Arthur S., Jr. *Criminal Interrogation*. 3rd ed. Springfield, Ill.: Charles C. Thomas, 1980.

Baker, J. Stannard. "A Framework for Assessment of Causes of Automobile Accidents." in Paul Lazarsfeld and Morris Rosenberg, eds., *The Language of Social Research: A Reader in the Methodology of Social Research* (pp. 438–48). Glencoe, Ill.: Free Press, 1955.

Becker, Howard S. "Studying Practitioners of Vice and Crime." In Robert W. Habenstein, ed. *Pathways to Data* (pp. 30–49). Chicago: Aldine, 1970.

Becker, Howard S., with a chapter by Pamela Richards. *Writing for Social Scientists: How to Start and Finish Your Thesis, Book or Article*. Chicago: University of Chicago Press, 1986.

Blauner, Bob. "Problems of editing 'First Person' Sociology." *Qualitative Sociology*, 10, no. 1 (Spring 1987): 46–64.

Blythe, Ronald. *Akenfield: Portrait of an English Village*. New York: Dell, 1969.

Briggs, Charles L. *Learning How to Ask*. New York: Cambridge University Press, 1986.

————. "Questions for the Ethnographer: A Critical Examination of the Role of the Interview in Field Work." *Semiotica*, 46–2/4 (1983): 233–61.

Brown, George W. "Some Thoughts on Grounded Theory." *Sociology*, 7 (1973): 1–16.

Carden, Maren Lockwood. *The New Feminist Movement*. New York: Russell Sage Foundation, 1974.

Cicourel, Aaron V. "Fertility, Family Planning, and the Social Organization of

Family Life: Some Methodological Issues.'' *Journal of Social Issues,* 23, no. 4 (1967): 57–81.

Cressey, Donald Ray. *Other People's Money.* Montclair, NJ: Patterson Smith, 1973.

Csikszentmihalyi, Mihaly. *Flow: The Psychology of Optimal Experience.* New York: Harper Collins, 1990.

Cuber, John F., and Peggy B. Harroff. *The Significant Americans: A Study of Sexual Behavior Among the Affluent.* New York: Appleton, 1965.

Daniels, Arlene. ''The Low-Caste Stranger in Social Research.'' In Gideon Sjoberg, ed., *Ethics, Politics, and Social Research* (pp. 267–96). Cambridge, Mass.: Schenkman, 1967.

Dean, John P., and William Foote Whyte. ''How Do You Know If the Informer Is Telling the Truth?'' *Human Organization,* 17, no. 2 (1958): 34–38.

DeVault, Marjorie L. ''Talking and Listening from Women's Standpoint: Feminist Strategies for Interviewing and Analysis.'' *Social Problems,* 37, no. 1 (February 1990): 96–120.

Dichter, Ernest. *Handbook of Consumer Motivations.* New York: McGraw-Hill, 1964.

Dunlap, Eloise, Bruce Johnson, and Harry Sanabria. ''Studying Crack Users and Their Criminal Careers.'' *Contemporary Drug Problems,* 17 (Spring 1990): 121–44.

Ehrensaft, Diane. *Parenting Together: Men and Women Sharing the Care of Their Children.* New York: Free Press, 1987.

Emerson, Ralph Waldo. ''The American Scholar.'' In *The Collected Works of Ralph Waldo Emerson* (vol. 1, pp. 49–80) Cambridge, Mass.: Belknap Press, 1971.

Emerson, Robert M. ''Four Ways to Improve the Craft of Field Work.'' *Journal of Contemporary Ethnography,* 16, no. 1 (April 1987): pp. 69–89.

Erikson, Kai T., *Everything in Its Path: Destruction of Community in the Buffalo Creek Flood.* New York: Simon & Schuster, 1976.

''Federal Policy for the Protection of Human Subjects: Notices and Rules,'' *Federal Register,* 56, no. 117 (June 18, 1991): 28001–28018.

Fielding, Nigel G., and Raymond M. Lee, eds. *Using Computers in Qualitative Research.* Newbury Park, Calif.: Sage, 1991.

Fraser, Ronald. *Blood of Spain: An Oral History of the Spanish Civil War.* New York: Pantheon Books, 1979.

Gerhardt, Uta. Department of Sociology, University of Heidelberg. ''The Use of Weberian Ideal-Type Methodology for Qualitative Data Analysis.'' In preparation, 1993.

———. ''Patient Careers in End-Stage Renal Failure.'' *Social Science and Medicine,* 30, no. 11 (1990): 1211–24.

Glaser, Barney G., and Anselm L. Strauss. *The Discovery of Grounded Theory: Strategies for Qualitative Research*. Chicago: Aldine, 1967.

————. *Time for Dying*. Chicago: Aldine, 1968.

Gorden, R. L. *Interviewing: Strategy, Techniques, and Tactics*. Homewood, Ill.: Dorsey Press, 1969.

Hammer, Dean, and Aaron Wildavsky. "The Open-Ended, Semi-Structured Interview: An (Almost) Operational Guide." In Aaron Wildavsky, ed., *Craftsways: On the Organization of Scholarly Work* (pp. 57–101). New Brunswick, N. J.: Transaction, 1989.

Hareven, Tamara K. *Family Time and Industrial Time: The Relationship Between the Family and Work in a New England Industrial Community*. New York: Cambridge University Press, 1982.

Herman, Judith Lewis. *Trauma and Recovery*. New York: Basic Books, 1992.

Hochschild, Arlie, with Anne Machung. *The Second Shift: Working Parents, and the Revolution at Home*. New York: Viking, 1989.

Hughes, Helen MacGill, ed. *The Fantastic Lodge: The Autobiography of a Girl Drug Addict*. Boston: Houghton Mifflin, 1961.

Ison, Chris, and Lou Kitzer. "The Art of the Confrontational Interview." *Writing Coach*, 1991. (A newsletter published in Milwaukee.)

Johnson, Timothy T., James G. Hougland, Jr., and Richard R. Clayton. "Obtaining Reports of Sensitive Behavior: A Comparison of Substance Use Reports from Telephone and Face-to-Face Interviews." *Social Science Quarterly*, 70, no. 1 (March 1989): 173–83.

Kidder, Tracy. *The Soul of a New Machine*. Boston: Little, Brown, 1981.

Kinsey, Alfred C., Wardell B. Pomeroy, and Clyde E. Martin. *Sexual Behavior in the Human Male*. Philadelphia: Saunders, 1948.

Komarovsky, Mirra. *The Unemployed Man and His Family*, New York: Dryden Press, 1940.

Komarovsky, Mirra, with Jane H. Philips. *Blue-Collar Marriage*. New York: Random House, 1962.

Laslett, Barbara, and Rhona Rapoport. "Collaborative Interviewing and Interactive Research." *Journal of Marriage and the Family*, 37 (November 1975): 968–77.

Lazarsfeld, Paul, and Morris Rosenberg, eds. *The Language of Social Research: A Reader in the Methodology of Social Research*. New York: Free Press, 1955.

Levinson, Daniel J., C. N. Darrow, E. B. Klein, M. H. Levinson, and B. McKee. *The Seasons of a Man's Life*. New York: Random House, 1978.

Lewis, Oscar. *The Children of Sanchez: Autobiography of a Mexican Family*. New York: Random House, 1961.

Liebow, Elliott. *Tally's Corner: A Study of Negro Streetcorner Men.* Boston: Little, Brown, 1967.

Maccoby, Michael. *The Gamesman: Winning and Losing the Career Game.* New York: Simon & Shuster, 1976.

Malcolm, Janet. *The Journalist and the Murderer.* New York: Knopf, 1990.

Merton, Robert K. "Insiders and Outsiders: A Chapter in the Sociology of Knowledge." *American Journal of Sociology,* 78 (1972): 9–42.

———. "Manifest and latent functions." In *Social Theory and Social Structure.* New York: Free Press, enlarged edition, 1968.

Merton, Robert K., Marjorie Fiske, and Patricia L. Kendall. *The Focused Interview: A Manual of Problems and Procedures.* 2nd ed. New York: Free Press, 1990.

Merton, Robert K., and Patricia L. Kendall. "The Focused Interview." *American Journal of Sociology,* 51 no. 6 (1946): 541–57.

Miles, Matthew B., and A. Michael Huberman. *Qualitative Data Analysis: A Sourcebook of New Methods.* Beverly Hills, Calif.: Sage, 1984.

Mishler, Elliot G. *Research Interviewing: Context and Narrative.* Cambridge, Mass.: Harvard University Press, 1986.

Mitford, Jessica. *Poison Penmanship: The Gentle Art of Muckraking.* New York: Knopf, 1979.

———. *The American Way of Death.* New York: Simon & Schuster, 1963.

Painter, Nell Irvin. *The Narrative of Hosea Hudson: His Life as a Negro Communist in the South.* Cambridge, Mass.: Harvard University Press, 1979.

Parkes, Colin M., and Robert S. Weiss. *Recovery From Bereavement.* New York: Basic Books, 1983.

Peattie, Lisa. "Economic Anthropology and Antrophologic Economics." In Robert Hinshaw, ed., *Currents in Anthropology: Essays in Honor of Sol Tax.* The Hague, Netherlands: Mouton, 1979.

Peneff, Jean. "The Observers Observed: French Survey Researchers at Work." *Social Problems,* 35, no. 5 (1988): 520.

Pennebaker, James W. *Opening Up.* New York: Morrow, 1990.

Piore, Michael J. "Qualitative Research Techniques in Economics." *Administrative Science Quarterly,* 24 (December 1979): 560–69.

Plummer, Ken. *Documents of Life: An Introduction to the Problems and Literature of a Humanistic Method.* London: George Allen and Unwin, 1983.

Pruett, Kyle D. *The Nurturing Father.* New York: Warner Books, 1987.

Riesman, David,, with Reuel Denney and Nathan Glazer. *The Lonely Crowd: A Study of the Changing American Character.* New Haven, Conn.: Yale University Press, 1950.

Riessman, Catherine K. *Divorce Talk: Women and Men Make Sense of Personal Relationships.* New Brunswick, N.J.: Rutgers University Press, 1990.

―――. "When Gender Is Not Enough: Women Interviewing Women." *Gender and Society,* 1, no. 2 (June 1987): 172–207.

Rothman, Barbara Katz. "Reflections: On Hard Work." *Qualitative Sociology,* 9, no. 1 (Spring 1986): 48–53.

Rubinstein, Robert L., Janet C. Kilbride, and Sharon Nagy. *Elders Living Alone: Frailty and the Perception of Choice.* New York: Aldine De Gruyter, 1992.

Scheff, Thomas J. *Catharsis in Healing, Ritual, and Drama.* Berkeley: University of California Press, 1979.

Schwartz, Howard, and Jerry Jacobs. *Qualitative Sociology: A Method to the Madness.* New York: Free Press, 1979.

Seidel, John. "Method and Madness in the Application of Computer Technology to Qualitative Data Analysis." In Nigel G. Fielding and Raymond M. Lee, eds. *Using Computers in Qualitatitve Research* (pp. 107–18). Newbury Park, Calif.: Sage, 1991.

Silverman, David. "Telling Convincing Stories: A Plea for Cautious Positivism in Case Studies." In Barry Glassner and Jonathan D. Moreno, eds., *The Qualitative–Quantitative Distinction in the Social Sciences* (p. 57–77). Dordrecht: Kluwer Academic Publishers, 1989.

Strauss, Anselm L. *Qualitative Analysis for Social Scientists.* New York: Cambridge University Press, 1987.

Suchman, Lucy, and Brigitte Jordan. "Interactional Troubles in Face-to-Face Survey Interviews." *Journal of the American Statistical Association,* 85, no. 409 (March 1990): 232–41.

Tausig, Jane E., and Ellen W. Freeman. "The Next Best Thing to Being There: Conducting the Clinical Research Interview by Telephone." *American Journal of Orthopsychiatry,* 58, no. 3 (July 1988): 418–27.

Terkel, Studs. *American Dreams, Lost and Found.* New York: Pantheon Books, 1980.

―――. *Hard Times: An Oral History of the Great Depression.* New York: Pantheon Books, 1970.

―――. *Working: People Talk About What They Do All Day and How They Feel About What They Do.* New York: Pantheon Books, 1974.

Tremblay, Marc-Adlard. "The Key Informant Technique: A Non-Ethnographic Application." *American Anthropologist,* 57, no. 4 (1957): 688–701.

Trost, Jan E. "Statistically Nonrepresentative Stratified Sampling: A Sampling Technique for Qualitative Studies." *Qualitative Sociology,* 9, no. 1 (Spring 1986): 54–57.

Van Maanen, John. *Tales of the Field: On Writing Ethnography.* Chicago: University of Chicago Press, 1988.

Waller, Willard W. *The Old Love and the New: Divorce and Readjustment.* New York: H. Liveright, 1930.

Wallerstein, Judith S., and Sandra Blakeslee. *Second Chances: Men, Women, and Children A Decade After Divorce.* New York: Tickner & Fields, 1989.

Weiss, Robert S. *Going It Alone: The Family Life and Social Situation of the Single Parent.* New York: Basic Books, 1979.

————. *Marital Separation.* New York: Basic Books, 1975.

————. *Staying the Course: The Emotional Life and Social Situation of Men Who Do Well at Work.* New York: Free Press, 1990.

Whyte, William F. *Streetcorner Society.* Chicago: University of Chicago Press, 1943.

Wildavsky, Aaron. *Craftways: On the Organization of Scholarly Work.* New Brunswick, N.J.: Transaction, 1989.

INDEX